INEQUALITY AND AMERICAN DEMOCRACY

INEQUALITY AND AMERICAN DEMOCRACY

What We Know and
What We Need to Learn

Lawrence R. Jacobs
Theda Skocpol
Editors

Russell Sage Foundation
New York

The Russell Sage Foundation

The Russell Sage Foundation, one of the oldest of America's general purpose foundations, was established in 1907 by Mrs. Margaret Olivia Sage for "the improvement of social and living conditions in the United States." The Foundation seeks to fulfill this mandate by fostering the development and dissemination of knowledge about the country's political, social, and economic problems. While the Foundation endeavors to assure the accuracy and objectivity of each book it publishes, the conclusions and interpretations in Russell Sage Foundation publications are those of the authors and not of the Foundation, its Trustees, or its staff. Publication by Russell Sage, therefore, does not imply Foundation endorsement.

Library of Congress Cataloging-in-Publication Data

Inequality and American democracy : what we know and what we need to learn / edited by Lawrence R. Jacobs and Theda Skocpol.
   p. cm.
Includes bibliographical references and index.
ISBN 0-87154-413-X
1. Equality—United States. 2. Democracy—United States. 3. United States—Politics and government. I. Jacobs, Lawrence R. II. Skocpol, Theda
JC575.I54 2005
323.42'0973—dc22

2005042897

The paper used in this publication meets the minimum requirements of American National Standard for Information Sciences—Permanence of Paper for Printed Library Materials. ANSI Z39.48-1992.

Text design by Genna Patacsil.

RUSSELL SAGE FOUNDATION
112 East 64th Street, New York, New York 10021
10 9 8 7 6 5 4 3 2 1

Contents

Contributors   vii

Acknowledgments   ix

Chapter 1   American Democracy in an Era of
Rising Inequality
Lawrence R. Jacobs and Theda Skocpol   1

Chapter 2   Inequalities of Political Voice
*Kay Lehman Schlozman, Benjamin I. Page,
Sidney Verba, and Morris P. Fiorina*   19

Chapter 3   Inequality and American Governance
*Larry M. Bartels, Hugh Heclo, Rodney E.
Hero, and Lawrence R. Jacobs*   88

Chapter 4   Inequality and Public Policy
*Jacob S. Hacker, Suzanne Mettler, and
Dianne Pinderhughes*   156

Chapter 5   Studying Inequality and American
Democracy: Findings and Challenges
Lawrence R. Jacobs and Theda Skocpol   214

Index   237

Contributors |

LAWRENCE R. JACOBS is Walter F. and Joan Mondale Chair for Political Studies and director of the Center for the Study of Politics and Governance at the Hubert H. Humphrey Institute and is professor in the Department of Political Science at the University of Minnesota.

THEDA SKOCPOL is Victor S. Thomas Professor of Government and Sociology and director of the Center for American Political Studies at Harvard University.

LARRY M. BARTELS is Donald E. Stokes Professor of Public and International Affairs and director of the Center for the Study of Democratic Politics at Princeton University.

MORRIS P. FIORINA is Wendt Family Professor of Political Science and senior fellow of the Hoover Institution at Stanford University.

JACOB S. HACKER is Peter Strauss Family Associate Professor of Political Science at Yale University.

HUGH HECLO is Clarence J. Robinson Professor of Public Affairs at George Mason University.

RODNEY E. HERO is Packey J. Dee Professor of American Democracy at Notre Dame University.

SUZANNE METTLER is Alumni Associate Professor in the Department of Political Science in the Maxwell School at Syracuse University.

BENJAMIN I. PAGE is Gordon S. Fulcher Professor of Decision Making and faculty associate of the Institute for Policy Research at Northwestern University.

DIANNE PINDERHUGHES is professor of political science and African American studies at the University of Illinois, Urbana-Champaign.

KAY LEHMAN SCHLOZMAN is J. Joseph Moakley Professor of Political Science at Boston College.

SIDNEY VERBA is Carl H. Pforzheimer University Professor and director of the University Libraries at Harvard University.

Acknowledgments |

In 1950, a task force sponsored by the American Political Science Association (APSA) published a seminal report, "Toward a More Responsible Two-Party System," that influenced generations of government officials and political observers. The association recently revived this tradition by launching a series of task forces designed to bring scholarly research to bear on pressing public issues. During Theda Skocpol's presidency in 2002 and 2003, the Task Force on Inequality and American Democracy was nominated to the APSA Council and appointed for a two-year term to run from early 2003 through early 2005. Larry Jacobs chaired and Theda Skocpol served and contributed to the group's direction. Thirteen other members were appointed, including two who later proved unable to serve. Ben Barber, Larry Bartels, Morris Fiorina, Jacob Hacker, Rodney Hero, Hugh Heclo, Suzanne Mettler, Benjamin Page, Dianne Pinderhughes, Kay Lehman Schlozman, and Sidney Verba participated as task force members.

The research and writing that laid the groundwork for this book included both focused writing and deliberation and collective decisionmaking. Three working groups drafted extensive reviews of research in American politics that form the basis of chapters 2, 3, and 4. Members of the task force gave the drafts of these working groups ongoing reviews and commentary, which were incorporated into the next round of drafting. In addition to the research reports that make up the core of this book, the task force also produced a relatively short report aimed at the general public and mass media and a set of materials geared to classroom instruction. Both can be found at www.apsanet.org. In our years in the academy, the level of involvement of task force members in the hard, shared work that went into this endeavor stands out for its collegiality and sense of urgent purpose.

As in any collective effort, a few people performed invaluable service to the task force as a whole. The three working groups were the hubs for much of our work; the coordinators of those groups—Kay Schlozman, Jacob Hacker, and Larry Bartels—deserve particular recognition for their extraordinary efforts.

We would also like to acknowledge Ben Barber for his stimulating and challenging contributions to our collective deliberations though he did not co-author one of the chapters.

Three outside peers with quite different backgrounds and expertise reviewed advanced drafts of the task force's reports and offered concrete suggestions for improvements that the task force then discussed and did its best to address. We would like to acknowledge and thank the constructive and valuable reviews of Larry Mishel, John DiIulio, and Linda Williams.

In preparing this book for publication, we are also grateful for the help of our editor at the Russell Sage Foundation, Suzanne Nichols, two anonymous reviewers, and our copyeditor, Helen Glenn Court. We are also appreciative of financial support provided by the Russell Sage Foundation under the leadership of Eric Wanner, which was critical and supplemented basic support from the American Political Science Association.

We are also indebted to the many individuals at the association who helped coordinate the task force and prepare and then publicly release its various materials. The task force and this book have benefited from the steady encouragement and assistance of Michael Brintnall, executive director of the American Political Science Association, and Rob Hauck, the association's deputy executive director. Association staff—especially Sean Twombly and Bahram Rajaee—committed tremendous energy and inventiveness to the project.

Although the task force was convened by the American Political Science Association and operated under the authority of the association's council, the authors of the task force materials and this book take responsibility for the evaluations and representations in them. The opinions expressed in the report are solely those of the task force members. No opinions, statements of fact or conclusions in the report should be attributed to the American Political Science Association, to the Russell Sage Foundation, or to any individual who offered assistance or comments.

Lawrence R. Jacobs and Theda Skocpol

Chapter One | American Democracy in an Era of Rising Inequality

Lawrence R. Jacobs
Theda Skocpol

EQUAL POLITICAL VOICE and democratically responsive government are widely cherished American ideals—yet as the United States aggressively promotes democracy abroad, these principles are under growing threat in an era of persistent and rising inequalities at home. Disparities of income, wealth, and access to opportunity are growing more sharply in the United States than in many other nations, and gaps between races and ethnic groups persist. Progress toward expanding democracy may have stalled, and in some arenas reversed.

Generations of Americans have worked to equalize citizen voice across lines of income, race, and gender. Today, however, the voices of American citizens are raised and heard unequally. The privileged participate more than others and are increasingly well organized to press their demands on government. Public officials, in turn, are much more responsive to the privileged than to average citizens and the less affluent. The voices of citizens with lower or moderate incomes are lost on the ears of inattentive government officials, while the advantaged roar with a clarity and consistency that policymakers readily hear and routinely follow. The scourge of overt discrimination against African Americans and women has been replaced by a more subtle but potent threat—the growing concentration of the country's wealth, income, and political influence in the hands of the few.

These are the conclusions that the Task Force on Inequality and American Democracy established by the American Political Science Association in 2002 reached. As one of several task forces recently formed to enhance the public relevance of political science, this group of scholars was charged with reviewing and assessing the best current scholarship about the health and functioning of U.S. democracy over recent decades, in a era of

1

expanding social rights yet rising economic inequality.[1] Speaking in its own voice and on the authority of the task force members alone, the group drew conclusions after surveying available evidence about three important, interlinked areas of concern: citizen participation, government responsiveness, and the impact of public policies on social inequalities and political participation. The core chapters of this book present in-depth reviews of research findings on these issues. With input and advice from other task force members, each chapter was prepared by a working group of scholars listed as the authors of that chapter.

This introduction sets the context for detailed explorations of citizen participation, government responsiveness, and public policymaking. We begin with evidence about the changing patterns of inequality in the United States, and then consider why recent rising economic inequality may be of special concern. Although Americans tolerate varied fortunes produced by the market, they worry when economic disparities threaten equal citizen voice and undermine government responsiveness to the needs and values of the majority. Americans want their democracy to ensure and expand equal opportunity for all citizens. The research reviewed in this book speaks to basic concerns about the health and prospects of U.S. democracy.

EXPANDING RIGHTS AND RISING ECONOMIC INEQUALITY

American society has become both more and less equal in recent decades. Following the Civil Rights movement of the 1950s and 1960s, racial segregation and exclusion were no longer legal or socially acceptable. Whites and African Americans began to participate together in schools and colleges, the job market, and political and civic organizations. Gender barriers have also been breached since the 1960s, with women now able to pursue most of the same economic and political opportunities as men. Many other previously marginalized groups have also gained rights to participate fully in American institutions and have begun to demand—and to varying degrees enjoy—the dignity of equal citizenship (Skrentny 2002).

But as U.S. society has become more integrated across the previous barriers of race, ethnicity, gender, and other long-standing forms of social exclusion, it has experienced growing gaps of income and wealth. This conclusion emerges from large bodies of authoritative government and nongovernment data, analyzed by researchers using diverse methodologies.[2] The critical questions we address here are how the relative share of income or wealth going to different segments of American society has changed over time and how it compares to distributions in other advanced industrialized countries committed to private enterprise. Numerous independent studies find that the distribution of economic resources in American society has become increasingly concentrated among the most affluent over the past three decades to a degree not found abroad. To be sure, the nation as a whole has become more affluent as absolute levels of income and wealth have risen. Alarmingly, however, rising affluence is sharply concentrated in the very top of American society. Gaps of income and wealth have grown not just between the poor and the rest of society, but also between privileged professionals, managers, and business owners on the one hand, and the middle strata of regular white-collar and blue-collar middle class on the other hand. The rich and the super-rich have appropriated a growing share of wealth and income since the mid-1970s.

Perfect income equality would mean that each fifth of the population (that is, each quintile) would receive 20 percent of the country's income.[3] In 2001, the most affluent fifth received 47.7 percent of family income; the middle class (the third and fourth fifths) earned 15.5 percent and 22.9 percent, respectively, and the bottom two quintiles each received less than 10 percent. Put simply, the richest 20 percent enjoyed nearly half of the country's income—and fully 21 percent of family income went to the top 5 percent of Americans.

The rich, of course, have always enjoyed a disproportionate hold over income. The top quintile has cornered more than 40 percent of the country's income since at least 1947. But patterns of income growth across segments of the American population have shifted radically over time. For twenty years after World War II, the hold of the top fifth on the country's income was slightly weakening—as income at the top grew less rapidly than income in the middle and at the bottom—but after 1973 the trend toward income equalization reversed. Figure 1.1 displays the sharply different distribution of income growth that prevailed in 1947 to 1973 versus 1973 to 2000. After 1973, income growth was clearly much more rapid for those in the top fifth than for all other Americans, and growth was especially anemic toward the bottom. What is more, even within the top fifth, rates of gain were especially fast for the richest 5 percent and fastest of all for the fabulously wealthy top 1 percent.

Even as the distribution of income has tilted sharply toward the top, the most affluent have amassed an even larger slice of the country's wealth (including stock holdings, mutual funds, retirement savings, ownership of property, and other assets). Table 1.1 is based on a survey of consumer finances conducted by the Federal Reserve Board in 1998 and shows the

Figure 1.1   U.S. Family Income Growth

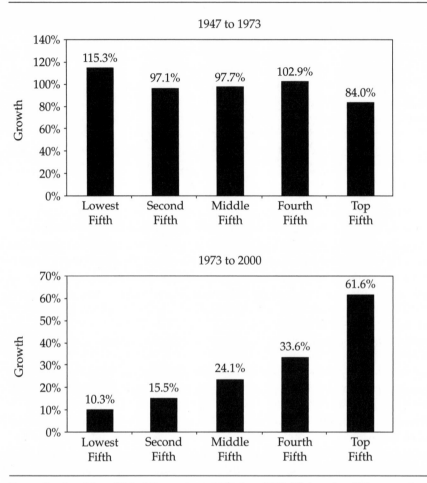

distribution of household income and net worth (total family assets minus its liabilities such as mortgages and other forms of debt). The top 1 percent of households drew 16.6 percent of all income but wielded control over more than double this percentage of the country's wealth (38.1 percent). By contrast, the supermajority of the country—the "bottom" 90 percent of households—earned the majority of household income (58.8 percent) but controlled less than half this percentage (29 percent).[4]

Table 1.1   Distribution of Income and Wealth, 1998

	Household Income (Percentage)	Net Worth (Percentage)
All	100.0	100.0
Top 1 percent	16.0	38.1
Bottom 90 percent	58.5	29.0

Source: Reprinted from Mishel, Bernstein, and Boushey (2003, 279), based on Federal Reserve Board Survey of Consumer Finances. Copyright © 2003 by Cornell University. Used by permission of the publisher, Cornell University Press.
Note: Net worth is the sum of all of a family's assets—checking and savings accounts, property ownership, stock holdings, retirement funds and other assets—minus all of the family's liabilities—debt owed for credit cards and loans for college, property, and other purchases.

Disparities in wealth and income in the United States are much sharper and have grown faster than in other advanced industrial Western democracies. Figure 1.2 presents information about income trends for American families compared against families in Britain and France. The proportion of income accruing to the top one-tenth of 1 percent of families ran along parallel tracks for much of the twentieth century. All three countries reduced inequality from the end of World War I through World War II and until the 1960s. But from the mid-1970s on, the United States rapidly diverged from both Britain and France and became far more unequal. By 1998, the share of income held by the very rich was two or three times higher in the United States than in Britain and France.

The bottom line is clear: the resident of an American penthouse on the top twentieth floor is doing much better than his neighbors not only in the basement but also on the sixteenth floor and, for that matter, any floor. The debate among analysts is no longer about whether inequality has risen and reached unparalleled levels in the United State. Discussion has shifted to pinpointing why economic inequality rose. A range of demographic, technological, and political factors have contributed to rising economic gaps, and we leave it to analysts of economic distributions to sort out their relative impact (see the discussions in Burtless 1999; and Mishel, Bernstein, and Boushey 2003, 56–82). In chapter 4, we will assess some of the ways in which government policies have contributed to the emergence and persistence of greater inequality in the United States compared with other advanced nations.

Economic disparities are particularly striking when it comes to comparisons across races. The Civil Rights era helped lift the absolute levels of income and wealth enjoyed by African Americans and Hispanics. These two groups, however, remain far behind white America. In the late 1980s, the median white household earned 62 percent more and had twelve

Figure 1.2   Top 0.1 Percent Income Shares

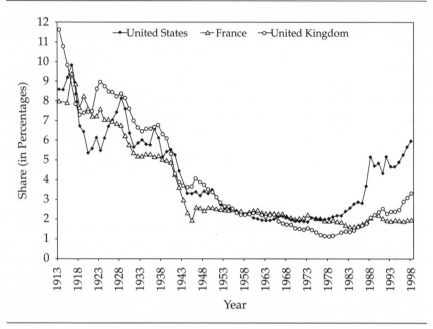

times the wealth of the median black household. Nearly two-thirds of black households (61 percent) and half of Hispanic households have no net worth, compared with only a quarter of their white counterparts.[5] Even young, married, black couples in which both adults work—the shining beacons of progress toward racial equality—still earn 20 percent less than their white counterparts and have a staggering 80 percent less net worth. These figures are based on an unfortunately all-too-infrequent in-depth analysis of income and wealth among African Americans from 1987 to 1989. More recent analyses, however, still show a similar pattern: improvement in absolute terms but continuing racial disparities. According to an analysis of the Federal Reserve Board's *Survey of Consumer Finances,* the median net worth of African Americans nearly quadrupled, from $5,300 in 1989 to $19,000 in 2001. Nonetheless, the median net worth of whites in 2001 was more than ten times greater ($121,000) than for African Americans ($19,000). At nearly every level of wealth, whites continued to enjoy much greater net worth than African Americans in 2001 (Kennickell 2003, 34–36).

Living conditions remain fragile even for the black middle class, and continue to lag far behind those experienced by their white counterparts. And, of course, the circumstances of African Americans who have not reached the middle class are even more precarious.

CONSEQUENCES FOR DEMOCRACY

How concerned should we be about persistent and rising socioeconomic inequalities? Few normative theorists propose a genuinely equal distribution of economic resources as either desirable or feasible. Most of the debate is about the consequences and tolerability of various degrees of economic inequality. Some theorists are comfortable with significant inequalities, which they see as a just reflection of greater rewards going to people who work harder and contribute specialized skills or capital investments to the economy. Those who accept high inequalities also fear that efforts to alter economic distributions will come at an excessive cost to liberty. Others are concerned whenever the life chances of citizens in a democracy become too divergent. If disparities become too great, how can people retain a sense of community and shared fate and engage in informed decisionmaking? And how can political equality be realized when citizens have increasingly divergent resources?

Theorists are not the only ones who disagree about the consequences of economic inequality. Citizens in various advanced-industrial societies differ as well. Our investigations take cues from the special concerns of Americans, which focus on the consequences of inequalities for democratic politics more than on the simple existence of economic disparities as such.

Concerns of Americans

According to opinion surveys, reviewed in chapter 2, Americans are much more likely than Europeans to accept substantial disparities of income and wealth. In the United States, unequal economic outcomes are seen as largely reflecting differences among individuals rather than flaws in the economic system. Americans support private property and free enterprise, and see much of the skewed distribution of wealth and income as a legitimate result of differences in individual talent and effort.

Tolerance of economic inequality by Americans is not unambiguous, however. Two caveats come into play (Page and Shapiro 1992; Weakliem, Andersen, and Heath 2003). First, Americans accept economic inequalities only when they are sure that everyone has an equal chance to get ahead—to achieve the best possible life for the individual and family. Research and news accounts document that the rise in economic inequality is short-circuiting the pathway to the American Dream—the hope that opportunities to prosper are within the reach of every individual willing to work hard and accept the sacrifice. Upward mobility continues, but the number of Americans who are able to enjoy the fruits of upward mobility are few in number and do not come close to offsetting the economic disparities among the many (Gottschalk 1997; Michaels 2004; Smeeding 2004). A narrowing of opportunities for getting ahead contradicts public hopes and expectations and raises concerns about what government is doing, or can do, to further equal opportunity.

Indeed, the second situation that raises public concern is when rising economic inequalities threaten to impinge on ideals of equal citizen voice and government responsiveness to the majority. Americans fervently believe that everyone should have an equal say in our democratic politics. They embrace wholeheartedly the ideal enunciated by the Declaration of Independence that "all men are created equal," which in our time means that every citizen, regardless of income, gender, race, or ethnicity, should have an equal voice in representative government.

According to the National Elections Studies (NES) and other evidence, Americans are increasingly worried about disparities of participation, voice, and government responsiveness.[6] Citizens are much less likely than they were four decades ago to trust government to "do the right thing." Between 1964 and 1994 the proportion of Americans who only trusted the federal government "some" or "none of the time" more than tripled from 22 percent to 78 percent. Although the terrorist attacks on September 11 precipitated a decline in distrust to 46 percent in 2002, distrust increased to 53 percent in 2004. The proportion of Americans who felt that the government is "run by a few big interests looking out only for themselves" more than doubled from 29 percent in 1964 to 76 percent in 1994. This proportion declined to 50 percent in 2002 following the 9/11 attacks (still nearly double the 1964 level) before rising to 56 percent in 2004. In addition, the number who believed that "public officials don't care about what people like me think" nearly doubled, growing from 36 percent in 1964 to 66 percent in 1994. While this proportion dropped to 29 percent in 2002 after the 9/11 attacks, the suspicion rebounded to 50 percent in 2004. Surveys in 1995 and 2000 found that more than six in ten respondents cited too much influence by special interests as a reason for not trusting government.[7]

Looking Ahead to Our Findings

The evidence suggests that citizens are right to be concerned about the health of American democracy. We find disturbing inequalities in the political voice expressed through elections and other avenues of participation. We find that our governing institutions are much more responsive to the privileged and well-organized narrow interests than to other Americans. And we find that the policies our government fashions today may be doing less than celebrated programs of the past to promote equal opportunity and security and enhance citizen dignity and participation, reinforcing the suspicion of many in the American public that government officials "don't care" about the needs and values of ordinary citizens.

As chapter 2 documents, only about a third of eligible voters regularly participate in mid-term congressional elections and only a little more than half regularly turn out for contemporary presidential elections. While the intensely competitive presidential election of 2004 increased turnout to its highest level since 1968—60 percent of individuals living in the United States who are 18 and over[8]—the United States remains a turnout laggard compared to other advanced industrialized countries. As Richard Freeman (2004, 703) puts it, on "a world scale, the United States ranks 138th in turnout among countries that hold elections—far below every other advanced democracy save for Switzerland." Overall, the U.S. electorate has contracted since the 1960s, and the well-educated and well-to-do are much more likely to vote than the least educated and economically privileged. Stratified voting was not, of course, created by any recent increases in economic disparities. But recently growing economic inequalities may reinforce voting differentials, counteracting major reforms that otherwise should have greatly expanded voter turnout. Reforms that should have done much to mitigate voting stratification include the Voting Rights Act of 1965, which brought millions of African Americans into the electorate; simplified processes for registering and casting absentee ballots; and the spread of formal education, which instills the skills and values that encourage voting. Analysts disagree as to whether voting has become more unequal by class over recent decades or has simply remained as it was (see Leighley and Nagler 1992 and the careful reanalysis by Freeman 2004). Certainly, however, voting has not become more equal, despite many factors that should have pushed it in that direction.

Despite all of the limitations in voter turnout, casting a ballot remains the most common political activity. Far fewer Americans take part in more demanding and costly political activities, from protest to giving money. The direct impact of rising economic inequality may be most directly apparent in campaign contributions. As wealth and income have become more concentrated and the flow of money into elections has grown, wealthy individuals and families have opportunities for political clout not open to those of more modest means. Stratification in participation is also evident in a range of other activities, such as joining and supporting a voluntary association or interest group, working in an electoral campaign, getting in touch with a public official, getting involved in an organization that takes political stands, and taking part in a protest or demonstration. Well-developed theory shows that exercising the rights of citizenship requires not only individual resources of income, time, and education, but also skills of the sort that privileged occupations disproportionately bestow on the economically well-off.[9] Managers, lawyers, doctors, and other professionals enjoy not only higher education and salaries but also greater confidence and abilities to speak and organize.

With socioeconomic inequality on the increase, there are some theoretical reasons to believe that the political participation of the less privileged should actually increase (see Brady 2004). But much depends on the role of organizations and political parties in mediating social interests. Although the sheer number of organizations in Washington that speak for once-underrepresented preferences and constituencies has grown, blue-collar trade unions have weakened and are thus less likely to mobilize working-class voters (Radcliff and Davis 2000). Corporate managers and professionals have also increased their organized presence in Washington and enhanced their capacities to speak loudly and clearly to government officials. Even political parties—which the APSA and generations of political activists and observers have held out as a vehicle for an inclusive form of democracy that counteracts the advantage of the better off—may nowadays skew participation in U.S. politics. Along with contemporary professionally managed interest groups, today's major parties target resources on recruiting those who are already the most privileged and involved (Schier 2000; Skocpol 2004a, 2004b). Democrats and Republicans alike have come to depend heavily on campaign contributors and middle-class activists, and have gotten used to competing for just over half of a shrinking universe of voters.

The stratification of political clout and voice interacts with the emergence of a new group of political activists harboring views more intense and extreme than the average citizen's. Operating through interest groups swirling in and around the major political parties, such activists are not only themselves likely to be higher-income and well-educated individuals. On a range of important matters from abortion to tax cuts, activists are also often resistant to government compromises that respond to the more ambiguous or middle of the road opinions of average citizens (Fiorina 1999; Skocpol 2003, chaps. 5 and 6). Even liberal "public interest" advocates, moreover, are likely to focus on the concerns and values of the middle class, than on those of the poor or working Americans (Berry 1999, 55–57).

Disparities in political participation and voice matter because they af-

fect who governs and how these elected officials respond to citizen preferences. Research surveyed in chapter 3 documents that campaign contributions influence who runs for government office—and therefore who sits
in the halls of government. The notion that monetary contributions can directly "buy" votes on the floor of Congress is *not* supported by rigorous
empirical research that controls for a variety of other relevant factors (Ansolabehere, Figueiredo, and Snyder 2003; Wright 1985, 1990). But wealthy
citizens and moneyed interests who make big contributions do gain privileged access to send clear signals about their political demands and support. Money and its increasingly unequal distribution buys the rare opportunity to present self-serving information or raise problems that can be
addressed through a host of helpful, low-profile actions—inserting a rider
into an omnibus bill, for example, expediting the scheduling of a bill that
has been languishing in committee, or making sure that threatening regulatory legislation receives minimal funding for implementation (Gopoian
1984; Hall and Wayman 1990; Kroszner and Stratmann 1998; Langbein
1986).

Scholars are beginning to document the exact degree to which skewed
political demands and support are converted by the governing process
into policies and activities that disproportionately respond to business,
the wealthy, and the organized and vocal. Recent research (Bartels 2002)
documents that the votes of U.S. senators are almost three times more
likely to correspond with the policy preferences of their most privileged
constituents than with the preferences of their least privileged constituents, even though the latter are of course much more numerous. Bias in
government responsiveness is evident not only in Congress but also in
national government policy more generally. Government officials who design policy changes are more than twice as responsive to the preferences
of the rich as to those of the least affluent (Gilens 2003). Business and other
elites also exert far more influence than the public on U.S. foreign policy,
which not only guides the country's diplomatic and defense affairs but
also has powerful consequences for domestic economic conditions
through decisions on trade and the protection and promotion of American
jobs and enterprise (Jacobs and Page 2005).

We also need to consider the impact of public policies, once enacted, on
social stratification and further political activities. The authors of chapter 4
not only examine the overall impact of U.S. social programs. They also discuss an impressive and growing body of contemporary research on "policy
feedbacks"—that is, the ways in which policies, once enacted, modify government capacities and future patterns of political participation.[10]

Dramatic changes in private markets have increased economic inequality in a number of advanced industrialized nations—yet nations differ

considerably in the degree to which, and ways in which, they use public policies to modify or counteract market-generated disparities. Governments in Canada, Germany, Sweden, France, and other U.S. trading partners have limited increases in economic inequality and built floors under the least privileged through the use of regulations and tax policy as well as social programs.[11] By contrast, government policies and actions in the United States have been especially responsive to the values and interests of the most privileged Americans and therefore have often not undertaken active and effective steps to mute or offset market inequalities.

What the U.S. government does—and does not do—about economic disparities and insecurities influences political participation as well as social outcomes. Research shows that broad social programs such as the G.I. Bill of 1944 and the Social Security Act (as updated through the early 1970s) not only distributed economic benefits, but also encouraged ordinary citizens to increase their political participation (Mettler 2002; Campbell 2003). Recent social programs are likely to be narrowly targeted and to work in complex and relatively invisible ways through the tax code. Such programs may do less than major social programs of the past to boost the political engagement of ordinary Americans, especially those who are not elderly.

The effects of government inaction in the face of rising market-generated inequality are particularly evident in the economic and political conditions of less privileged minorities and women. One of the great stories of the past century in the United States has been the reduction of overt discrimination that once excluded millions of Americans from the core of political, economic, and social life. Well-educated women and minorities have benefited greatly from the removal of discriminatory barriers. In recent years, however, the reduction of overt discrimination has been countered by growing gaps in income and wealth, which have undermined economic progress and political inclusion for many, nonelite African Americans, Latinos, and women, even as equal opportunity and citizenship is also imperiled for many white men. Subsequent chapters demonstrate a general pattern of stalled progress and persistent political disparities: The political playing field remains highly unequal, and the immediate gains of the rights revolution have not yielded a sustained widening of political voice and influence in the governing process.

The chapters to come discuss many more developments and assess the contributions of many more factors than we have been able to mention in this brief overview. Furthermore, and as these snapshots suggest, this book does not present a simple picture of the impact of widening economic disparities on U.S. politics and government. Some relationships are relatively direct. Individual participation is socially stratified, for reasons that are increasingly well understood. And in a period when monetary contributions to politicians, parties, and interest groups are more and more important, the ability to give large chunks of money equips the growing ranks of the most affluent with a potent mechanism to express individual voice. Less privileged citizens may (or may not) find ways to band together to give money as well as votes, but as individuals their clout is less.

Other ways in which rising economic disparities may matter are less clear-cut, however, because socioeconomic shifts often work in complex interaction with slowly changing political institutions or with other ongoing changes that cannot be reduced to economic trends. New information technologies, for example, may magnify the effects of individuals and groups that are economically privileged enough to deploy them intensively. And long-standing "checks and balances" built into U.S. political institutions might promote pluralism under some socioeconomic conditions, but further entrench privilege under others—especially if the majority needs new government initiatives to mitigate effects of rising economic inequality and insecurity.

Indeed, in the final analysis, rising economic inequalities may have served primarily to counteract otherwise equalizing influences. As we have suggested, stasis in the situation of many African Americans may have resulted from the ways in which relative economic losses for less-privileged people have undercut the undoubted democratic gains of the Civil Rights movement.

An overriding theme of this volume is examination of the interconnections among economic and social inequalities, politics and governance, and public policies. This volume resists the all-too-common tendency of social science research to compartmentalize the study of American politics into discrete cubby holes (for research developments in political science see Task Force on Inequality and American Democracy 2004). We investigate the discrete aspects of American politics to assess the overall vitality and health of U.S. democracy in an age of rising inequality. Understanding the democratic political system requires persistent investigation into complex interrelationships with an eye toward consequences for society and polity.

The various ways in which rising inequality matters, either directly or indirectly, require careful unpacking with the benefit of the latest empirical research. The next three chapters make a solid start in pursuing such analyses, drawing together current findings from political science and neighboring disciplines. As the discussions of existing evidence and currently developed literatures make clear, the data we have to answer important questions are incomplete. Much additional theorizing and analysis remains for those who would unpack the complex, two-way relationships between socioeconomic change and politics. In our conclusion to this volume, we look toward the future, offering thoughts on the challenges that remain to be tackled by scholars determined to continue to probe the health and functioning of American democracy in an era of rising inequality.

NOTES

1. Nominated by Theda Skocpol, president of the American Political Science Association (APSA) from 2002 to 2003, and chaired by Lawrence Jacobs of the University of Minnesota, the Task Force on Inequality and American Democracy was appointed by the APSA in the fall of 2002. With support from the APSA and the Russell Sage Foundation, it began meeting in January 2003 and issued its report in June 2004. Fifteen scholars were appointed, of whom two were eventually unable to participate for personal reasons. In addition to Jacobs and Skocpol, the members were Ben Barber (University of Maryland); Larry Bartels (Princeton University); Morris Fiorina (Stanford University); Jacob Hacker (Yale University); Rodney Hero (Notre Dame University); Hugh Heclo (George Mason University); Suzanne Mettler (Syracuse University); Benjamin Page (Northwestern University); Dianne Pinderhughes (University of Illinois at Urbana-Champaign); Kay Lehman Schlozman (Boston College); and Sidney Verba (Harvard University).

2. Data on economic inequality has been collected from a number of authoritative sources including the U.S. government (for example, U.S. Bureau of the Census, U.S. Bureau of Labor Statistics, U.S. Bureau of Economic Analysis, and U.S. Internal Revenue Service) and the Luxembourg Income Study. Information on the distribution of income and other economic rewards in the United States can be found in Mishel, Bernstein, and Boushey (2003). Evidence that compares income and wealth distributions in the United States and other advanced-industrial democracies can be found in the Luxembourg Income Study (http://www.lisproject.org).

3. Unless otherwise noted, the next three paragraphs are based on Mishel, Bernstein, and Boushey (2003, 52–57, 86–94, 277–307, and table 1.8).

4. Although the Federal Reserve's Survey was conducted near the stock market's peak (1999), the value of the stock market remained at or near record levels even after its sharp decline (1999 to 2001) with the top 10 percent of households continuing to own over 69 percent of the country's net worth in 2001 compared to 2.8 percent among the bottom half, according to a study of the Federal Reserve Board's Survey of Consumer Finances (Kennickell 2003, table 5).

5. This analysis is based on Oliver and Shapiro (1997, 86–90, 96–103), a survey

of income and wealth among African Americans from 1987 to 1989. The survey shows that the median income for white households during that period was $25,384 as compared with $15,630 for their black counterparts; the net financial assets of whites was $43,800 compared with $3,700 for blacks. In terms of two-earner young couples (25 to 35 years old), white couples enjoyed a median income of $36,435 and a median net worth of $23,165 compared with an income of $29,377 for black couples and a net worth of $4,124.

6. Unless otherwise noted, the data cited in this paragraph is from NES. A valuable discussion of these patterns appears in Nye, Zelikow, and King (1997), especially the chapters by Gary Orren (1997), "Fall from Grace: The Public's Loss of Faith in Government," and Robert J. Blendon and others (1997), "Changing Attitudes in America."

7. 1995 survey is discussed in Blendon and others (1997, 210), and the 2000 poll was conducted by International Communications Research.

8. Most media discussion of turnout focuses on the number of ballots that are cast as a proportion of the number of individuals living in the United States who are 18 and older (Committee for the Study of the American Electorate 2004). The disenfranchisement of felons and other factors reduce the number of Americans who are actually eligible to vote (McDonald and Popkin 2001). Voter turnout in 2004 did rise, however, regardless of which method is used.

9. Relevant research is reviewed and synthesized in chapter 2. See especially Verba, Schlozman, and Brady (1995).

10. On the concept of policy feedback, see especially Hacker (2002); Heclo (1974); Mettler (2002) and Pierson (1993).

11. Many references appear in chapter 4. See also Freeman (1994) and Smeeding (2004).

REFERENCES

Ansolabehere, Stephen, John M. Figueiredo, and James M. Snyder. 2003. "Why Is There So Little Money in U.S. Politics?" *Journal of Economic Perspectives* 17(1): 105–30.

Bartels, Larry. 2002. "Economic Inequality and Political Representation." Paper presented at the Annual Meeting of the American Political Science Association, Boston, Mass. Available at: http://www.princeton.edu/~bartels/papers (accessed April 20, 2005).

Berry, Jeffrey M. 1999. *The New Liberalism: The Rising Power of Citizen Groups*. Washington, D.C.: Brookings Institution Press.

Blendon, Robert J., John M. Bensons, Richard Morin, Drew E. Altman, Mollyann Brodie, Marios Brossard, and Matt James. 1997. "Changing Attitudes in America." In *Why People Don't Trust Government*, edited by Joseph S. Nye Jr., Philip D. Zelikow, and David C. King. Cambridge, Mass.: Harvard University Press.

Brady, Henry E. 2004. "An Analytical Perspective on Participatory Inequality and Income Inequality." In *Social Inequality*, edited by Kathryn M. Neckerman. New York: Russell Sage Foundation.

Burtless, Gary. 1999. "Growing American Inequality: Sources and Remedies." In *Setting National Priorities: The 2000 Election and Beyond*, edited by Henry J. Aaron and Robert D. Reischauer. Washington, D.C.: Brookings Institution Press.

Campbell, Andrea Louise. 2003. *How Policies Make Citizens: Senior Political Activism and the American Welfare State*. Princeton, N.J.: Princeton University Press.

Committee for the Study of the American Electorate. 2004. "President Bush, Mobilization Drives, Propel Turnout to Post-1968 High." November. Available at: http://www.fairvote.org/reports/CSAE2004electionreport.pdf (accessed April 20, 2005).

Fiorina, Morris P. 1999. "Extreme Voices: A Dark Side of Civic Engagement." In *Civic Engagement in the United States*, edited by Theda Skocpol and Morris P. Fiorina. Washington, D.C., and New York: Brookings Institution Press and the Russell Sage Foundation.

Freeman, Richard, ed. 1994. *Working Under Different Rules*. A National Bureau of Economic Research project report. New York: Russell Sage Foundation.

———. 2004. "What, Me Vote?" In *Social Inequality*, edited by Kathryn M. Neckerman. New York: Russell Sage Foundation.

Gilens, Martin. 2003. "Unequal Responsiveness." Paper presented at conference on Inequality and American Democracy, Princeton University. November. Available at: http://www.princeton.edu/~csdp/events/pdfs/Gilens.pdf (accessed April 20, 2005).

Gopoian, J. David. 1984. "What Makes PACs Tick? An Analysis of the Allocation Patterns of Economic Interest Groups." *American Journal of Political Science* 28(2): 259–81.

Gottschalk, Peter. 1997. "Inequality, Income Growth, and Mobility: The Basic Facts." *Journal of Economic Perspectives* 11(2): 21–40.

Hacker, Jacob S. 2002. *The Divided Welfare State: The Battle over Public and Private Benefits in the United States*. New York: Cambridge University Press.

Hall, Richard L., and Frank W. Wayman. 1990. "Buying Time: Moneyed Interests and the Mobilization of Bias in Congressional Committees." *American Political Science Review* 84(3): 797–820

Heclo, Hugh. 1974. *Modern Social Politics in Britain and Sweden*. New Haven, Conn.: Yale University Press.

Jacobs, Lawrence, and Benjamin Page. 2005. "Who Influences U.S. Foreign Policy Over Time?" *American Political Science Review* 99(1): 107–24.

Kennickell, Arthur. 2003. "A Rolling Tide: Changes in the Distribution of Wealth in the U.S., 1989–2001." Federal Reserve Board, September 2003. Available at:

http://www.federalreserve.gov/pubs/oss/oss2/papers/concentration.2001.
10.pdf (accessed April 20, 2005).

Kroszner, Randall S., and Thomas Stratmann. 1998. "Interest Group Competition and the Organization of Congress: Theory and Evidence from Financial Services Political Action Committees." *American Economic Review* 88(5): 1163–87.

Langbein, Laura. 1986. "Money and Access: Some Empirical Evidence." *Journal of Politics* 48(4): 1052–62.

Leighley, Jan, and Jonathan Nagler. 1992. "Socioeconomic Class Bias in Turnout, 1964–1988: The Voters Remain the Same." *American Political Science Review* 86(3): 725–36.

McDonald, Michael P., and Samuel Popkin. 2001. "The Myth of the Vanishing Voter." *American Political Science Review* 95(4): 963–74.

Mettler, Suzanne. 2002. "Bringing the State Back In to Civic Engagement: Policy Feedback Effects of the G.I. Bill for World War II Veterans." *American Political Science Review* 96(2): 351–65.

Michaels, Walter Benn. 2004. "Diversity's False Solace." *New York Times Magazine*, April 11: 12–14.

Mishel, Larry, Jared Bernstein, and Heather Boushey. 2003. *The State of Working America, 2002–2003.* Ithaca, N.Y.: Cornell University Press.

Nye, Joseph S., Jr., Philip D. Zelikow, and David C. King, eds. *Why People Don't Trust Government.* Cambridge, Mass.: Harvard University Press.

Oliver, Melvin, and Thomas Shapiro. 1997. *Black Wealth, White Wealth.* New York: Routledge.

Orren, Gary. 1997. "Fall from Grace: The Public's Loss of Faith in Government." In *Why People Don't Trust Government*, edited by Joseph S. Nye Jr., Philip D. Zelikow, and David C. King. Cambridge, Mass.: Harvard University Press.

Page, Benjamin I., and Robert Y. Shapiro. 1992. *The Rational Public: Fifty Years of Trends in Americans' Policy Preferences.* Chicago: University of Chicago Press.

Pierson, Paul. 1993. "When Effect Becomes Cause: Policy Feedback and Political Change." *World Politics* 45(4): 595–628.

Piketty, Thomas, and Emmanuel Saez. 2003. "Income Inequality in the United States, 1913–1998." *Quarterly Journal of Economics* 118(1): 1–39.

Radcliff, Benjamin, and Patricia Davis. 2000. "Labor Organization and Electoral Participation in Industrial Democracies." *American Journal of Political Science* 44(1): 132–41.

Schier, Steven E. 2000. *By Invitation Only: The Rise of Exclusive Politics in the United States.* Pittsburgh, Penn.: University of Pittsburgh Press.

Skocpol, Theda. 2003. *Diminished Democracy: From Membership to Management in American Civic Life.* Norman: University of Oklahoma Press.

———. 2004a. "Voice and Inequality: The Transformation of American Civic Democracy." *Perspectives on Politics* 2(1): 3–20.

———. 2004b. "Civic Transformation and Inequality in the Contemporary United

States." In *Social Inequality*, edited by Kathryn M. Neckerman. New York: Russell Sage Foundation.

Skrentny, John D. 2002. *The Minority Rights Revolution*. Cambridge, Mass.: Harvard University Press.

Smeeding, Timothy. 2004. "Public Policy, Economic Inequality, and Poverty: The United States in Comparative Perspective." Revised version of paper presented at the conference on Inequality and American Politics, Maxwell School, Syracuse University (February). Available at: http://www-cpr.maxwell.syr.edu/faculty/smeeding/pdf/campbell%20paper_5.17.04.pdf (accessed April 21, 2005).

Task Force on Inequality and American Democracy. 2004. "American Democracy in an Age of Rising Inequality." *Perspectives on Politics* 2(4): 651–66.

Verba, Sidney, Kay Lehman Schlozman, and Henry E. Brady. 1995. *Voice and Equality: Civic Voluntarism in American Politics*. Cambridge, Mass.: Harvard University Press.

Weakliem, David L., Robert Andersen, and Anthony F. Heath. 2003. "The Directing Power? A Comparative Study of Public Opinion and Income Distribution." Unpublished paper, University of Connecticut, Storrs.

Wright, John R. 1985. "PACs, Contributions, and Roll Calls: An Organizational Perspective." *American Political Science Review* 79(2): 400–14.

———. 1990. "Contributions, Lobbying, and Committee Voting in the U.S. House of Representatives." *American Political Science Review* 84(2): 417–38.

Chapter Two | Inequalities of Political Voice

Kay Lehman Schlozman
Benjamin I. Page
Sidney Verba
Morris P. Fiorina

THE EXERCISE OF political voice goes to the heart of democracy. By their political participation citizens seek to control who will hold public office and to influence what policymakers do when they govern. In voting and other political participation, citizens communicate information about their preferences and needs and generate pressure on public officials to respond. Although politicians in America have many ways to learn what is on the minds of citizens by parsing the polls, reading the newspaper, listening to talk radio, or watching the evening news, the messages conveyed through citizen participation are essential to democratic governance. Beyond being instrumental in permitting activists to communicate their politically relevant concerns, participation itself is a value, conferring on the individual the dignity that comes with being a full member of the political community.

American citizens who wish to have an impact on politics have a variety of options for exercising political voice. They can communicate their concerns and opinions to policymakers to affect public policy directly, or they can seek to affect policy indirectly by influencing electoral outcomes. They can act on their own or work with others in informal efforts, formal organizations, political parties, or social movements. They can donate their time or their money. They can use conventional techniques or protest tactics. They can work locally or nationally. They can even have political input when, for reasons entirely outside politics, they become affiliated with a politically active organization or institution.

Students of civic involvement in America are unanimous in characterizing political input through political participation as being extremely unequal. The exercise of political voice is related most fundamentally to social class. Those who enjoy high levels of income, occupational status, and

19

especially education are much more likely to take part politically than are those who are less well endowed with these resources. Paralleling class differences in political participation are disparities on the basis of both gender and race or ethnicity.

What is much less clear is whether these inequalities have been exacerbated in recent decades. The last quarter century has seen a substantial increase in economic inequalities. Since the stagflation of the late 1970s gave way to relatively sustained periods of expansion, the fruits of economic growth have accrued disproportionately to those at the top of the economic hierarchy. There is, however, difference of opinion as to whether political inequalities have correspondingly become more pronounced. That is, the consensus about the extent of class-based inequalities in political voice does not extend to whether those political inequalities have grown in tandem with economic inequalities.

In this chapter we explore these matters with respect to the level of inequality of political voice and recent changes, if any, in the stratification of political voice. Our argument unfolds as follows. We begin by placing our concerns in the framework of public opinion by reviewing briefly what surveys can tell us about American attitudes toward inequality. We then proceed to examine inequalities of political voice paying attention to the representativeness of citizen communications in terms of both who takes part and what they say. In sequence we treat the expression of political voice through individual participation, organized interests, political parties, and social movements. In each case we investigate both the extent of political inequality and the way that the extent of political inequality has changed in recent years.

WHAT AMERICANS THINK ABOUT INEQUALITY

A central part of the background for our consideration of how the U.S. political system has responded, or failed to respond, to rising economic inequality and long-entrenched racial, ethnic, and gender inequalities is an understanding of what ordinary Americans think about these matters. Knowledge of the public's attitudes may help inform our normative thinking about what sorts of inequalities should be considered acceptable or unacceptable. To the extent that government policy responds to citizens' wishes, knowledge about public opinion on issues involving inequality may also affect our understanding of why the political system has reacted as it has.

Evidence about the public's views of inequality is complicated by the fact that the subject is complex. Sidney Verba and Gary Orren (1985, chap. 1) make several important distinctions that are useful in developing a full and nuanced portrait of the views of the American public. For example, with respect to the acceptable limits of inequality, members of the public might differ depending whether what is at stake is *economic* inequalities in income, wealth, or other benefits for which one would need to pay or *political* inequalities in power and influence. Moreover, it would be necessary to differentiate inequalities of opportunity from inequalities of result. That is, we would need to ask whether inequalities of condition reflecting individual differences in talent, industriousness, and perseverance are judged differently if, regardless of background, we are all equal at the starting line. It would also be necessary to investigate attitudes toward the ways that these inequalities—whether political or economic inequalities, or those of opportunity or condition—are enhanced or reduced by the operations of politics and markets. Actions taken by individuals, by private, nonprofit, and religious institutions, and by public authorities have consequences for levels of inequality; in its responses, the public is likely to differentiate among the sources of inequality and among the policies that affect inequality. Finally, it would be essential to distinguish between inequalities among *individuals* and among *groups* defined along a variety of dimensions—most notably for our purposes, class, race or ethnicity, and gender. That is, levels of inequality among individuals might be deemed less tolerable if those individual inequalities cumulate in such a way as to produce aggregate differences between women and men or among Asian Americans, Hispanics, African Americans, and non-Hispanic whites.

We sketch the outlines of Americans' views of inequality based on data from opinion surveys. Over time, large majorities of Americans have come to reject most legally enforced inequality or discrimination against particular social groups, even though support is uneven when it comes to government remedies for past discrimination. Particularly relevant to our concern with equal political voice, most Americans favor a high degree of political equality and seek a democracy in which people's voices weigh equally. In the economic realm, support for equality of opportunity is qualified by reluctance to embrace equality of result. Nevertheless, in spite of certain antiegalitarian biases in survey results, polls indicate that large majorities favor certain concrete policies (such as closing tax loopholes, generous funding of Social Security, and government help with education and medical care) that can have substantial egalitarian effects. Thus, evidence from surveys raises questions about whether inequalities of political voice may lead to government policies that do not fully reflect ordinary citizens' wishes.

Inequalities Among Social Groups

One of the great stories of the past century in the United States has been the gradual rejection of inequalities based on such social characteristics as race, gender, ethnicity, disability, or sexual orientation. More and more, Americans have come to oppose any government-enforced discrimination on such grounds. Most now say they oppose private prejudice and discrimination as well. The chief remaining areas of controversy concern whether and how laws and regulations should prohibit, or counteract the effects of, private discrimination.

The change in public attitudes about African Americans has been particularly dramatic. Between 1942 and 1985, the proportion of Americans saying that black and white children should go to the same schools (rather than "separate schools") rose in a steady, linear fashion, from a meager 31 percent to an overwhelming 93 percent. Similarly, the proportion of whites who opposed "separate sections for Negroes" on streetcars and buses grew from 46 percent in 1942 to 88 percent in 1970. The 45 percent minority who said in 1944 that "Negroes should have as good a chance as white people to get any kind of job" grew to a near-unanimous, 97 percent majority in 1972. Opinion also turned against the segregation of public accommodations and housing. Between 1963 and 1990, opposition to "laws against marriages between blacks and whites" rose from 38 percent to 79 percent.[1]

Still, even now, public support for federal government policies that enforce pro-integration principles is mixed. Only a minority of Americans—a proportion that declined in the 1970s and 1980s—has said that the government in Washington should "see to it" that schools are integrated. Large majorities oppose school busing or job quotas. Reactions to affirmative action depend on the details. Support for open housing laws has increased, reaching a small majority (57 percent) in favor by 1990. But only with respect to public accommodations, where racial interactions are transient and casual, have substantial and growing majorities of whites favored government action.[2]

Does this opposition to concrete measures for achieving integration and remedying past discrimination result from continuing racism? Or does it reflect broader, "race-neutral" principles, like individualism and color-blind application of the law? This question continues to provoke scholarly controversy. Some scholars tend to blame "symbolic racism" or "racial resentment." Others point toward ideological principles.[3]

With respect to gender discrimination, public opinion has also moved strongly in favor of legal equality for women. In 1937, only 18 percent of Americans said they approved of a woman "earning money in business or industry" if she had a "husband capable of supporting her." This figure rose markedly over the years to 82 percent in 1990. Large majorities oppose job discrimination and favor equal pay for equal work. The proposed Equal Rights Amendment regularly won 60 percent support, and fully 77 percent when the text was read to respondents.[4]

By 1982, affirmative action programs in *industry* ("provided there are no rigid quotas") won 72 percent support or higher with respect to women, "Spanish-Americans," blacks, and especially the physically handicapped. Support for "affirmative action programs in *higher education*" was a bit stronger. After hitting a plateau in the 1980s, support for such programs remains high. Even in the case of homosexuality, which many Americans still call "wrong," majorities do not think it should be illegal and oppose job discrimination—with some distinctions among occupations (Page and Shapiro 1992, 97–100). Moreover, Americans' attitudes toward homosexuality have become substantially more tolerant over the past two decades (Fiorina 2005, chap. 5).

Economic Inequalities

Americans' views of inequalities in the economic domain are multidimensional. Most Americans say that all people are "created equal" and strongly favor equality of opportunity. However, there is considerably more tolerance of inequality of economic results—especially when people perceive extensive opportunities to get ahead, or when economic inequality can be plausibly justified as providing incentives to work and invest in ways that may benefit everyone. At the same time, most Americans oppose what they see as unfair economic disparities that do not reflect merit or effort, and most favor a number of government programs with egalitarian effects.

Large majorities of Americans approve of private property and free enterprise. They believe that hard work and ambition are rewarded, that their children will be better off than they are, and that it benefits the country to have a class of rich people. But most Americans also think that the rich have too much political power and do not pay enough taxes. They consider lawyers, CEOs, doctors, investment bankers, and various celebrities to be "overpaid," while restaurant workers, school teachers, secretaries, policemen, nurses, and factory workers "underpaid." Most feel that "money and wealth in this country should be more evenly distributed."[5] These attitudes appear to vary somewhat with the business cycle and with international events. Economic downturns tend to produce more egalitarian sentiments, and extra sacrifices are sought from the affluent during major wars.

Government Action Against Economic Inequality   According to opinion surveys, although Americans are not necessarily more likely to embrace economic inequalities than are citizens of other advanced democracies, they are much more likely than Europeans to blame individuals rather than government for disparities of income and wealth. Perhaps reflecting a general skepticism about government, they also express little enthusiasm—less than people elsewhere—for redistribution of income or wealth by the government, at least when the issue is posed in the abstract.[6] For example, very few favor "a law limiting the amount of money any individual is allowed to earn in a year," and most agree that "people should be allowed to accumulate as much wealth as they can, even if some make millions while others live in poverty." On a 7-point scale, responses tilt only slightly more toward the sentiment that "Washington ought to reduce income differences between rich and poor," than toward the feeling that the "government should not concern itself" with such matters.[7]

At the same time, there has long been a difference between Americans' "ideological conservatism" and their "operational liberalism."[8] Considerable majorities favor a number of concrete policies that would have, or actually do have, substantial redistributive effects. Large numbers of Americans support having moderately—though not highly—progressive taxes. Most favor closing tax "loopholes" used by the wealthy. While most people call their own taxes "too high," antitax fervor among ordinary Americans is considerably weaker than politicians sometimes imply. Substantial majorities of the public are willing to pay the taxes needed to fund popular spending programs. In 2001 and 2003, for example, when large, regressive cuts in income and estate taxes were enacted, polls showed that substantial majorities of Americans would have preferred to keep the money and bolster the Social Security system or reduce the budget deficit. In 2004 as well, most said that they preferred budget balancing and more progressive taxes.[9]

It is noteworthy that Social Security—the largest single program in the federal budget—is extremely popular. The primary effect of Social Security is to smooth out middle-class people's incomes over their lifetimes, but it also redistributes incomes among individuals by providing substantial benefits even for those who had low incomes during their working lives. For that reason, poverty experts have called Social Security "crucial" in reducing poverty among the elderly (Blank 1997, 228; Page and Simmons 2000, chap. 4). Year after year, the overwhelming majority of Americans have said that they want to keep Social Security at its present level or spend more on it; only a tiny minority wants to cut back. There has been considerable resistance to any "reforms" that would reduce guaranteed Social Security benefits in any way, even through reduced cost-of-living increases or stretched-out retirement ages. What appears to be high public support for partial privatization of the program (for example, allowing individuals to invest part of their payroll taxes in personal retirement accounts) drops sharply when it is made clear that such a change would imply cuts in guaranteed benefits. This pattern remained unchanged in early 2005, as President Bush began his serious push for private accounts.[10]

The American public also generally favors universalistic government help with education (including day care and pre-schooling), which can be a major equalizing force in society. Most Americans want government help with jobs and employment, including a surprising (though seldom surveyed) level of support for job creation through public works programs. Large majorities want to help the uninsured get health care, and favor a variety of possible methods including the expansion of Medicare to younger people, providing catastrophic health insurance coverage to everyone, expanding community health clinics, and subsidizing private health insurance. The term "welfare" is despised, but a wide range of programs for the "deserving" poor win public approval, so long as the able-bodied are willing to work. Public support has been high, for example, for Supplemental Security Income, Unemployment Insurance, and even the former Aid for Families with Dependent Children. Well into the George W. Bush administration, large majorities of Americans said they favored universal, government-run health insurance.[11]

Political Inequalities

In contrast to the economic realm, substantial majorities of Americans endorse a high degree of equality in the realm of politics—in terms of both abstract principles and concrete legal arrangements. For example, in an early study with a local sample, as many as 95 percent of Americans endorsed the idea that "every citizen should have an equal chance to influence government policy"; and 91 percent said that everyone should have an equal right to hold public office. True, roughly half of Americans have said that government should pay most attention to "people of intelligence and character" or to "the people who really know something about the subject." But large majorities have said that elected officials would "badly misuse their power" if they were not watched by voters, and that elections are one of the best ways to keep officials on their toes. A large majority of Americans have said that all adult citizens should be allowed to vote, "regardless of how ignorant they may be" (McClosky and Zaller 1984, 74, 75, 79).

When it comes to specific institutional arrangements, most Americans favor a variety of reforms aimed at reducing political inequalities in the control of government. Even before the controversies surrounding the 2000 presidential election, solid majorities of Americans (73 percent or 86 percent in different polls) favored abolishing the Electoral College and electing the president by popular vote. Equally large majorities of 70 percent or 80 percent have also favored choosing presidential candidates in a nationwide primary rather than through party conventions. Before the 1971 ratification of the Twenty-sixth Amendment, 60 percent to 70 percent of Americans favored granting the vote to eighteen-year-olds. Concerned about the power of money in politics, substantial majorities of Americans favor limits on private campaign contributions and on campaign spending—not, however, public financing of elections (Page and Shapiro 1992, 166–67).

UNEQUAL VOICES IN SURVEYS WEIGHING PUBLIC OPTION

These opinions are mostly those expressed in national public opinion surveys—which, by interviewing random samples of adult Americans, try to ascertain what all Americans think. In such surveys, everyone is supposed to have an equal voice. Yet there is evidence that surveys do not in fact report the opinions of all citizens equally, and that the results are biased in the direction of making Americans' opinions seem less egalitarian than they actually are.

The problem is that in forming political opinions, and expressing them to survey interviewers, is easier for those who have abundant resources in skills, income, and, especially, education. Less advantaged people—who also have real political wants and needs—are more likely to be uncertain or confused or to say "don't know" when interviewers ask their opinions. Natural supporters of egalitarian social welfare policies are also the least likely to register their opinions. By contrast, the very people who have abundant resources and make their voices most heard in surveys are the same people who are least concerned about gaps between the rich and the poor.

As a result, survey data appear to be subject to a consistent "exclusion bias" that tends to make Americans look, on average, somewhat more conservative and antiegalitarian (less likely, for example, to say that government should "reduce income differences between the rich and the poor") than they actually are. This bias has been estimated to be rather small—smaller, for example, than the resource-related biases, discussed later in this report, in voting and nearly every other form of individual or collective political input. Still, the exclusion bias appears to reinforce other political barriers faced by disadvantaged.[12] The survey results presented here reveal substantial proegalitarian sentiments despite this bias. Data corrected for the bias would probably move further in the same direction, especially on issues of economic inequality and redistribution.

Public Opinion as Effect Rather than Cause

In democratic political systems it is natural to think of public opinion as a cause, or at least a possible cause, of what governments do. We tend to judge how well democracy works partly in terms of how well government policies correspond with what citizens say they want. But this way of thinking neglects the possibility that public opinion may be an effect as well as a cause of political processes. Charles E. Lindblom referred to this as the problem of "circularity."[13] If political leaders, organized interest groups, large corporations or others can manipulate the opinions of ordinary citizens, democracy will be compromised even though the government responds perfectly to those opinions. If public opinion can be manipulated, and if the tools of opinion manipulation are most available to the wealthy and powerful—who tend to occupy "bully pulpits" and to have the rhetorical skills or money needed to persuade others—the result may be a subtle, indirect, but pervasive kind of inequality in political influence.

It is fairly well established that the political contents of the mass media—especially the reported views of ostensibly nonpartisan commentators and "experts"—tend to affect the priorities and policy preferences of the public (Iyengar and Kinder 1987; Page, Shapiro, and Dempsey 1987). It is also well known that what appears in the media is heavily influenced by public officials, who are major sources of political news, and that business corporations spend a great deal of money funding the think-tanks, universities, and foundations that produce and publicize "expert" opinions. Corporations and others have also spent large amounts of money on issue advocacy advertisements, often trying to turn the public against egalitarian policies (Saloma 1984; Stefancic and Delgado 1996; West and Loomis 1998). Still, it is very difficult to ascertain the net impact, if any, of this activity on public opinion. And even when there are measurable effects, the interpretation is often disputed. If ordinary citizens change their opinions in response to persuasion by public officials or other policy elites, how are we to discern whether the process is one of "education" or "manipulation"? At minimum, it seems important to bear in mind the possibility that the wealthier and more powerful members of American society have been able to influence the opinions of the less affluent, reducing public support for policies that would combat economic inequality and adding to inequalities of political voice.

Similar problems arise in attempting to assess the possibility that recent increases in economic inequality have themselves affected public opinion, perhaps by making people angry, cynical, and distrustful of government, which they may see as not doing much about—or, even, as exacerbating—their troubles. Seymour Martin Lipset and William Schneider (1983) demonstrate that much of the sharp decline in Americans' trust and confidence in government and other institutions occurred very early—in the late 1960s and early 1970s—before economic inequality began to increase. The causes of these declines, then, may have had more to do with political disenchantment over Vietnam and Watergate than with economic trends. But the long subsequent history of negative political attitudes, punctuated by protest candidates and rejections of incumbent officials, suggests that economic stagnation and increased gaps between rich and poor may indeed have contributed to the souring of the political views of many Americans or, at a minimum, reinforced the distrust that was precipitated by Vietnam and Watergate. We cannot be sure.

Public Opinion and Egalitarian Policies

This broad framework of opinion should be taken into account as we think about the reasons for egalitarian and antiegalitarian public policies. To recapitulate, although most Americans support a high level of equality among social groups and favor equality of opportunity, they appear to be less concerned about inequality in economic outcomes. For example, there is little public support for a massive redistribution of income or wealth. At the same time, however, there can be little doubt that large majorities of Americans prefer a democracy with a high level of political equality among citizens. Moreover, most support a number of concrete government policies that have, or would have, substantially egalitarian economic effects.

To anticipate issues that will be raised later in this book, if we wish to judge the extent to which political equality among citizens does or does not prevail in policymaking, it can be useful to compare policies that are actually enacted and implemented with policies that majorities of Americans say they favor. Evidence indicates that most Americans favor a number of policies that would tax the wealthy and upper-income people at higher levels, and spend more money to help middle- and lower-income people, than is currently the case. In other words, there are indications of something other than perfect political equality in U.S. policymaking. It is not the case that every citizen has one effective vote, one equal amount of influence upon political outcomes.[14] If this leads to a tilt against egalitarian public policies, political inequality in the United States may tend to reinforce economic inequalities.

WHY DO WE CARE ABOUT EQUAL POLITICAL VOICE?

Discussions about democratic participation are ordinarily conducted as if the reasons why we care about it are self-evident. Rather than make such presumptions, it seems appropriate to make it explicit why political voice matters. Political participation is often placed in the context of civic engagement construed more generally. Voluntary activity benefits both the community by cultivating democratic virtues and cooperation in the name of the common good as well as the individual by developing capacities and skills and by instilling a sense of dignity as a full member of the community.

Equal Protection of Interests

When we separate political involvement from other forms of civic engagement a different rationale emerges, one that focuses on equal protection of interests. This perspective acknowledges the conflicting interests of individuals and groups and reflects James Madison's fundamental insight in *Federalist* No.10 that differences of opinion are sown in the nature of humankind, especially in the unequal acquisition of property. Through the medium of political participation, citizens communicate information about their preferences and needs for government action and generate pressure on public officials to heed what they hear. Of course, we know that public officials act for many reasons only one of which is their assessment of what the public wants and needs. And policymakers have ways other than the medium of citizen participation of learning what citizens want and need from the government. Nonetheless, what public officials hear clearly influences what they do. Therefore, so long as citizens differ in their opinions and interests, the level playing field of democracy requires that we take seriously the fact that citizens differ in their capacity, and desire, to exercise political voice. The democratic principle of one-person, one-vote is the most obvious manifestation of the link between voluntary participation and equal protection of interests. However, for forms of voluntary political participation beyond the vote—for example, writing letters to public officials, attending protests, making political contributions, joining organizations, working for a political party—there is no such mandated equality of participatory input. When placed in the context of equal protection of interests in a democracy, concerns about the aggregate quantity of civic engagement become less significant and questions of representation come to the fore. What matters is not only the amount of civic activity but its distribution, not just how many people take part but who they are and what they say.

Although the evidence about public opinion that we have just seen suggests that Americans are, on average, less comfortable with political inequalities than with economic inequalities, theorists of democracy raise normative and practical concerns about political equality as a democratic value. One perspective, which has been present in various guises throughout American history, implicitly endorses inequalities of political voice. Underlying property requirements for the franchise in the colonies and the early days of the republic and intermittent demands for educational requirements or literacy tests thereafter is a fear of the mob and an understanding that political voice is appropriately exercised by those who can be trusted to do so with wisdom and respect for democratic process.[15] A different approach is more utilitarian. While inequalities of political voice may be regrettable from the perspective of democratic theory, the costs of addressing those inequalities—whether measured in economic terms or construed in terms of tradeoffs among competing democratic values such as liberty—do not justify the effort.

Others raise the difficulty of reconciling concern about political equality with some deference to views that are intensely held. The question of how to weight the strength of collective preferences is a problematic one in democratic theory. To ignore the fact that some people care deeply about a particular issue while the large majority is more or less indifferent would seem to be perverse and unreasonable. In fact, as Madison makes clear, once again in *Federalist* No. 10, the structure of the American government was established to ensure that majority factions do not always prevail. Yet, unless some mechanism is designed to equalize political voice across multiple issues, to allow an intense minority to prevail over and over risks violating the principle of political equality. In the abstract, the principle of political equality can be harmonized with respect for intensity of preferences by insisting that everyone have the same amount of total political influence while allowing the individual to specify the issues—one, a few, or many—over which that equal allocation of influence will be spent.

What About the Satisfied and Indifferent?

Specifying this ideal version of political equality—equal inputs from all citizens distributed among issues as each individual sees fit—immediately raises another question. What about people who are genuinely content with the policy status quo or who really do not care about political outcomes? Do the dictates of equality of political voice require equal input from the satisfied and the indifferent? From the perspective of democratic theory, are inequalities of political voice that are related to differences in how much people care about politics or in how they appraise what is good for them politically less worrisome that inequalities arising from other sources—in particular, group-based differences in resources? That is, if hairdressers, convenience store clerks, secretaries, and gas station attendants do not take part in politics and do not have organized representation because they are satisfied with current public policies or would rather spend their time and energy going hiking or fishing than attending school board meetings, then should their lack of political voice be deemed less consequential? Or does the principle of equal protection of interests require equal voice for all regardless of the level of political interest or awareness?

One perspective that is more congenial to political inequalities of result draws an implicit analogy between economic and political life. According to this construction, the requirements of democracy are essentially procedural and what are needed are equal rights for all citizens. So long as all enjoy equal opportunity in the political realm—a condition that has often been violated in American history—inequalities of political voice may be considered acceptable. A variant of this argument concedes that equal rights may not confer equal capacity to exercise political voice. However, if inequalities in political voice reflect differences in taste, rather than differences in the resources of time, money and skills that make effective participation possible, they are easier to justify.

The normative issue of how we assess political silence that arises from satisfaction with or indifference to policy outcomes raises an empirical one: does a lack of activity or organization inevitably imply a lack of political concern? The absence of advocacy or organized representation for what would seem to be a politically relevant interest is sometimes construed as prima facie evidence for an absence of political concern on the part of those who might be presumed to have political interests. However, as we shall see, there are multiple barriers to political mobilization, most of which have nothing to do with lack of concern.

Understanding Collective Action

Scholars have paid a great deal of attention to the problem of collective action and have pointed to the hurdles to group mobilization, especially when the group in question is relatively large and not well endowed with political resources. In particular, Mancur Olson (1965) has pointed out that large, diffuse groups lacking the capacity to coerce cooperation or to provide selective benefits often face severe collective action problems that prevent them from organizing on behalf of their joint political concerns.[16] According to Olson, the rational individual has an incentive not to spend scarce resources of money and time in support of favored causes but rather to free ride on the efforts of others. Only when an organization has the capacity to force a potential free rider to support group efforts or when it supplies benefits available only to those who assist in the collective effort will an organization emerge and prosper.

Others have pointed out that Olson's argument neglects the significance of the costs of organization, costs that not all potential constituencies are in a position to bear. These costs are not simply financial although money is surely a necessity. The affluent and well-educated are not only able to afford the financial costs of organizational support but they are in a better position to command the skills, acquire the information, and take advantage of connections that are helpful in getting an organization off the ground or keeping it going. In short, a group of jointly interested citizens that is well endowed with a variety of kinds of resources is more likely to overcome the hurdle posed by the logic of collective action than is a group of similar size and similar intensity of concern that is resource-poor. For all these reasons, it is erroneous to assume that the amount of organization activity is a surrogate for intensity of group political preferences or that the underrepresentation in organized political groups of those with fewer resources indicates indifference to political outcomes.

POLITICAL PARTICIPATION AND EQUALITY OF POLITICAL VOICE

Citizens in American democracy have many options for expressing their political voice including the sending of messages directly to policymakers or seeking indirect influence through the electoral process. It is widely known, however, that participation in American politics is anything but universal and that those who do take part are, in important ways, not representative of the public at large.[17] These days, only about half of Americans vote in a presidential election. Much smaller proportions take part in more demanding and costly activities such as working in an electoral campaign, getting in touch with a public official, making a campaign contribution, getting involved in an organization that takes political stands, or taking part in a protest or demonstration. Not only are many citizens politically inactive, but the processes by which people come to take part imply that, taken together, activists are not representative of the American public and, thus, that public officials are disproportionately likely to hear from people with certain politically relevant characteristics.

Various political acts differ with respect to the extent to which the participatory public is representative. At one end of the continuum is the vote.[18] Although once construed as a privilege rather than a right of citizens, the vote is now widely considered to be fundamental to democracy. Through their votes, citizens in a democracy choose their leaders and hold them accountable for their conduct in office. Democratizing regimes inevitably establish procedures for national elections even if they neglect other guarantees—for example, the right to dissent—that are usually deemed essential to a functioning democracy. Voters are not only the most numerous but also the most representative group of political activists. As

Table 2.1   Voter Registration and Turnout

	Percentage Reporting They Registered		Percentage Reporting They Voted	
	1998	2000	1998	2000
Education				
Eight years or less	40.2%	36.1%	24.6%	26.8%
High school				
One to three years	43.4	45.9	25.0	33.6
Four years	58.6	60.1	37.1	49.4
College				
One to three years	68.3	70.0	46.2	60.3
Four years or more	75.1	77.3	57.2	72.0
Race				
White	63.9	65.6	43.3	56.4
Black	60.2	63.6	39.6	53.5
Hispanic	33.7	34.9	20.0	27.5
Sex				
Male	60.6	62.2	41.4	53.1
Female	63.5	65.6	42.4	56.2
Age				
Eighteen to twenty years old	32.1	40.5	13.5	28.4
Twenty-one to twenty-four years old	43.1	49.3	19.2	24.2
Twenty-five to thirty-four years old	52.4	54.7	28.0	43.7
Thirty-five to forty-four years old	62.4	63.8	40.7	55.0
Forty-five to sixty-four years old	71.1	71.2	53.6	64.1
Sixty-five years old and over	75.4	76.1	59.5	67.6

Source: U.S. Census Bureau, *Statistical Abstract.*

shown in table 2.1, there are significant group differences in turnout. Nevertheless, the extent of participatory inequality is much less pronounced when it comes to voting than it is for political activities that demand more in the way of resources or skills—for example, contacting a public official, getting involved in a campaign, or sitting on the local zoning board.

At the other end of the continuum, campaign contributors, especially those who make large donations, are the least representative group of activists. Not only are campaign donors an unrepresentative group of individuals but, unlike voters, they can easily raise the volume of their political voice. In spite of campaign finance laws placing upward boundaries on campaign contributions, the amount of individual political input through the medium of campaign contributions can be multiplied to an extent that is unique among political acts. When it comes to voting, the principle of democratic equality is legally mandated: we each get only one per election. Even the most prolific of letter writers or the most industrious of meeting goers cannot multiply participatory input to the extent that a generous donor can. In 2000, when 26 percent of Americans age twenty-five and over had completed at least a bachelor's degree, fully 85 percent of those who made donations of over $1,000 to a presidential candidate had at least a bachelor's degree. In fact, 58 percent of that group of significant donors, compared with only 9 percent of Americans twenty-five and over, had attained a graduate degree. While only 12 percent of American households had incomes over $100,000 in 2000, 95 percent of the substantial donors did.[19]

Group Differences in Participation

As the evidence just presented suggests, foremost among the characteristics associated with political participation is socioeconomic status. Study after study has demonstrated that individuals with high socio-economic status—that is, those who have high levels of education, income, and occupational status—are much more likely to be politically active. This relationship, which obtains for all democracies, is especially pronounced in the United States. Figure 2.1 uses data from a 1990 survey of the American public to contrast the political activity of two income groups, each of which constituted roughly one fifth of the sample—those having family incomes below $15,000 and those at the top of the income ladder with family incomes over $75,000.[20] For instance, nearly nine out of ten individuals in families with incomes over $75,000 reported voting in presidential elections while only half of those in families with incomes under $15,000 reported voting. This pattern of class structuring of voter turnout has been documented in a variety of analyses including those based on census data and validated votes.[21] The gap in voting between the well-off and the poor is also evident, or even greater, for the other seven political activities listed in figure 2.1: working in a campaign; making a campaign contribution; getting in touch with a public official; taking part in a protest, march, or demonstration; getting involved in an informal effort to solve a community problem; serving as an unpaid volunteer on a local governing board such as a school board or city council; and being affiliated with an organization that takes stands in politics. While there are different ways to measure the magnitude of the differences, it is clear that the disparity in activ-

Figure 2.1   Percentage Active in Various Activities: High and Low
Income Groups

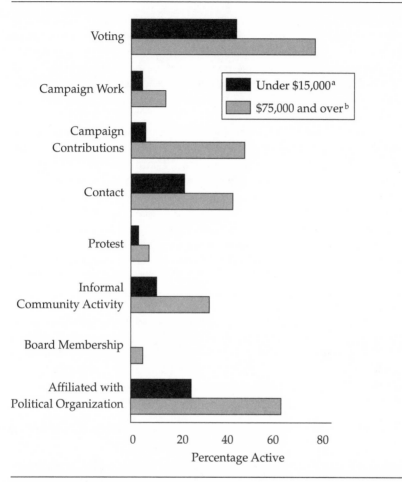

Source: Verba, Schlozman, and Brady (1995, 190). Reprinted by permission of the publisher
from *Voice and Equality: Civic Voluntarism in American Politics* by Sidney Verba, Kay Lehman
Schlozman, and Henry E. Brady, Cambridge, Mass.: Harvard University Press, Copyright ©
1995 by the President and Fellows of Harvard College.
[a] N = 483 weighted cases
[b] N = 224 weighted cases

ity between the two income groups is especially wide when it comes to
making campaign contributions.

Interestingly, even protesting—which demands little in the way of
skills or money and is often thought of as "the weapon of the weak"—is

characterized by the pattern of socioeconomic bias. The successes of the labor and civil rights movements illustrate the possibilities for the disadvantaged when they mobilize collectively. However, the United States also has a long tradition of middle-class protest movements ranging from abolition and temperance to environmentalism and disarmament. The bottom line is that, even when it comes to protest, the well-educated and well-heeled are more likely to take part. In fact, when the protesters in this survey were asked about the issue or problem at stake in their activity, those who had demonstrated about a national issue were far more likely to mention abortion than any other issue.

Participatory input is associated not only with socioeconomic status but also with race or ethnicity, gender, and age. In terms of overall participation, non-Hispanic whites are more politically active than African Americans and, especially, Hispanics. However, as shown in table 2.2, this rank order does not always obtain when we consider particular forms of political activity, and the differences between African Americans and non-Hispanic whites are, for most activities, small in magnitude and inconsistent in direction. Blacks are more likely to have reported taking part in a protest, engaging in informal community activity and, perhaps, reflecting the timing of the survey in the aftermath of Jesse Jackson's 1988 presidential bid, working in a political campaign. In contrast, for most of the activities, Hispanics, even Hispanic citizens, were less likely to report having taken part.

When it comes to gender, as shown in figure 2.2, the differences are small in magnitude and consistent in direction: except for protesting, men

Table 2.2   Political Activities by Race and Ethnicity

Activity	Non-Hispanic Whites	African Americans	Hispanics	Hispanic Citizens
Vote	73%	65%	41%	52%
Campaign work	8	12	7	8
Campaign contributions	25	22	11	12
Contact	37	24	14	17
Protest	5	9	4	4
Informal community activity	17	19	12	14
Board member	4	2	4	5
Affiliated with a political organization	52	38	24	27

Source: Verba, Schlozman, and Brady (1995, 233). Reprinted by permission of the publisher from *Voice and Equality: Civic Voluntarism in American Politics* by Sidney Verba, Kay Lehman Schlozman, and Henry E. Brady, Cambridge, Mass.: Harvard University Press, Copyright © 1995 by the President and Fellows of Harvard College.

Figure 2.2   Political Activities by Gender

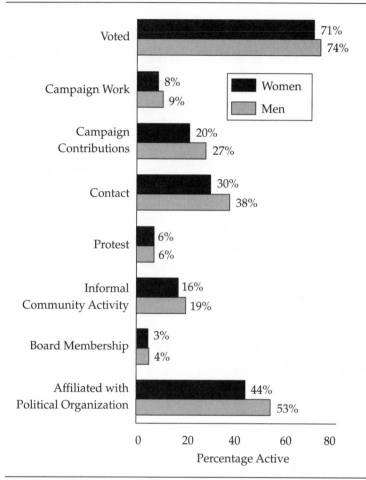

Source: Verba, Schlozman, and Brady (1995, 255). Reprinted by permission of the publisher from *Voice and Equality: Civic Voluntarism in American Politics* by Sidney Verba, Kay Lehman Schlozman, and Henry E. Brady, Cambridge, Mass.: Harvard University Press, Copyright © 1995 by the President and Fellows of Harvard College.

were slightly more likely than women to have taken part in each of the political activities on the list.[22] The pattern of gender differences in figure 2.2 is, however, somewhat unexpected. It has sometimes been argued that the masculine advantage with respect to political participation derives from an emphasis on electoral forms of activity. However, when the definition of political activity is expanded to encompass informal community activity and organizational affiliation—forms of involvement in which women

Figure 2.3   Overall Political Activity by Race or Ethnicity

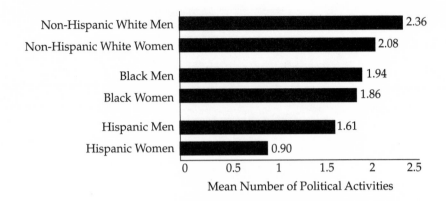

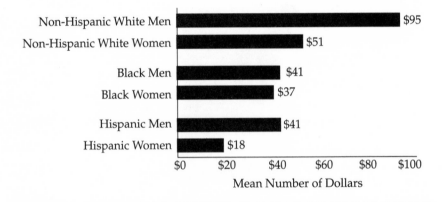

Source: Burns, Schlozman, and Verba (2001, 278). Reprinted by permission of the publisher from *The Private Roots of Public Action,* by Nancy E. Burns, Kay Lehman Schlozman, and Sidney Verba, Cambridge, Mass.: Harvard University Press, Copyright © 2001 by the President and Fellows of Harvard College.

have been presumed to specialize—the gender gap in participation does not disappear.

Figure 2.3 considers the overall activity, as measured by the average score on an additive scale of these eight activities and the average number of dollars donated to political campaigns and causes, of the groups defined by race or ethnicity and gender. When it comes to various kinds of political activity, both race or ethnicity and gender play a role. In a pattern that is repeated over and over, when the scale is taken apart into its individual components, non-Hispanic white men are the most active, Latina

Figure 2.4   Mean Number of Political Acts by Age

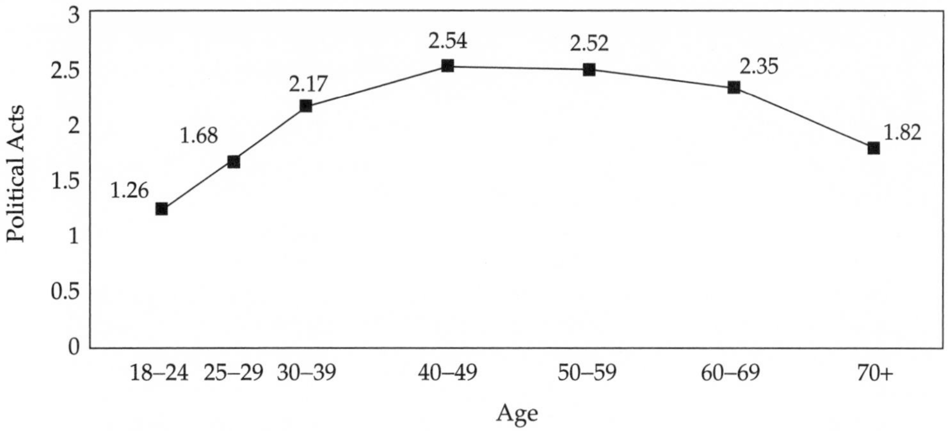

Source: Schlozman et al. (2001).

women the least. Overall, non-Hispanic whites are more active than African Americans, who are, in turn, more active than Hispanics. Within each group defined by race or ethnicity, women are less active than men. However, the size of the gender gap varies across the groups defined by their race or ethnicity and is widest, by far, among Latinos and narrowest among African Americans. With respect to political giving, non-Hispanic white men donate the largest amounts, and the gender disparity is widest in absolute dollars among non-Hispanic whites, whose levels of contributions are highest, and in relative terms among Latinos.

Figure 2.4 confirms the widely observed pattern of life-cycle variation in political activity: participation rates are low among younger citizens, rise steadily before peaking in middle age, and drop off somewhat among the elderly. The age disparities are substantial: the gap in activity between those under twenty-five and the forty-somethings is wider than that between non-Hispanic white men and Latina women. This curvilinear pattern is remarkably consistent when particular political acts are considered separately. However, as usual, there are variations. While those under thirty generally post very low rates of political activity, they are about average in their rate of campaign participation and are the age group most likely to take part in a protest. At the other end of the life cycle, as we saw in table 2.1, the elderly continue to go to the polls. In contrast, the decline in senior participation is especially steep when it comes to informal community activity and contacts with public officials.

Explaining Group Differences

Cataloguing the groups that are under- or overrepresented among activists does not, however, *explain* group differences in activity. It is essential to understand what it is about being, say, well-educated, non-Hispanic white, male, or middle-aged that leads to higher levels of participation. With respect to the substantial, and widely noted, socioeconomic bias in political participation, political scientists have begun to elaborate the causal links between political activity and high levels of income, occupation, and education.[23] In particular, they have demonstrated why education is so central to the relationship between socioeconomic status and participation. Not only does education have a direct impact on political activity, but more important, education has indirect effects through its consequences for the acquisition of nearly every other participatory factor. The well-educated earn higher incomes on the job; are more likely to develop civic skills at work, in organizations, and, to a lesser extent, in church; are more likely to receive requests for political activity; and are more politically interested and knowledgeable.

The explanation for the relationship between socioeconomic status and political donations is, not unexpectedly, quite straightforward. In contrast to forms of political involvement for which command of civic skills or location in the networks through which requests for political activity are mediated, or for which political interest and information help to predict who will take part, what really matters when it comes to making political contributions is the size of the bank balance. Family income plays an overwhelming role in explaining not only who will make political contributions but how large those contributions will be.

With respect to participatory disparities among groups defined by race or ethnicity, once group differences in participatory resources—in particular, education, income, and job-related civic skills—are taken into account, the disparities in participation among non-Hispanic whites, African Americans, and Latinos disappear. Although systematic national data are not readily available, it seems that this analysis does not hold for Asian Americans, who are less politically active than would be expected on the basis of their class-based participatory factors (Citrin and Highton 2002, chap. 2).[24]

Disparities in class-based participatory resources are also front-and-center when it comes to gender differences in activity. However, in contrast to the circumstance for non-Hispanic whites, African Americans, and Latinos, they do not fully explain the gap between women and men in political activity. Several factors contribute to the disparity in participation between men and women. First, men have, on average, higher levels of education than women do. In addition, because they are more likely than women to be in the work force and, if employed, more likely to hold jobs that permit the acquisition of organizational and communications skills useful in politics and exposure to requests for political participation, men have an advantage when it comes to work-based participatory factors. Moreover, men are more likely than women to be psychologically engaged with politics—that is, to be politically interested, informed, and efficacious. Once these factors are taken into account, the gender gap in political activity closes.

The deficit in activity of the young is both more complicated and more difficult to explain. It is commonly asserted that the younger citizens are less likely to take part because they have not yet settled down. According to this story, once they acquire the roles and responsibilities of adulthood—full-time jobs, families, and mortgages—they will become more active. In fact, the acquisition of adult statuses works in very complex ways to influence political participation. With other factors taken into account, these adult roles and responsibilities do not have an independent impact on participation. That is, going to work, getting a job, and having children do not themselves raise participation. Indeed, those who leave school early and get married, have children, and work full time in their teens or early twenties are likely to be less, not more, active than their peers. Furthermore, the nexus among marriage, children, and work force status is different for men and women: a spouse and children operate to push men into the work force; for women, the effect is the opposite. Still, some of these adult statuses are associated with the resources, recruitment, and political orientations that predict political activity. In particular, having work that is well paid and highly skill-endowing is central to the cultivation of the factors that foster participation. Nonetheless, in contrast to the circumstance for gender or race, differences in participatory endowments among age groups do not fully explain the gap in participation between the young and their elders. Indeed, even after all the factors we have been discussing have been taken into account, the unexplained difference in activity between those in their twenties and those in their forties is actually larger than the initial disparity between blacks and whites or between women and men.

What Do Policymakers Hear?

Understanding the origins of group differences in participation, however, does not put the matter of equal political voice to rest. Although memberships in demographic groups may not be the key to causal understanding of political activity, they are fundamental to politics. It is not enough simply to understand, for example, that disparities in participation among Latinos, African Americans, and non-Hispanic whites stem not from race or ethnicity but from group differences in participatory factors, most of which are rooted in class differences. For one thing, focusing on the way that class differences among racial and ethnic groups account for participatory differences does not obviate the fundamental question of why there are such enduring and pronounced socioeconomic differences among groups defined by their race or ethnicity. Class differences along racial or ethnic lines reflect the legacy of historical and social processes that have everything to do with racial or ethnic status.

Furthermore, the fact that socioeconomic differences are behind differences in participation among racial and ethnic groups does not obviate the fact that policymakers are hearing less from African Americans or, especially, Latinos. These are groups with distinctive political preferences and participatory agendas: they differ in their opinions on public matters and, when they are active, they are concerned with a different mix of issues. Hence, it makes a difference with respect to equal protection of interests if participatory messages to policymakers underrepresent input from African Americans and Latinos. That the sources of these group differences in activity lie in characteristics other than race or ethnicity does not vitiate the political significance of disparities in participation. The same logic obtains for participatory differences rooted in groups defined by gender, age, or such politically relevant characteristics as citizenship status or dependence upon government benefits. When the messages to public officials are skewed, then the democratic norm of equal responsiveness to all is potentially compromised.

Do Demographic Differences in Political Voice Matter?

One important line of reasoning suggests that participatory differences among demographic groups do not really matter. In a significant analysis of the representativeness of the electorate, Raymond Wolfinger and Steven Rosenstone (1980, chap. 6) demonstrate that, although the electorate is not demographically representative of the public at large, voters do not differ from nonvoters in their partisan leanings or their opinions on policy matters as expressed in surveys. That is, although those who go to the polls differ from those who stay home in many ways—for example, in age, race or ethnicity, or level of income and education—their answers to questions in public opinion polls are quite similar.

However, taking a broader view of the attributes of citizens that matter for politics—encompassing not just demographics and policy positions as expressed in response to survey questions but also other circumstances that are relevant for policy and the actual content of participatory input—sheds a different light on this finding.[25] Political participants can be distinguished from inactives in many ways that are politically very significant:

although similar in their attitudes, activists are distinctive in their personal circumstances and dependence upon government benefits, in their priorities for government action, and in what they say when they get involved. These disparities are exacerbated when we move from the most common political act, voting, to acts that are more difficult, convey more information, and can be multiplied in their volume.

Consider, for example, economic needs and circumstances. Compared with those who are politically quiescent, those who take part in politics are much less likely to have experienced a need to trim their sails economically—to have been forced to work extra hours to get by, to have delayed medical treatment for economic reasons, or to have cut back on spending on food. Predictably, almost no one among substantial campaign donors reported having cut back financially to make ends meet. Not only are there differences in economic circumstances, there are differences in their need for various kinds of government assistance. Those who receive such means-tested government benefits as food stamps and housing subsidies are underrepresented among political activists, even among those who undertake participatory acts that might be expected to be especially relevant to their circumstances—getting in touch with public officials, taking part in protests, and getting involved in informal community efforts. Their inactivity has consequences for the messages sent to public officials about government programs. The government hears more from those on some programs than on others, and the ones it hears from are systematically among the more advantaged citizens; for example, Medicare recipients are *more* likely than Medicaid recipients to get in touch with a public official about their medical benefits.

Furthermore, in spite of the fact that inactive citizens do not differ substantially from activists in their responses when survey researchers choose the issues, when it comes to what political activists actually say when they take part, members of various underrepresented groups have distinctive participatory agendas. When asked about the issues and problems that animated their political activity those who engage in the kinds of participatory acts that permit the communication of explicit messages to policymakers—for example, contacting, protesting, or serving as a volunteer on a local board—more advantaged and less advantaged activists have distinctive policy agendas attached to their participation. Compared with those who are more advantaged, those who have limited income and education are considerably more likely to discuss issues of basic human need—that is, matters like poverty, jobs, health, and housing—in association with their participation. These matters, not surprisingly, figure especially importantly in the participatory agendas of those who receive means-tested government benefits like food stamps or Medicaid. However, because the disadvantaged are so inactive, public officials actually hear less about these matters from them than from more advantaged activists. In short, when we consider what policymakers actually hear, the association between socioeconomic status and participation has potential political consequences.

Changing Participatory Representation: Conflicting Expectations

The widespread agreement about the extent to which political voice is unequal is not matched by consensus as to whether the extent of that inequality has changed over the last generation. Part of the reason for the absence of agreement is that, as is so often the case, scholarly inquiries do not always reach the same conclusion when investigating the same subject. A more important explanation, however, derives from the fact that political voice is multi-faceted, and developments with respect to various modes of expressing political voice—for example, campaign giving, protest, or activity in political organizations—need not operate in tandem. Thus, the inability to reach a single conclusion about changing inequality of political voice reflects the multiple dimensions of the subject as well as scholarly disputation.[26]

Recent decades have witnessed several trends with potential and potentially contradictory implications for participatory inequalities. Some of these trends might possibly be expected to have had an ameliorative impact on the strength of the relationship between participation and education or income. Consider, for example, the recent decline in political activity. The widely noted erosion in voting turnout that began after the recent high in 1960 was the first, and most immediately visible, manifestation of a more general trend.[27] It turns out that the decay in turnout, a complex matter that we shall discuss in greater detail later, is part of a more general decline in political participation as well as in civic involvement construed more broadly (Rosenstone and Hansen 1993; Putnam 2000). Because those on the lowest rungs of the socioeconomic ladder have traditionally been so politically inactive, the recent decline in overall rates of political activity cannot come solely from erosion at the bottom. Thus, participatory decline might actually decrease participatory stratification. Inequality in political voice may have also been reduced by the rise in education during recent decades. Because education is such a powerful predictor of political engagement, rising absolute levels of education might be expected to facilitate the political activation of those at the bottom of the SES hierarchy and produce class convergence in participation. In fact, however, Norman Nie, Jane Junn, and Kenneth Stehlik-Barry (1996) demonstrate that increasing education does not necessarily yield commensurate increases in activity.

In contrast, other developments might lead to the aggravation of inequalities in political voice. Most important, in recent decades economic inequalities have become more pronounced. Since 1980, several factors— among them the attenuation of the labor movement and economic processes such that most of the fruits of economic expansion have accrued to those at the top—have conspired to exacerbate class stratification, though not class conflict. These trends would suggest increasing inequality in political activity. Moreover, the institutions that link citizens to policymakers have been transformed in ways that have the capacity to enhance the voice of the well-off and well-educated. Reflecting a trend that characterizes many institutions of American society, the domain of citizen politics has become increasingly professionalized in the past generation. Roles in political parties and interest groups that would once have been taken on by volunteers are now assumed by professional staff with expertise in such matters as campaign management, polling, direct mail, and public relations. To keep such political operations going requires that citizen supporters provide voluntary contributions of cash rather than of expertise or sweat equity. Under the circumstances, those who have the wherewithal to write large checks would be expected to enjoy enhanced political voice.

Changing Participatory Representation: The Evidence

Has there been a change in whose voices are heard? Studies of various forms of participation, including voting, are unanimous in finding that the strong association between political activity and socioeconomic status has not been ameliorated in recent decades. Beyond that, however, there are no easy conclusions when it comes to changing inequality of political voice.

Consider, first, one of the most basic rights and responsibilities of the citizen, the vote. The enfranchisement of blacks in the South as the result of the civil rights movement and the Voting Rights Act of 1965 coupled with increasing levels of education within the public might be expected to have rendered the electorate more representative not only in racial but also in socioeconomic terms. In contrast to other forms of participation, for which those in the lowest SES ranks register such low rates that not much decline is possible, erosion at the bottom is possible when it comes to voting.

Scholars differ on whether voting stratification has changed over recent decades and the numerous studies have conflicting findings.[28] In the most recent contribution to the literature, Richard B. Freeman (2004) concludes that, despite many efforts to expand the electorate and make voting easier, the decline in turnout since the late 1960s has come disproportionately from those at the bottom of the SES hierarchy, thus, exacerbating the demographic bias of the electorate. Furthermore, whatever the disagreements among scholars, no one suggests that the U.S. electorate is less stratified today than it was when turnout peaked most recently in 1960.

Only rarely does an overtime study consider a broad range of activities beyond voting. The only study to encompass a variety of modes of political activity (Brady et al. 2002) finds that the socioeconomic bias in political participation fluctuated somewhat in the two decades separating the early 1970s and early 1990s, but was more or less the same at the end of the period as at the beginning. Figure 2.5A shows the average amount of participation as measured by an additive scale of twelve political acts for five equal groups (quintiles) ranked on the basis of education and income. For every quintile, there is an overall decline in participation between 1973 and 1994. Figure 2.5A also makes clear the striking degree to which political activity is structured by SES. The five quintiles array themselves neatly in order with discernible differences between adjacent quintiles. The lines move more or less in tandem and never cross. Those at the highest level of SES are roughly five times more active than those at the bottom—undertaking, on average, about 2.1 acts compared to 0.4 acts for the lowest quintile.

Figure 2.5B measures representational inequality by presenting a "representation ratio"—namely, the ratio of average participation by the top SES quintile to the average participation by the bottom SES quintile. A ratio of 1 indicates representational equality between the two quintiles (or any two groups). It is hardly surprising that the representation ratios presented in figure 2.5B, which range between 4 and 7, show an ongoing pattern of participatory dominance by the highest-SES quintile. What is surprising, however, is the absence of any clear trend over time. Participatory inequality rises somewhat in the late 1970s, falls during the early 1980s and ends the two-decade period almost exactly where it started. It might be argued that the recent increase in political activity by the elderly—who do not command high levels of income or, especially education—might obscure increased inequality on the basis of SES among younger cohorts. However, when the elderly are eliminated from the analysis, the findings are unchanged.

These data suggest that we tread carefully before assuming that greater economic inequality implies commensurate increases in class-based inequalities in political participation. However, they leave many questions unanswered. Because the additive scale in figure 2.5 combines numerous activities, it obscures developments with respect to particular forms of participation. Consider, for example, the domain of organizational involvement. Activity in voluntary associations is significant for political voice in two ways.

Figure 2.5   Has the Class Stratification of Political Activity Changed?

A. Political Activities, by SES Quintile
   Mean Number of Activities

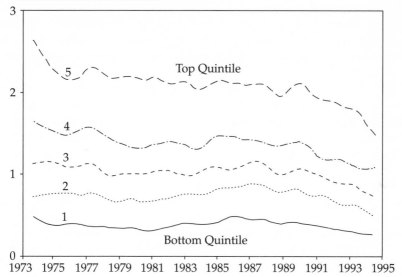

B. Political Activities Ratio, Top Fifth to Bottom Fifth

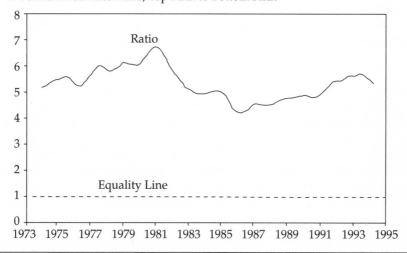

Source: Roper Social and Political Trends Data, 1973–1994 as reported in Brady et al. (2002, 227, 299).

First, regardless of whether the organizations in question take stands in politics, people who are active in membership associations are more likely to take part in politics because, through their organizational involvement, they develop politically useful civic skills and they are exposed to political cues and to requests for political participation. Second, voluntary associations themselves are an important vehicle for the expression of political voice. Theda Skocpol's work (2003; 2004a; 2004b) demonstrates that recent decades have witnessed not only erosion but also transformation in this sphere.

The decline in membership in voluntary associations has not been uniform across different kinds of groups. Instead, organizations that traditionally enrolled working-class as well as middle-class members have fared especially badly: in the period between World War II and the late 1990s, the median decrease in membership for a group of twenty-one cross-class, chapter federations was 60 percent; the analogous figure for a group of seven elite professional societies was only 28 percent. Furthermore, with the erosion of the share of workers enrolled in unions, the gap between the proportion of college-educated Americans who are members of a professional society and the proportion of non–college-educated Americans who are union members has grown substantially (Skocpol 2003, 212–19). In addition, increasing numbers of professionally managed national organizations that require little of their members other than financial support draw their members very disproportionately from among the well educated (Skocpol 2004b, fig. 3). These developments have consequences for the experience of democratic governance and cultivation of democratic habits. We must, however, add a cautionary note. As we shall soon see, we cannot extrapolate directly from changes in membership in voluntary associations to changes in political voice through organized interests. Many voluntary associations, even large ones, are not involved in politics. Moreover, voluntary associations of individuals are not the sum total of organized interest politics. This arena also includes membership organizations such as trade associations that have organizations rather than individuals as members as well as institutions—ranging from corporations to public interest law firms to hospitals—that have no members in the ordinary sense. In short, not all membership groups are active in pressure politics and pressure politics involves many kinds of organizations and institutions that are not membership groups.

Another problem with drawing inferences about changing political voice from the data considered earlier is that evidence based on the enumeration of activities does not take into account how much people do when they take part. This concern is especially relevant when it comes to giving to campaigns and to other political causes. As we have discussed, political contributors, especially those who make large donations, are the least representative of the participant publics. Studies indicate that the social characteristics of campaign contributors have not changed in recent decades (Shields and Goidel 2000; Wilcox 2003). Although increasing levels of education and income and inflationary erosion of the value of the dollar imply that such comparisons are difficult to make, table 2.3 shows considerable continuity in a variety of characteristics—education, income, race, gender, and age—of those who contributed more than $200 to a presidential candidate in three election years: 1972, 1988, and 2000.[29] What these figures cannot reveal, however, is that political contributions have become a more important component of the participatory mix over the period. It is well known that, even when measured in constant dollars, campaign giving has risen rapidly over the last generation at a time when other forms of political activity are declining. In particular, soft money donations, which until recently have not been subject to limits, have increased especially dramatically. Although there are no longitudinal data to assess the consequences of this configuration of circumstances, there is reason to suspect that the changing mix of modes of activity—in particular, a participatory system in which large-scale campaign giving is increasingly important—exacerbates inequalities in participatory input.

At the same time there has been a change in the ideological composition of activist publics. Survey data confirm the impression gleaned from journalistic accounts, that citizen politics in America has become more polarized. Studies find that the decline in civic engagement has been especially pronounced within the large, and growing, sector of the public that describes its political views as moderate, thus producing a circumstance such that political activists are drawn disproportionately from the ranks of those at both ends of the political spectrum (Putnam 2000, 342; Fiorina 1999).

POLITICAL VOICE THROUGH ORGANIZED INTERESTS

Citizens in American democracy seek political voice not only individually but jointly—through organized interests, political parties, and social movements. Collective political efforts raise the same kinds of questions about inequalities of political voice we have been considering with respect to individual activity. Who is talking? How loudly? About what subjects? What are they saying?

Although the evidence for this proposition is not simply incomplete but impossible to gather, it is probably fair to say that, of the various forms of collective political voice, expressions of preference through organized interest activity are least likely to represent all citizens equally, and that

Table 2.3   Characteristics of Significant Presidential Donors

	1972	1988	2000
Education			
High school or less	9%	6%	2%
Some college	16	15	14
College degree	24	22	28
Some graduate	16	11	11
Graduate or professional	36	45	46
	101%	99%	101%
Income			
Under $30,000	22%		
$30,000 to $49,999	22		
$50,000 to $99,999	31		
$100,000 and up	26		
	101%		
Under $50,000		18%	
$51,000 to $99,999		22	
$100,000 to $250,000		30	
Over $250,000		31	
		101%	
Under $100,000			14%
$100,000 to $249,999			42
$250,000 to $500,000			21
Over $500,000			23
			100%
Race			
White	99%	95%	96%
African American	1	2	2
Hispanic		na	2
Asian		1	1
Other		1	1
	100%	99%	102%
Sex			
Male	83%	73%	70%
Female	17	27	30
	100%	100%	100%
Age			
Eighteen to thirty	7%	5%	1%
Thirty-one to forty-five	24	30	17
Forty-six to sixty	48	35	43
Sixty-one or older	21	30	40
	100%	100%	101%

Source: Wilcox (2003).

the economically advantaged speak especially loudly and clearly in organized interest politics.[30] Once again, while it is unambiguous that not all
individuals—and, consequently, not all points of view—are equally well
represented through organized interest politics, it is less clear whether
those inequalities of political voice have been exacerbated during a period
of marked increases in economic inequality among Americans.

Representation by Organized Interests

The set of organizations that represent Americans' political interests and
preferences—which, as we have discussed, is not coterminous with the
vast set of voluntary associations that individuals can join—is remarkable
in its breadth and diversity. The 2001 *Washington Representatives* directory
lists more than six hundred organizations with names beginning with the
word "American," among them:

- American Automobile Association
- American Academy of Pediatrics
- American Airlines
- American Civil Liberties Union
- American Corn Growers Association
- American Council of Korean Travel Agents
- American Enterprise Institute
- American Express
- American Federation of Teachers
- American Friends of the Czech Republic
- American Frozen Food Institute
- American Greyhound Track Operators Association
- American Hiking Society
- American Kennel Club
- American Legion
- American Muslim Council
- American University

As indicated by this brief list, these organizations include membership
groups with many, many members, groups with few members, and institutions—most notably, corporations but also universities and think tanks—

with no members in the ordinary sense; organizations based on how people earn a living, how they spend their leisure, and how they define themselves in religious or ethnic terms; organizations, especially corporations,
with billions in assets and others that operate from hand to mouth; organizations with liberal views and organizations with conservative views. In
view of the stunning array of organizations that take part in American politics, it makes sense to ask: Is everyone represented? Is everyone represented equally?

To the extent that organizations have an impact on public policy (an issue dealt with in chapter 4), unequal representation by organizations may
imply unequal influence upon policy. After taking many political factors
into account, one sophisticated study of controversies in four policy domains found it difficult to predict which of the players will prevail in influencing policy, but reported that it is essential to be at the table (Heinz et
al. 1993, 344–60). Absence of representation is, obviously, especially detri-
mental at the critical phase before policy controversies emerge—when the
political agenda is being set.[31] In short, although we should not equate the
organizational representation of an interest with political influence, representation is fundamental.

What Would Equal Representation by Organizations Look Like?

At the individual level it is possible to specify in the abstract what a representative sample of Americans would look like. It would contain pro-
portionate numbers of individuals with particular characteristics: occupation, income, race, religion, gender, veteran status, health, immigrant status,
attitudes on school prayer, taxes, and national health care, and so on.
Questions of representativeness become much more complicated when
we move from consideration of individuals to consideration of groups ar-
rayed along a variety of dimensions of political cleavage and having radically different numbers of members—and, sometimes, no members at all
in the ordinary sense.[32]

With respect to the problem of how to measure equal voice in the domain of organizational politics, how do we compare the relative political
weight of AARP (formerly the American Association of Retired Persons),
which has 35 million members, and the American Coalition for Filipino
Veterans, which has four thousand? Or the American Furniture Manufacturers Association, which has companies as members, rather than individuals? Or American Airlines and American University, which are not
membership groups at all? For that matter, when representation is by institutions like corporations or universities, whose concerns and prefer-

ences are being represented: the stockholders, managers, employees, or customers of a corporation? The administration, professors, staff, graduates, or students of a university?

Furthermore, beyond the obvious differences in numbers of members are differences in resources, especially money. Such disparities in resources are not proportional to the number of members, the number of politically relevant issues, or the intensity of political concerns. Budgetary resources are especially important because they can be converted into a wide variety of inputs into the policymaking process: ranging from traditional lobbying activities to making campaign contributions to grassroots lobbying. Moreover, organizations with deep pockets can spend more generously in hiring the talent to undertake these activities.

An additional complexity is that the set of organizations that take stands in politics is structured around multiple axes of cleavage. It is complicated enough to characterize political equality considering only the dimension around which the largest portion of organized interest representation takes place, economic interests associated with making a living. It becomes even more so when the framework includes the many other dimensions around which interests are organized. In achieving equality of political voice, how much of the space should be occupied by organizations based on race? On sexual orientation? On attitudes toward capital punishment or policy in the Middle East? On hobbies?

What Does the Set of Organized Interests Actually Look Like?

For all the conceptual difficulties in specifying what political equality would look like when political input arises from organizations rather than from individuals, there is widespread agreement that whatever an unbiased set of organized interests would look like, it would not very closely resemble what we have ever had in the United States. E. E. Schattschneider (1960, 35) observed famously that "the flaw in the [organized interest] heaven is that the heavenly chorus sings with a strong upper-class accent." He argued that what he called the "pressure system" is biased in favor of groups representing the well off, especially business, and against groups representing broad public interests (or public goods) and the disadvantaged.

The essential outlines of Schattschneider's analysis of the pressure system still hold today. The set of organized political interests continues to be organized principally around economic matters—in particular, around the joint political concerns attendant to making a living—and to be dominated by business and the professions. As we shall see, significant changes in how broad public interests are represented have taken place over the past generation or two. Still, the proportion of people who take part in an organization seeking public goods like safer streets or safer consumer products, cleaner water or cleaner government, enhanced domestic security or reduced domestic violence is far smaller than the proportion who would benefit from those conditions. This brief list of public goods sought by interest organizations should make clear that these broad public interests are not inevitably liberal. In many cases, opposing conceptions of the public interest compete with each other. A liberal vision of the public interest (involving, for example, wilderness preservation or consumer product safety) may vie with a conservative one (perhaps economic growth or low prices). These competing visions do not necessarily always balance one another. In particular, advocates of conservative public interests are more likely than their liberal counterparts to find themselves on the same side of a policy controversy as an intense private interest (for example, a corporation or trade association representing real estate developers or the manufacturers of infant car seats).

Moreover, the economically disadvantaged continue to be underrepresented in pressure politics. Organizations of the poor themselves are extremely rare, if not nonexistent, and organizations that advocate on behalf of the poor are relatively scarce (Imig 1996). Furthermore, as Jeffrey Berry (2003, 65) points out, the health and human service nonprofits that have as clients "constituencies that are too poor, unskilled, ignorant, incapacitated, or overwhelmed with their problems to organize on their own" are constrained by the 501(c)3 provisions in the tax code from undertaking significant lobbying.[33] However, in an era when economic gains have flowed very disproportionately to those at the top, it is not simply the poor whose economic interests receive little direct representation. If they are not members of a labor union, those who work in occupations having modest pay, benefits, and status are very unlikely to have direct organizational representation in politics. Furthermore, the economic interests of many other groups that are not economically privileged—for example, students, holders of company pensions, working people without health care benefits, women at home—receive little direct organizational representation.

We should, however, note an important qualification to the generalization that the organized interest community is biased in favor of the well-off, especially business, at the expense of the economically disadvantaged and broad publics. When it comes to the sets of groups that coalesce around non-economic axes of cleavage—for example, race, ethnicity, age, or gender—it is not the dominant groups in society that receive the lion's share of explicit organizational representation. Few, if any, groups are explicitly organized around the interests of, for example, men, the middle aged, or WASPs, but numerous groups represent the interests of women, the elderly, Muslims, Asian Americans, or African Americans. Still, for all their numbers, such groups constitute only a small fraction of the universe of organized interests. Furthermore, the interests of middle-aged white men are surely well represented in the mainstream economic organizations—corporations, business associations, professional associations, and unions—that form the bulk of the organized interest community. When it comes to economic issues, the bias of organized interests toward the well-off seems quite clear.

Changing Organized Interest Representation

At the same time that there has been continuity, the organized interest community has also changed in important ways in the decades since Schattschneider warned about the "upper-class accent " of the "heavenly chorus." First, even though, on average, individual membership in voluntary associations has diminished, the pressure community has grown substantially. Many new political organizations have come into being—not all of them, by any means, membership associations—and many existing organizations that were hitherto outside of politics have come to take part in politics. With this growth in the number of politically active organizations has come the representation of new groups and interests—for example, gays and the disabled—not previously included in organized interest politics and enhanced representation for many others such as African Americans and women (Minkoff 1995). This circumstance may reflect the fact that social movements in the United States often leave organizations in their wake. In contrast to protest politics in other democracies, American social movements are likely to generate an organizational legacy.

Moreover, the bias against groups representing broad public interests has almost certainly been ameliorated. Organizations that advocate on behalf of such public goods as environmental preservation, national security, safe streets, durable consumer products, clean government, or low taxes have increased in numbers and in resources. The presence of all these new organizations in national politics—the result, in part, of infusions of initial resources from foundations and other patrons—might be seen as reducing the political inequalities in the set of organized interests active in politics.[34]

At the same time, several developments would have the opposite effect, shoring up the dominance of organizations traditionally well-represented in organized interest politics. At least in part in reaction to the explosion in the number of consumer and environmental groups that became active in national politics in the late 1960s and early 1970s, previously apolitical corporations and professional associations began a massive mobilization into politics. Large numbers of existing corporations and professional associations augmented their political efforts beginning in the late 1970s, often by establishing an independent office in Washington rather than relying on trade associations and lobbyists-for-hire to manage their political affairs.[35]

Furthermore, after a union-backed measure in the 1974 amendments to the Federal Election Campaign Act preserved political action committees (PACs) as part of the campaign finance system, the Federal Election Commission issued an advisory opinion in the 1975 *Sun Oil* case that permitted corporations to use corporate funds to set up and administer PACs and to solicit voluntary contributions from managers and stockholders. Since then, there has been sharp growth in the number of PACs associated with corporations and professional associations and in the number of dollars flowing through them. Since the elections of 1994 that ended Democratic control of Congress and, therefore, the right to chair committees and subcommittees, business-related PACs have no longer had a strong incentive to channel funds to Democrats. Increasingly, they have focused their giving on Republicans.

Over the past half century, while business interests have gained new antagonists—as well, of course, as new allies—in the public interest community, their traditional adversary, organized labor, has become progressively weaker, both politically and economically. This development has significant consequences for the political representation of the interests of less affluent Americans (Goldfield 1987; Radcliff and Davis 2000). In contrast to the substantial growth in the numbers of politically active organizations of various kinds—ranging from corporations to environmental groups to civil rights groups—the number of labor unions has remained relatively stable. The attrition in the power of labor unions, which were traditionally part of the coalition backing egalitarian social programs, has been particularly pronounced in the years since the late 1970s. The proportion of the work force that is now unionized, 13.5 percent, is roughly half what it was in 1970. The erosion in union membership has come entirely from the ranks of private-sector workers. Currently, only 9 percent of workers in the private sector are union members.[36]

The implications of the weakening of labor unions are thrown into relief when we note that, while the membership associations, public interest law firms, and think tanks that represent diffuse public interests in politics broaden the perspectives brought to the political process, they do not broaden the socioeconomic base of citizen politics. Even when they provide political opposition to the business interests that have traditionally been so powerful in pressure politics, and they frequently do not, these public interest organizations tend to be staffed and supported by the well-educated and privileged and, thus, do not diminish class-based inequalities in political voice.

Some scholars have made an interesting, but controversial, argument about another change in pressure politics that has potential implications for policies affecting social and economic equality. According to this line of reasoning, certain segments of the business community played an active part in shaping key social welfare policies under the New Deal and provided support crucial to overcoming the bias intrinsic to a business-dominated interest group system.[37] Perhaps in response to heightened international economic competition, by the end of the 1970s, the bulk of formerly liberal businesses and investors had turned sharply against the tax and regulatory policies needed for social programs. Since then, according to this argument, American businesses have constituted a much more consistently conservative voice in American politics.[38] Such a transformation in the political aims of some businesses might help to explain the failure of the United States, in contrast to other advanced industrial democracies, to enact public policies to ameliorate the recent rise in economic inequality.

Thus, recent decades have witnessed a series of opposing processes—some of which have reinforced the political voice of interests traditionally well represented in organized interest politics and some of which have strengthened less traditional interests. On the one hand, many relatively marginal groups—including racial and ethnic minorities, women, gays, and the disabled—have become organized, and business has new antagonists (and allies) among public interest groups. On the other, labor unions have grown substantially weaker, and the economically disadvantaged have been left behind in the explosion of organized interest representation. The bottom line would be extremely difficult to calculate. Whether these contradictory trends have had an impact in either direction on the inequalities that have long characterized organized interest politics may be impossible to measure. What is clear is that, in this realm of citizen politics, substantial inequalities of political voice remain.

POLITICAL PARTIES AND POLITICAL VOICE

No account of political voice in a democracy can neglect the role of political parties. In democracies around the world political parties serve to shape political voice in two ways—influencing not only whose voices are heard but also what is said. First, in seeking support for the candidates for political office running under their banner, parties mobilize citizens to vote or otherwise to get involved in politics, especially by giving time or money to electoral campaigns. When parties reach deeply into the citizenry to mobilize the less advantaged, they may have an equalizing impact. In addition, they present party programs that appeal to contrasting coalitions of citizens. Related to our concern with equality of political voice, parties are widely agreed to be a potential vehicle for the political organization of the disadvantaged. Where there are strong working class, peasant, or social-democratic parties, the class-based needs of the economically disadvantaged are more likely to be well represented.[39]

The American political parties were once more potent in mobilizing voters. As shown in figure 2.6, during the nineteenth century voting turnout was high, well above current levels and quite similar to turnout rates in other democracies today.[40] An important part of the explanation for the high levels of voter participation was the role played by political parties. And, of necessity, a more fully mobilized electorate was a less unequal electorate. However, the eligible electorate from whom the parties mobilized support so fully was a very limited electorate containing white, adult males only and encompassing perhaps 40 percent of those who would be eligible today. Thus, what is described by the textbooks as a Golden Age of citizen engagement cannot be celebrated as a Golden Age of equal participation.[41] After 1896, voter turnout fell off significantly, a development that can be explained, at least in part, by the reduced role of parties as political mobilizers. Concerned about party machines and corruption, reformers introduced a variety of measures including civil service, registration laws, and the Australian ballot that neutralized the leverage that party machines used to mobilize voters and activists and limited their ability to dominate elections.[42]

The Recent Demobilization of Citizens

Electoral turnout rebounded somewhat during the New Deal but has eroded fairly steadily since the 1960s, a development that has generated a great deal of attention among observers of American politics and society. In fact, the widely noted decrease in turnout is a complex phenomenon. Although turnout did decline during the 1960s, since 1972 the apparent decline results partially, if not fully, from the increase in the proportion of the voting age population (VAP) that is disqualified from voting by virtue of incarceration or lack of citizenship.[43] That turnout in presidential elections has fallen rather than risen since the 1960s is somewhat surprising. For a variety of reasons, we might have expected turnout to increase. First, African Americans in the South—who were included in the population eligible by virtue of their age to vote, but not permitted to do so—have been brought into the electorate. In addition, the population has become more educated. Furthermore, legal changes including the easing of residency requirements and provisions making it easier to register and to acquire an

Figure 2.6   Turnout in American Elections

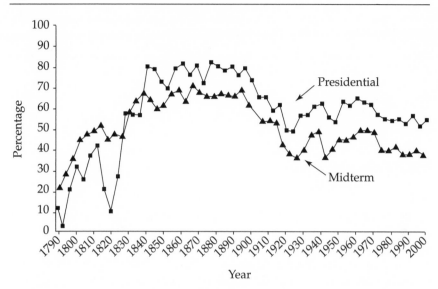

Year

Source: Hershey and Beck (2003, 143). Fig. 8.1, p. 143 "Turnout in American Elections" from *Party Politics in America,* 11th ed. by Marjorie Randon Hershey. Copyright © 2005 by Pearson Education, Inc. Reprinted by permission.
Note: These are votes for president and for the office with the highest vote in midterm elections.

absentee ballot were designed to raise turnout. One factor that has operated in a contrary direction and may have contributed to downward pressure on turnout is the erosion in union power and in the share of American workers who are union members.[44]

Our political parties are in many ways enjoying a period of revitalization: party voting in Congress has risen over the past two decades, and the parties are more ideologically coherent at both the elite and the mass level. The party organizations provide services and funding for candidates. Still, an important part of the explanation for the erosion in electoral turnout one is the weakened role of the political parties as vote mobilizers. Efforts by party workers to contact potential voters to urge them to vote have declined.[45] Campaigns are increasingly run by professionals rather than party activists.[46] Using poll data, campaign consultants have the technological wherewithal to target carefully selected small groups of citizens with targeted messages that seek to raise money or to activate voters to turn out.

The weakness of parties as mass institutions results in greater stratification of the activists who get involved in elections as campaign workers

Table 2.4   Party Mobilization for Political Activity: Who is Asked?

All Respondents $40,300	Average Family Income	
	Republican	Democratic
Party identifiers	$45,400	$36,900
Regular voters	$48,000	$38,500
Those asked to work in a campaign by a fellow partisan	$51,700	$49,800
Those asked to contribute to a campaign by a fellow partisan	$56,700	$54,700

Source: Citizen Participation Study.

and contributors. Those who ask others to take part in political campaigns act as "rational prospectors" recruiting from among those who have the resources to make a substantial contribution of time, effort, or money and who are likely to say yes if asked. In particular, they will ask people who have demonstrated those attributes by having taken part in the past (Brady, Schlozman, and Verba 1999).[47]

As table 2.4 shows, the result of these processes of targeted recruitment is to exacerbate the bias of the electoral process toward the more advantaged citizens rather than to correct it. The two parties differ in their support bases: in terms of average family income, Democratic identifiers and voters are substantially less affluent than their Republican counterparts. However, when party activists, whether Republican or Democratic, seek campaign workers and campaign contributors, they search among the more affluent members of their support bases. The Democratic identifiers and voters may be different from their Republican counterparts, but the economic profiles of those asked by a fellow partisan to get involved in a campaign—or, especially, to make a campaign donation—are much more similar.

The search for political money by both political parties has turned upside down the role of electoral politics as entertainment. In the nineteenth century, the rallies and parades stimulated political interest and activity among Americans of all classes, perhaps disproportionately among the poorer members of society for whom political spectacle was one of the few forms of entertainment available and for whom patronage and the other benefits that parties provided were particularly valuable. Today, the entertainment is likely to be a fund raiser where affluent guests are wined and dined and given an opportunity to rub elbows with political celebrities. At the same time, in a media-saturated society, mass political communications no longer stimulate political engagement among ordinary citizens. In fact, when they take the form of negative advertising and negative television coverage, they may depress political involvement (Ansolabehere and Iyengar 1995, chap. 5).

Whom Do Parties Represent?

Parties shape political voice not only by mobilizing citizens to take part in politics but also by presenting alternatives as they compete for voters in order to win elections. This competition leads them to support policies that will garner the needed votes. From the perspective of equal political voice we are led to ask: From what coalition of supporters will each party seek support? And what policies does each party or its candidates espouse as a way of attracting a winning coalition? In other words: whom does each party represent?

A leading theory of party competition argues that both parties will try to satisfy the median voter—that is, the voter in the dead center of the political issue space whose vote might go either way. By this logic, the tweedledum and tweedledee parties would offer little or no choice to the public, a circumstance that would not necessarily favor the advantaged over the disadvantaged. Rather it would be equally unfavorable to the truly advantaged and to the truly disadvantaged, both of whom are far from the median voter.[48]

Consistent with the logic of the median voter, both parties do court the moderate middle. However, there is more to the story. In order for candidates to succeed in primaries and to field increasingly expensive campaigns, they need to attract the support of partisan primary electorates and the party activists who work in and fund campaigns. In each of the parties, the median campaign worker and, especially, the median contributor are more affluent than the median voter, a circumstance that works against the representation of the disadvantaged by either of the parties. Seeking to satisfy the median contributor or activist also pushes the parties apart ideologically: although similar in their affluence, Democratic and Republican party activists differ substantially in their preferences on a variety of policy matters, including economic policies with special consequences for disadvantaged groups.[49] In this way, the needs of groups that exercise less voice on their own might gain attention.

The Social Class Basis of Party Conflict

The New Deal alignment of the 1930s organized class interests into politics in a way not seen before or since, and the 1936 election was the high-water mark of class polarization in voting. Except in the solid Democratic

South, where virtually all whites supported the Democrats and blacks were not represented by either party, the less advantaged economically lined up with the Democrats and more affluent citizens with the Republicans. Over the past half century, a series of changes has altered the coalitions underlying the parties and the issue basis on which they compete.[50] Members of the electorate are less likely to identify with one of the parties.[51] New groups have entered the electorate, most notably, southern blacks and large numbers of immigrants, especially Latinos. The coalitions underlying the parties have been modified; most important, southern whites, especially southern white men, have increasingly left the Democratic Party. The parties have become more distinctive ideologically and new issues—for example, environmental preservation, affirmative action, abortion, and identity politics of various kinds—have emerged as fodder for partisan competition. [52]

Although students of American politics agree in their descriptions of many of the aspects of recent changes in the parties, consensus is more elusive when it comes to the extent to which the parties continue either to organize voters on the basis of social class or to offer contrasting policy proposals on class-relevant economic issues. As party coalitions and partisan competition has evolved, how has the relationship of class to party changed?

Class differences in party coalitions remain. Surveys of voters, including the data already presented in table 2.4, invariably show a relationship between income and party choice with the affluent preferring the Republicans and the less well heeled the Democrats. In addition, Republican and Democratic partisans differ more substantially in their opinions on economic and welfare issues than in their opinions on cultural and foreign policy issues (Shafer and Claggett 1995, chap. 3). In the nation as a whole, there also seems to be some tendency for increasing class division between the parties. In particular, the parties in the South have become more class-based than at the time of the New Deal when all white southerners were Democrats.[53]

Moreover, the parties do continue to offer contrasting programs on economic issues that meet the distinctive needs of their partially class-based constituencies. They differ regularly on such matters as taxation, social welfare programs, and economic regulation. However, even as far back as the 1950s, the Democrats backed away from the populist economic rhetoric, with its denunciations of the "interests" and the "rich", they had used during the Roosevelt and Truman years (Gerring 1998, chap. 7). More recently, in their attempt to attract a majority of voters, Republicans have broadened their economic appeal by stressing tax cutting and economic performance—policies presented as serving all Americans—and some

Democrats have sought to pursue more moderate economic policies that appeal to a broader middle class. Overall, the result is a shift to the right in the economic agenda.[54]

The Rise of Elite Activism   In an era when the role of the parties as mass organizations has become attenuated, one development is clear, however. Elite issue activists in both parties have gained ascendance at the expense of traditional party activists.[55] Long-term changes in American politics— from the development of the civil service to public sector unionization to welfare state entitlements—have deprived traditional party organizations of the kinds of benefits that once generated support among ordinary citizens (Fiorina 2001). These long-term developments are reinforced by more recent institutional changes that have opened the political process to constituencies with intense issue preferences that operate increasingly within the parties as well as within interest groups and local politics. Examples of such changes include a primary-dominated presidential nominating process, sunshine laws for meetings, expanded rules of standing in the courts, and increased use of ballot propositions. These activists have brought new attributes to the stratum of the middle management of party leadership. Among the Democrats at least, they are more affluent and better educated.[56] Furthermore, in both parties, they have made politics more issue based and less moderate. And their issue concerns are new ones that do not fit easily into the contours of a New Deal party alignment anchored in competition over economic issues. Still, these party activists continue to differ over, among other things, the economic issues that have divided the parties since the 1930s.[57] What is, once again, less clear is the extent to which a party politics based on the multiple issue concerns of upper-status issue activists has compromised the capacity of the parties to bring about greater equality of political voice.[58]

SOCIAL MOVEMENTS

Social movements provide an important vehicle, sometimes the only vehicle, for the mobilization of citizens previously outside politics and the collective expression of nonmainstream opinions.[59] From the outset, protest has enjoyed a central position in American mythology. The Boston Tea Party figures importantly in our narratives of the American Revolution, Shays' Rebellion in our narratives of the shortcomings of the Articles of Confederation. More recently, during the Civil Rights movement of the 1950s and 1960s, politically disenfranchised southern blacks engaged in direct action campaigns in order to secure basic rights, including the right to vote. Movement participants took to the streets because conventional channels of political participation were closed to them. Indeed, a chief purpose of the movement was to pry these channels open (Morris 1984).

Social movements bring into politics previously ignored points of view. They may also bring into politics relatively resource-poor groups that use movement activities to attract third-party support (Lipsky 1968) or to influence the policymaking process through disruptive collective action (Piven and Cloward 1971, 1977). For groups whose social and economic disadvantage tends to restrict their conventional political access, then, a social movement can serve as an alternative means for gaining and expressing political voice, thereby potentially mitigating the impact of inequality upon democratic participation. Just as we could not specify what political equality would look like with respect to representation through organized interests, it is impossible to define some universe of potential social movements to which the set of actual movements could be compared in order to determine whether it is representative. Earlier we saw that data about individual participation show that taking part in protests, marches or demonstrations is related to SES—a finding that might have been different had the survey been conducted in the mid-1960s rather than in 1990. Even without being able to specify some measure of political skew, however, it seems reasonable to conclude that the domain of social movement activity is characterized by a lesser degree of inequality of political voice than the other realms of citizen activity we have discussed.

The boundaries between social movement activity and rioting, on the one hand, and between social movement activity and conventional politics, on the other, are notably blurry. Was the Los Angeles civil unrest of 1992 a politically motivated rebellion or a riotous spree of criminal behavior? What about the rioting by whites in opposition to James Meredith's attempt to matriculate at the University of Mississippi in 1962? With respect to more conventional modes of activity, just about all movements combine conventional and extra-conventional resources and tactics in pursuit of their goals.[60] For example, the story of the civil rights movement in the American South includes lunchroom sit-ins, the Freedom Rides, the Montgomery bus boycott, the march on Selma, and the legal test cases filed by the NAACP. A hallmark of successful social movements in the United States is that they almost inevitably produce advocacy organizations—for example, the National Organization for Women or the Mexican-American Legal Defense and Educational Fund—that behave like other organized interests and gain semi-insider status in Washington. Social movements may also find themselves welcomed, or co-opted, by one of the major political parties. In fact, many of the changes in the party coalitions discussed earlier represent the incorporation of a social movement into a political party. The incorporation of the pro-choice forces into the

Democrats and the Christian right into the Republicans are good examples. In addition, collective political efforts that entail substantial grassroots organizing and activity (such as antismoking campaigns) may rely solely on conventional forms of participation such as petition drives without necessarily involving protest activity. Each of these examples illustrates the permeability of the borders between social movement and other forms of activity.

Social Movement in Action: Changing Policy, Changing Hearts and Minds

Social movements seek to realize their objectives not only by influencing public policy but also by changing private behaviors, challenging accepted cultural understandings, and transforming the lives of their adherents.[61] Indeed, social movements offer citizens the opportunity to articulate alternative collective visions of what society should look like and to aim discussion not just at policymakers but at the public as well. Such nonpolicy-related approaches were important in the early days of the revival of the women's movement—both because significant aspects of the relations between the sexes lie deep in private life beyond the reach of the state, and because gender roles have deep cultural resonance in societies throughout history and around the world. Thus, the women's movement, especially its radical wing, supplemented strategic efforts to influence specific policy with a focus on consciousness-raising and efforts to win over the hearts and minds of the members of the public, transform their values, and alter their lifestyles.[62] Social movements also influence the people who participate in them. Activists come to see themselves as effective political actors: they interpret their experiences in political terms and politicize their actions both in movement contexts and in everyday life. Civil rights veterans of the lunch-counter sit-ins in Greensboro have noted what it meant to them personally to have taken responsibility for changing the segregated South. It transformed their sense of identity and, thus, changed their lives forever (Sitkoff 1981, 90).

The multiple seemingly extrapolitical ways that social movements operate do, however, have a variety of consequences for politics, conventionally understood. When hearts and minds are changed in the course of cultural transformation, previously nonpolitical issues may be politicized and policymakers may construe social conflicts in new ways. The process of forming new identities may create new constituencies for explicitly political advocacy. Movement activity, even on behalf of nonpolitical objectives, can create skills and cultivate self-confidence that may easily be transported to political settings. In short, even when they do not focus on having an impact on public outcomes, social movements have secondary effects with potential for ameliorating inequalities of political voice.

EQUALIZING POLITICAL VOICE THROUGH SOCIAL MOVEMENTS: POSSIBILITIES AND LIMITS

Of the various forms of citizen involvement we have reviewed in this chapter, social movements are the most likely to mobilize those who have been outside of politics by dint of resource deprivation. Many of the most prominent social movements in U.S. history have been undertaken by groups suffering some sort of social, economic, or political disadvantage relative to the majority. Among them are the labor movement, the welfare rights movement, the women's movement and American Indian Movement. However, it is simplistic to view social movements solely as a means through which the socially and economically disadvantaged gain a political voice. To begin with, the United States boasts a long tradition of middle-class protest movements. The nineteenth-century abolition and temperance movements, the peace movement of the 1960s, and the contemporary environmental and animal rights movements are examples of movements that involved oppositional activism on behalf of initially overlooked or unpopular ideas by foot soldiers drawn from the middle class. While the individual supporters of each of these movements were not socially or economically disadvantaged, they were collectively politically disadvantaged compared with their well-organized and resource-rich adversaries both inside and outside the government.   ●

Even when a movement mobilizes the disadvantaged, it usually engages not those who are worst off in absolute terms but rather those who have some stake in the political and economic system. Resource mobilization theorists have argued convincingly that certain basic resources—for example, organizational networks, leadership capacity, and access to some financial backing—are required to launch and sustain a movement (McCarthy and Zald 1977). The leadership of the contemporary African American reparations movement, for instance, consists of individuals who have substantial resources: among the players are lawyers, elected officials, business executives, and academics. Lacking a stake in the system, a sense that they can make a difference, and the skills and resources that facilitate political participation, the worst-off in disadvantaged groups usually do not join social movements. They may, however, engage in other forms of spontaneous collective actions, such as the urban civil disturbances during the 1960s. Thus, even though social movements serve as vehicles for those without conventional political resources, participation in them is characterized by the same kinds of stratification we have seen in other forms of political activity.

Moreover, the internal dynamics of social movements often mirror power relations in the larger society. For example, in the student movements of the left during the 1960s, women resented the dominance of men, who occupied the leadership positions. Within the civil rights movement, African American members of SNCC chafed under the leadership of white counterparts as black women fought against sexual stereotyping by both black and white men (Freeman 1975, chap. 2; Robnett 1997). During the Asian American movement of the 1960s and 1970s, Filipino Americans complained that the movement was being run by the numerically dominant Chinese and Japanese Americans, who presumed, inappropriately, to speak for all Asian Americans (Espiritu 1992). Although social movements often challenge the status quo from the vantage point of disadvantaged groups, they inevitably favor some voices within these groups over others.

Although there is a longstanding tradition of social movement activism on the left in the United States and elsewhere, we should note that the causes on behalf of which social movements advocate span the ideological spectrum. In fact, a number of important recent social movements—including the pro-life movement, the Christian right, and the militia movement—are on the right, not the left. Like many of their progressive counterparts, they mobilize alienated nonelites to activity in contentious politics and face entrenched adversaries.

Social Movements in an Era of Increasing Economic Inequality

In our examination of various realms of citizen activity, we have asked repeatedly whether there has been an increase in political inequality corresponding to the recent increase in economic inequality. When it comes to social movements, we have not been inclined to ask about the extent of political inequality in this realm of citizen politics. Instead, we have inquired about the extent to which social movement activity compensates for other political inequalities.

Social movement activity in the United States has been cyclical, peaking most recently in the decades between the 1950s and the 1970s. Although our mass politics are currently less contentious than they were a generation or two ago, a variety of social movements are making themselves heard. Some, the animal rights movement, for example, do not have an obvious place on a traditional left-right continuum. Others, such as the antiglobalization protests against the WTO and the scattered demonstrations against the invasion of Iraq, have affinities with the left. Arguably, the energy in social movement politics seems concentrated disproportionately on the opposite end of the political spectrum in such conservative movements as the pro-life and Christian conservative movements, movements that draw from groups that are not privileged.

However the net ideological pitch of political expressions emanating from social movements is evaluated, one conclusion seems inescapable. An era when the fruits of prosperity accrue so disproportionately to those at the top of the economic hierarchy has not spawned a social movement on behalf of the economically disadvantaged. The kind of class-based oppositional politics once associated with the labor movement has not materialized in response to increasing economic inequality.

THE INTERNET AND POLITICAL EQUALITY

What are the implications for political equality of the revolutionary changes in communications and information acquisition produced by the Internet? In spite of early predictions about the capacity of the Internet to broaden the base of citizen politics, it has become apparent that Internet use is highly stratified, a phenomenon sufficiently pervasive as to acquire a descriptive moniker, the "digital divide."[63] Although computer use and web access are increasingly widespread, they are not universal in America and are structured in by-now-familiar patterns. Inequalities in access are not simply a function of the uneven distribution of computer skills or the inability to afford an Internet connection. Rather they are rooted in the patterns of social stratification that structure so much of what we have already discussed. Internet use does not stand apart from other forms of information acquisition; instead, it correlates strongly with exposure to traditional media, including newspapers. Moreover, the demographic attributes associated with Internet use are familiar as correlates of political participation. The well-educated, the affluent, and non-Hispanic whites are much more likely to be online.[64] Although patterns of computer use and Internet access replicate the racial, ethnic, and socioeconomic stratification we have seen for political activity, they are, in one important respect, very different: the young are much more likely to be online than are their elders. Presumably, the aging of this wired generation, and its successors, will speed the diffusion of these technological innovations. What is less clear is the extent to which the racial and SES stratification in Internet use that characterizes the population as a whole obtains for the younger generation.

The implications of Internet-based political mobilizations for equality of political voice are analogous to those of the middle-class social movements discussed earlier: they involve new issues and new ideas but not new kinds of people. Thus, the experience so far is that the Internet is not overcoming the social stratification of political participation. Indeed, it may simply "activate the active" (Norris 2001, 229), and thus widen the disparity between participants and the politically disengaged by making it easier for the already interested to gain political information and to make political connections. Furthermore, as demonstrated in the 2004 elections, the utility of the Internet in raising political money—the form of participation most closely related to SES—raises an additional concern about whether cyber-politics will promote political equality.

In addition, it is not clear whether the Internet will channel Americans into or away from politics. As more Americans go online, will they use its capacities to keep current with political developments, to acquire political information, to engage in political discussion, and to become politically connected, or will their activity be confined to emailing friends, planning vacations, and going shopping? Internet use need not be political in content. In short, conclusions about the meaning of the Internet for inequalities of political voice are premature, but there is reason for caution.

CONCLUSION

In the course of our discussion of inequalities of political voice, certain themes have emerged repeatedly. Most important, the level of political inequality in America is high. The expression of political voice is strongly related to social class. Those with high levels of income, occupational status and, especially, education are much more likely to be politically articulate. with unambiguous implications for what policymakers hear. The socioeconomic bias in citizen politics implies as well that the concerns of members of disadvantaged groups are systematically less likely to make themselves heard. Once again, there are clear consequences for the sorts of messages conveyed to policymakers.

The various domains of citizen politics differ in the extent to which the group of activists and the messages they send are unrepresentative. Social movement politics has the clearest capacity to bring into politics previously quiescent publics and hitherto ignored points of view. In the realm of conventional politics, party politics functions more effectively in this way than does organized interest politics. Still, all forms of citizen participation, including the alleged weapon of the weak, social movements and protests, are characterized by some degree of socioeconomic bias.

In an era of increasing economic inequality and increasing educational attainment, have these inequalities of political voice changed in any way? One important development is the increasing overrepresentation of extreme viewpoints at the expense of moderate opinions. This trend toward ideological polarization was noted in various domains of citizen politics including political party leadership and overall political participation. What is more complicated is how class-based political inequalities have been altered as economic inequalities have grown and educational levels have risen. That the fruits of late twentieth-century prosperity accrued so disproportionately to those at the top of the economic ladder might be expected to exacerbate inequalities of political voice. In contrast, higher levels of popular education might have been expected to yield reduced levels of political inequality, a circumstance that has surely not materialized. In no aspect of the multifaceted phenomenon of political voice have inequalities been ameliorated in recent decades.

Whether political voice has become even more unrepresentative in socioeconomic terms seems to depend upon the realm of citizen politics under scrutiny. With respect to voting, the evidence is unclear. Scholars differ in their assessments, but there may well be some aggravation of political inequality. When it comes to organized interest activity, it is difficult to specify what a level playing field would look like, and adequate data about the changes over the past few decades do not exist. Among the contradictory trends are, on the one hand, the overall increase in the number of organized interests and enhanced advocacy on behalf of a number of underrepresented interests such as racial and ethnic minorities, women, gays, the disabled, and such public goods as environmental preservation and lower taxes. On the other hand, advocacy on behalf of the economically disadvantaged has not been correspondingly expanded. When coupled with the weakening of the labor unions, the organized representation of the economic needs of the less well off has suffered in relative terms.

In terms of various kinds of individual activity, a study using an additive scale of numerous kinds of political participation found fluctuations in the association between political activity and socioeconomic status over a twenty-year period but no net change from the beginning of the period to the end. However, the increasing dominance of political giving, a form of activity that permits the affluent to achieve disproportionate political voice, among the modes of citizen involvement would seem to have the consequence of aggravating inequalities of political voice.

In short, there is variation across domains of political involvement with respect to whether inequalities of political voice have been exacerbated in recent decades and no evidence that those inequalities have been reduced. If we cannot be sure that they have become more pronounced in an era of widening disparities of income and wealth, we are certain that those political inequalities have long been and continue to be substantial, a challenge to the democratic ideal of citizen equality.

We are grateful to our colleagues on the task force for the stimulating conversations that guided our work, to Mark Fennell for research assistance, to Claire Kim and David Meyer for their generous help on the section on social movements, to Theda Skocpol for an insightful reading and countless helpful suggestions, and to Larry Jacobs for his steady hand at the helm in guiding this project from launch to landing.

NOTES

1. On this point, which is confirmed by more recent surveys, see Schuman, Steeh, and Bobo (1985, 74–76); and Page and Shapiro (1992, 63, 68–71). These and other generalizations about public opinion are based not only on the published sources cited but also on the most recent data available (early 2005) on such web sites as PollingReport.com, ropercenter.uconn.edu, and those of particular news and polling organizations.
2. See Schuman, Steeh, and Bobo (1985, esp. 88–90); and Page and Shapiro (1992, 71–75).
3. For the former perspective, see, for example, Sears (1988); Kinder and Sanders (1996); and Gilens (1999); for the latter, see, for example, Sniderman and Piazza (1993). Sears, Sidanius, and Bobo (2000) bring together a variety of positions.
4. On public attitudes toward the ERA, see Mansbridge (1986); and Page and Shapiro (1992, 64, 100–2, 105–10).
5. On Americans' attitudes toward economic equality, see Hochschild (1981); McClosky and Zaller (1984, 108, 116, 133, 140); and Ladd and Bowman (1998, esp. 17, 18, 20–21, 97–98, 110).
6. For example, data from the International Social Survey Programme indicate that the average American's position on whether it should be "the government's responsibility to reduce income differences" between rich and poor is less favorable to redistribution than is that of citizens of any of the thirteen other countries studied, even though there is little indication of American exceptionalism concerning desired income discrepancies across occupations (Osberg and Smeeding, 2003, 31, 37, 41). See also, Kleugel, Mason, and Wegener (1995); Weakliem, Andersen, and Heath (2003, 47–48); and Mehrtens (2004).
7. See, Lipset and Schneider (1983); McClosky and Zaller (1984, 120, 141, 1430; and Ladd and Bowman (1998, 108–9, 111).
8. On the distinction between "ideological" and "operational" liberalism, see Free and Cantril (1968).
9. A June 2003 Harris survey found a solid 65 percent majority saying that that year's tax cuts were generally "unfair" in incidence among income groups.

An AP/Ipsos survey at the time of the 2004 election (November 3 through 5, 2004) found much more support for balancing the budget (66 percent) than for cutting taxes (31 percent). Although sentiment for tax progressivity may have declined somewhat since the early 1990s, 63 percent of respondents said that upper-income people were paying "too little"—but only 12 percent said that lower-income people were paying "too little"—in a recent Gallup study (April 5 through 8, 2004) asking about the fairness of the federal tax burden on various income groups. For earlier data, see Hansen (1983); and Page and Shapiro (1992, 160–66).

10. On public opinion and Social Security, see Page (2000); and Cook and Jacobs (2001). A CNN/USA Today/Gallup poll (January 1 through 5, 2005) asked, "As you may know, one idea to address concerns with the Social Security system would allow people who retire in future decades to invest some of their Social Security in the stock market and bonds, but would reduce the guaranteed benefits they get when they retire. Do you think this is a good idea or a bad idea?" Forty percent responded that it is a good idea, 55 percent that it is a bad idea. To a similar question in a PSRA poll for Pew (January 1 through 5, 2005) that emphasized choice (noting possible rises or falls in investment values) versus guaranteed monthly benefits linked to past earnings, 65 percent preferred guaranteed benefits and only 29 percent favored younger workers deciding for themselves how to invest part of their Social Security taxes.

11. For example, an October 2003 ABC/*WP* survey found that a large majority of Americans (79 percent to 17 percent) said that it was important to get health coverage for everyone, even if it meant raising taxes. A majority (62 percent to 33 percent) preferred universal, government-provided health insurance over the current provision by employers or no one, and similar majorities favored it even if this limited their own choice of doctors or meant waiting lists for some nonemergency treatments. On public attitudes toward programs of government income support, see also Cook (1979); McClosky and Zaller (1984, 272–76); Page and Shapiro (1992, chap. 4); Cook and Barrett (1992, esp. 62); and Page (2001).

12. Berinsky (2002, 285) estimates that in 1996 the exclusion bias led to a .11 point overestimation of the average respondent's opinion on the 7 point "reduce income differences between the rich and the poor" scale. See also Brehm (1993); Bartels (1996); Althaus (1998); and Berinsky (2004).

13. See Lindblom (1977, chap. 15) for a discussion of the "circularity" problem.

14. An entry point to the extensive literature on the extent to which public opinion has an influence upon public policy is Manza, Cook, and Page (2002).

15. On the history of the right to vote and, more specifically, on the arguments used to justify political exclusion, see Keyssar (2000).

16. For discussion of the problem of organizational maintenance and the diffi-

culties confronting someone who wishes to found a membership group or keep one going, see Wilson (1973, esp. chaps. 2, 3).

17. The academic literature on citizen participation in America is extensive. A number of helpful sources contain general discussions of political participation and extensive bibliographical references. Among them are Milbrath and Goel (1977); Bennett and Bennett (1986); Leighley (1995); Brady (1999); Conway (2000); and Schlozman (2002).

18. The classic work on voting and the representativeness of those who go to the polls is Wolfinger and Rosenstone (1980).

19. Figures for those who made donations over $1,000 to a presidential candidate are taken from Campaign Finance Institute (2003). Figures for the American public are calculated from the Web site of the U.S. Census.

20. The data in figure 2.1—as well as those in table 2.2 and figures 2.2 and 2.3—are taken from Verba, Schlozman, and Brady (1995). See their appendices A and B for information on the nature of the sample and the wording of questions. It would be preferable if there were more recent data that would permit the investigation of these matters. These 1990 data remain the most comprehensive information on citizen participation.

21. It has long been observed that a higher proportion of survey respondents claim to have gone to the polls than would have been possible on the basis of election returns. However, evidence that the American electorate is stratified by class holds regardless of whether the self-reported or the validated electorate is considered. See Traugott and Katosh (1979); Leighley and Nagler (1992a and 1992b); and Freeman (2004).

Some analyses *seem* to suggest that the well educated and affluent are not overrepresented among voters. Presser and Traugott (1992) report that education is not a significant predictor of validated turnout in multivariate models of validated voting (but see Katosh and Traugott 1981), a finding that is probably an artifact of model specification. (Attitudinal variables such as political efficacy and political interest, which are included in these analyses and retain their predictive power and their statistical significance, are strongly associated with educational attainment, and they probably mediate the impacts of education.) In addition, Silver, Anderson, and Abramson (1986, 615) demonstrate that among those who did not go to the polls, "education is positively related to overreporting."

These findings related to overreporting are not as relevant to our concern with equality of political voice as might be supposed. Among non-voters, the proportion of well-educated and affluent citizens who falsely claim to have voted is relatively high. However, the critical finding for our analysis is that privileged Americans turn out to vote at such high rates that the misreporting is only a relatively minor proportion of their overall level of participation.

Conversely, the turnout of less privileged Americans is sufficiently modest that misreporting by this group is a relatively large share of its turnout. Indeed, Traugott and Katosh (1979, 366) find that misreporting turnout is related not to sex or education but to age, race, and income—with "the younger, nonwhite, and low income groups more likely to misreport their registration and voting."

The bottom line is that vote turnout is skewed toward upper-income groups, which would come as no surprise to politicians who know that affluent precincts are much more likely than poor ones to deliver high turnout as measured by voting returns.

22. With respect to gender differences in voter turnout, the data in figure 2.2, which are based on the Citizen Participation Study, contradict those in table 2.1, which are based on larger—and presumably more trustworthy—samples in the Current Population Survey. For at least two decades, the Current Population Survey has showed women to be slightly more likely than men to go the polls.

23. Unless otherwise noted, the discussion of how group differences in participation are explained is drawn from Verba, Schlozman, and Brady (1995); Burns, Schlozman, and Verba (2001); and Schlozman et al. (2001). For additional perspectives, discussion, and bibliographical references, see Verba and Nie (1972); Strate et al. (1989); de la Garza et al. (1992); Nie, Junn, and Stehlik-Barry (1996); Harris (1999); Leighley and Vedlitz (1999); Hritzuk and Park (2000); and Leighley (2001).

24 Lien, Conway, and Wong (2004) use the Pilot National Asian American Political Survey to study in detail the participatory profiles of various Asian American nationality groups. Unfortunately, because they do not have data about other ethnic groups, they are unable to shed light on the issue of whether Asian Americans in the aggregate, or particular groups of Asian Americans, are less active than would be expected on the basis of their socioeconomic characteristics.

25. The discussion in this section draws on Verba, Schlozman, and Brady (1995, chaps. 7–8).

26. In considering a related subject, Robert Wuthnow (2002) demonstrates that to understand whether social capital has declined, it is necessary to unpack the concept and examine each of its multiple dimensions separately.

27. On the erosion in voter turnout, see Brody (1978) and Teixeira (1992).

28. Among recent works, contrast Rosenstone and Hansen (1993, 241–45) and Freeman (2004), who (on the basis of data that end in 1988) find an increase in SES stratification of voters, with Leighley and Nagler (1992a, 1992b) and Shields and Goidel (1997), who do not. Those who report increased stratification of the electorate tie that change to erosion in turnout rather than to increased economic inequality. In fact, Freeman (2004, 722) shows the greatest

increase in the stratification of the electorate to have occurred between 1968 and 1972, *before* economic inequalities began to rise sharply. In addition, Rosenstone and Hansen (1993, 243) show the 1960s to be the distinctive era with income and educational inequality of the electorate at lower levels than either before or after. See Shields and Goidel (1997) and Freeman (2004) for summaries of the relevant studies and bibliographical references.

29. While it might be argued that $200 is not a very large donation—mere peanuts compared to the aggregate sums donated by high-rolling contributors—only a small fraction of contributors to a presidential campaign give as much as $200.

30. The study of organized interest politics has a venerable history in political science. Important works include Schattschneider (1960); Bauer, Pool and Dexter (1963); McConnell (1966); Lowi (1969); Truman (1971); Wilson (1973); Lindblom (1977); and Walker (1991). Baumgartner and Leech (1998) present useful discussions of the political science literature and many references. Further discussion of the specific issue of the representation of interests through organized interest politics and additional bibliography can be found in Schlozman and Tierney (1986, chap. 4) and McFarland (1992).

31. On the role of organized interests in agenda setting, see Baumgartner and Jones (1993, esp. chap. 9), who show the impact on the political agenda of the emergence of new environmental groups.

32. On the complexities in understanding equal voice when political representation is by organized interests, see Schlozman and Tierney (1986, esp. chap. 4).

33. In his analysis of the impact of the tax code on lobbying by nonprofits, Berry points out that a little-known tax provision of which nonprofits are not aware, the possibility of H election, permits them autonomy in undertaking political action.

34. On the implications for politics of the growth of new citizens' groups, see Berry (1999). On the role of foundations and other patrons in stimulating these developments, see Walker (1991, esp. chap. 5). Discussions of the role of patronage in stimulating the growth of public interest organizations have tended to focus on the cultivation of liberal groups. However, conservative advocates for broad public interests, especially conservative think tanks and legal foundations, have also benefited from this kind of sponsorship. See Ferguson and Rogers (1986, 86–7).

35. David Vogel (1989, chap. 8) documents the massive increase in the government relations capacity of business.

36. Figures taken from the *Statistical Abstract* on the website of the U.S. Bureau of the Census.

37. Although they disagree about the motivations of business people, both Ferguson (1995, esp. chap. 2), and Swenson (2002) emphasize their importance to the New Deal.

38. An especially articulate, though controversial, version of this argument is contained in Ferguson and Rogers (1986).
39. Discussions in the comparative literature include Verba, Nie, and Kim (1979) and Powell (1986).
40. On the role of the nineteenth century political parties in mobilizing voters, see Burnham (1965), McGerr (1986), and Schier (2000, 54–64).
41. The political parties were never in the vanguard of efforts to enfranchise the single largest group of citizens who lacked the right to vote, women, and urban party organizations actually opposed suffrage for women (Scott and Scott 1975, 26). Furthermore, this was a period of constriction of the eligible electorate, most significantly through the Jim Crow disenfranchisement of blacks in the South.
42. Although the vast literature on the changing shape of the American political universe around the turn of the twentieth century contains many controversies, there is agreement on the overall contours of the change. See Burnham (1965); Rusk (1970); McGerr (1986); and Silbey (1991). These changes that had a disproportionate effect on poorer citizens are usually dated from this period of progressive reform. Keyssar (2000, chap. 5) presents evidence that similar efforts were made even earlier with the same effect.
43. McDonald and Popkin (2001) discredit the common wisdom about falling turnout rates. They consider turnout as a proportion of the voting eligible population (VEP) and conclude that turnout has fluctuated, but not declined, since 1972. While Freeman (2004) agrees that higher rates of ineligibility within the VEP are responsible for some of the apparent decline in rates of turnout, he argues that McDonald and Popkin overestimate the impact of these factors and finds that turnout has continued to decline since 1972.
44. See Radcliff and Davis (2000) for a discussion of why unions enhance turnout even among non-members. Both cross-national and state-level American data demonstrate the significance of levels of union membership for rates of turnout.
45. Rosenstone and Hansen (1993, chap. 7) emphasize the consequences for political activity of the decline in voter mobilization by parties (as well as social movements). In their discussion of the origins of the decline in turnout, Abramson, Aldrich, and Rohde (1999, 85) point out that the decline in contacts from political parties has not tracked turnout very well. In fact, even though turnout was falling, party contacts rose during the first part of the 1960s and rose again in the 1990s, a period of fluctuating turnout.
46. For an expanded version of this argument, and extensive references, see Aldrich (1995, chap. 8).
47. Rosenstone and Hansen (1993) make a similar point about the strategic elites that seek to get others involved in politics.
48. The fact that the income distribution in most societies is skewed has led to the

prediction that the median voter will vote to expropriate the wealth of the affluent. However, see Meltzer and Richard (1981, 914) for an economic analysis of the factors that might offset that prediction.

49. On the logic of how the requirements for getting nominated and running a campaign push candidates and parties away from the dead center of the political spectrum, see Schlozman and Verba (1987), Aldrich (1995), and Verba, Brady, and Schlozman (2004).

50. For a helpful summary that places changes in the coalitions underlying the parties in the context of party dealignment, see Beck (2003).

51. For a strong statement about partisan dealignment, see Wattenberg (1991).

52. On the emergence of abortion as a partisan issue, see Adams (1997). On the exchange of positions between the parties on the ERA, in particular, and issues of women's rights more generally, see Freeman (1987).

53. McCarty, Poole, and Rosenthal (1997, 20–23) and Stonecash (2000) present extensive data to show increasing class differences between the parties. However, Flanigan and Zingale (2002, 110–12) give evidence that suggest the opposite. See Stonecash (2000) for bibliography about this debate.

54. Although the extent and the sources of any rightward movement in the political agenda are debated among analysts of American politics, Radcliff and Davis (2000) demonstrate that the attenuation of union strength has ideological consequences.

55. This development was first observed about the Democrats by Wilson (1960).

56. Kirkpatrick (1976, chap. 3) demonstrates that while political reforms have made Democratic convention delegates more representative of the rank and file in terms of race and gender, they are less representative in terms of income and occupation.

57. In fact, in their survey-based study Jackson, Bigelow, and Green (2003, 68) show that, while Democratic convention delegates are quite uniformly liberal across a variety of issues, "welfare liberalism" is the dimension that most strongly structures opinion among them.

58. The common assertion is that party elites in both parties are less moderate than their respective rank and file. However, Shafer and Claggett (1995, chap. 7) argue that disparities are not uniform across issues: Democratic party elites are more liberal than Democratic supporters on what they call the "cultural/national" dimension and Republican party elites are more conservative than Republican supporters on the "economic" dimension.

59. The literature on protest and social movements is extensive. For varying perspectives and bibliographical references, see Lipsky (1968); Lowi (1971); McCarthy and Zald (1977); Tilly (1978); McAdam (1982); Meyer, Whittier, and Robnett (2002); Morris and Mueller (1992); Snow, Rochford, Worden, and Benford (1986); and Tarrow (1998a).

60. Sidney Tarrow (1998b) points out that social movements in America have al-

ways used political institutions as part of their strategy. In response to the puzzling failure of the social movement literature to differentiate between an SMO (social movement organization) and an interest group, Paul Burstein (1998, 39) argues that "they are actually the *same thing* (his emphasis) . . . social scientists . . . have often thought that they were studying different things when in fact they were studying the same thing under different labels."

61. On this theme, see Snow et al. (1986), Snow and Benford (1988), and Meyer (2000).
62. See, for example, the writings collected in Morgan (1970).
63. The discussion in this section draws from the analysis and data in Norris (2001, esp. chaps. 4 and 11).
64. The initial gender gap in Internet use seems now to have closed (Norris 2001, 72). With respect to race and ethnicity, a 1997 report (NTIA, 1997, chart 13) by the National Telecommunications and Information Administration demonstrates that, even within rough income groups, blacks and Hispanics are less likely to own computers than are non-Hispanic whites or, especially, other non-Hispanics (who are, presumably, principally Asian American). In the brief period between 1994 and 1997, when computer ownership was expanding rapidly in the United States, the proportion of PC owners in each racial or ethnic group increased. Nonetheless, at the same time that the number of black households with computers grew, the number of non-Hispanic white households with computers grew even faster. Thus, in 1997 the racial gap in PC ownership was larger than it had been three years earlier, a result that obtains within each of the four income groups.

REFERENCES

Abramson, Paul R., John Aldrich, and David W. Rohde. 1999. *Change and Continuity in the 1996 and 1998 Elections*. Washington, D.C.: CQ Press.

Adams, Greg D. 1997. "Abortion: Evidence of an Issue Evolution." *American Journal of Political Science* 41(3): 718–37.

Aldrich, John H. 1995. *Why Parties?* Chicago: University of Chicago Press.

Althaus, Scott. 1998. "Information Effects in Collective Preferences." *American Political Science Review* 92(2): 545–58.

Ansolabehere, Steven, and Shanto Iyengar. 1995. *Going Negative: How Political Advertisements Shrink and Polarize the Electorate*. New York: Free Press.

Bartels, Larry M. 1996. "Uninformed Votes: Information Effects in Presidential Elections." *American Journal of Political Science* 40(1): 194–230.

Bauer, Raymond A., Ithiel de Sola Pool, and Lewis Anthony Dexter. 1963. *American Business and Public Policy: The Politics of Foreign Trade*. Chicago: Aldine.

Baumgartner, Frank R., and Bryan D. Jones. 1993. *Agendas and Instability in American Politics*. Chicago: University of Chicago Press.

Baumgartner, Frank R., and Beth L. Leech. 1998. *Basic Interests: The Importance of Groups in Politics and in Political Science*. Princeton, N.J.: Princeton University Press.

Beck, Paul Allen. 2003. "A Tale of Two Electorates: The Changing American Party Coalitions, 1952–2000." In *The State of the Parties*, 4th ed., edited by John C. Green and Rick Farmer. Lanham, Md.: Rowman and Littlefield.

Bennett, Linda, and Stephen Earl Bennett. 1986. "Political Participation: Meaning and Measurement." In *Annual Review of Political Science*, edited by Samuel Long. Norwood, N.J.: Ablex Publishing.

Berinsky, Adam J. 2002. "Silent Voices: Social Welfare Policy Opinions and Political Equality in America." *American Journal of Political Science* 46(2): 276–87.

———. 2004. *Silent Voices: Public Opinion and Political Participation in America*. Princeton, N.J.: Princeton University Press.

Berry, Jeffrey. 1999. *The New Liberalism: The Rising Power of Citizen Groups*. Washington, D.C.: Brookings Institution.

———. 2003. *A Voice for Nonprofits*. Washington, D.C.: Brookings Institution.

Blank, Rebecca M. 1997. *It Takes a Nation: A New Agenda for Fighting Poverty*. Princeton, N.J.: Princeton University Press.

Brady, Henry E. 1999. "Political Participation." In *Measures of Political Attitudes*, edited by John P. Robinson, Phillip R. Shaver, and Lawrence Wrightsman. San Diego, Calif.: Academic Press.

Brady, Henry E., Kay Lehman Schlozman, and Sidney Verba. 1999. "Prospecting for Participants: Rational Expectations and the Recruitment of Political Activists." *American Political Science Review* 93(1): 153–68.

Brady, Henry E., Kay Lehman Schlozman, Sidney Verba, and Laurel Elms. 2002. "Who Bowls?: The (Un)Changing Stratification of Participation." In *Understanding Public Opinion*, edited by Barbara Norrander and Clyde Wilcox. Washington, D.C.: CQ Press.

Brehm, John. 1993. *The Phantom Respondents*. Ann Arbor: University of Michigan Press.

Brody, Richard A. 1978. "The Puzzle of Participation in America." In *The New American Political System*, edited by Anthony King. Washington, D.C.: AEI Press.

Burnham, Walter Dean. 1965. "The Changing Shape of the American Political Universe." *American Political Science Review* 59(1): 7–28.

Burns, Nancy, Kay Lehman Schlozman, and Sidney Verba. 2001. *The Private Roots of Public Action: Gender, Equality, and Political Participation*. Cambridge, Mass.: Harvard University Press.

Burstein, Paul. 1998. "Interest Organizations, Political Parties, and the Study of Democratic Politics." In *Social Movements and American Political Institutions*, edited by Anne N. Costain and Andrew S. McFarland. Lanham, Md.: Rowman and Littlefield.

Campaign Finance Institute. Task Force on Presidential Nomination Financing. 2003. *Participation, Competition, and Engagement: How to Revive and Improve Public Funding for Presidential Nomination Politics*. Washington, D.C.: Campaign Finance Institute.

Citrin, Jack, and Ben Highton. 2002. *How Race, Ethnicity, and Immigration Shape the California Electorate*. San Francisco: Public Policy Institute of California.

Conway, M. Margaret. 2000. *Political Participation in the United States*, 3rd ed. Washington, D.C.: CQ Press.

Cook, Fay Lomax. 1979. *Who Should be Helped? Public Support for Social Services*. Beverly Hills, Calif.: Sage Publications.

Cook, Fay Lomax, and Edith J. Barrett. 1992. *Support for the American Welfare State: The Views of Congress and the Public*. New York: Columbia University Press.

Cook, Fay Lomax, and Lawrence R. Jacobs. 2001. "Assessing Assumptions about Americans' Attitudes Toward Social Security: Popular Claims Meet Hard Data." Paper presented at the Annual Conference of the National Academy of Social Insurance. National Press Club, Washington, D.C. (January 24).

de la Garza, Rodolfo O., Louis De Sipio, F. Chris Garcia, John Garcia, and Angelo Falcon. 1992. *Latino Voices: Mexican, Puerto Rican, and Cuban Perspectives on American Politics*. Boulder, Colo.: Westview Press.

Espiritu, Yen Le. 1992. *Asian American Panethnicity: Bridging Institutions and Identities*. Philadelphia: Temple University Press.

Ferguson, Thomas. 1995. *Golden Rule: The Investment Theory of Party Competition and the Logic of Money-Driven Political Systems*. Chicago: University of Chicago Press.

Ferguson, Thomas, and Joel Rogers. 1986. *Right Turn: The Decline of the Democrats and the Future of American Politics*. New York: Hill and Wang.

Fiorina, Morris P. 1999. "Extreme Voices: A Dark Side of Civic Engagement." In *Civic Engagement in American Democracy*, edited by Theda Skocpol and Morris Fiorina. Washington, D.C.: Brookings Institution.

———. 2001. "Parties, Participation, and Representation in America: Old Theories Face New Realities." In *Political Science: State of the Discipline*, edited by Ira Katznelson and Helen V. Milner. New York: W. W. Norton.

———. 2005. *Culture War: The Myth of a Polarized America*. New York: Pearson Longman.

Flanigan, William H., and Nancy H. Zingale. 2002. *Political Behavior of the American Electorate*, 10th ed. Washington, D.C.: CQ Press.

Free, Lloyd A., and Hadley Cantril. 1968. *The Political Beliefs of Americans: A Study of Public Opinion*. New York: Simon & Schuster.

Freeman, Jo. 1975. *The Politics of Women's Liberation*. New York: David McKay.

———. 1987. "What You Know versus Whom You Represent: Feminist Influence in the Democratic and Republican Parties." In *The Women's Movements of the United States and Western Europe*, edited by Mary Fainsod Katzenstein and Carol McClurg Mueller. Philadelphia: Temple University Press.

Freeman, Richard B. 2004. "What, Me Vote?" In *Social Inequality*, edited by Kathryn M. Neckerman. New York: Russell Sage Foundation.

Gerring, John. 1998. *Party Ideologies in America: 1828–1996*. New York: Cambridge University Press.

Gilens, Martin. 1999. *Why Americans Hate Welfare: Race, Media, and the Politics of Antipoverty Policy*. Chicago: University of Chicago Press.

Goldfield, Michael. 1987. *The Decline of Organized Labor in the United States*. Chicago: University of Chicago Press.

Hansen, Susan B. 1983. *The Politics of Taxation: Revenue without Representation*. New York: Praeger.

Harris, Frederick C. 1999. *Something Within: Religion in African-American Political Activism*. New York: Oxford University Press.

Heinz, John P., Edward O. Laumann, Robert L. Nelson, and Robert H. Salisbury. 1993. *The Hollow Core: Private Interests in National Policymaking*. Cambridge, Mass.: Harvard University Press.

Hershey, Marjorie R., and Paul A. Beck. 2003. *Party Politics in America*. 10th ed. New York: Longman.

Hochschild, Jennifer L. 1981. *What's Fair: American Beliefs about Distributive Justice*. Cambridge, Mass.: Harvard University Press.

Hritzuk, Natasha, and David K. Park. 2000. "The Question of Latino Participation: From an SES to a Social Structural Explanation." *Social Science Quarterly* 81(1): 151–66.

Imig, Douglas R. 1996. *Poverty and Power: The Political Representation of Poor Americans*. Lincoln: University of Nebraska Press.

Iyengar, Shanto, and Donald R. Kinder. 1987. *News that Matters*. Chicago: University of Chicago Press.

Jackson, John S., Nathan S. Bigelow, and John C. Green. 2003. "The State of the Party Elites: National Convention Delegates, 1992–2000." In *The State of the Parties*, 4th ed, edited by John C. Green and Rick Farmer.. Lanham, Md.: Rowman and Littlefield.

Katosh, John P., and Michael W. Traugott. 1981. "The Consequences of Validated and Self-Reported Voting Measures." *Public Opinion Quarterly* 45(4): 519–35.

Keyssar, Alexander. 2000. *The Right to Vote*. New York: Basic Books.

Kinder, Donald R., and Lynn M. Sanders. 1996. *Divided by Color: Racial Politics and Democratic Ideals*. Chicago: University of Chicago Press.

Kirkpatrick, Jeane. 1976. *The New Presidential Elite*. New York: Russell Sage Foundation.

Kluegel, James R., David S. Mason, and Bernd Wegener, eds. 1995. *Social Justice and Political Change: Public Opinion in Capitalist and Post-Communist States*. New York: Aldine de Gruyter.

Ladd, Everett Carll, and Karlyn H. Bowman. 1998. *Attitudes Toward Economic Inequality*. Washington, D.C.: AEI Press.

Leighley, Jan E. 1995. "Attitudes, Opportunities, and Incentives: A Field Essay on Political Participation." *Political Research Quarterly* 48: 181–209.

———. 2001. *Strength in Numbers?: The Political Mobilization of Racial and Ethnic Minorities*. Princeton, N.J.: Princeton University Press.

Leighley, Jan E., and Jonathan Nagler. 1992a. "Socioeconomic Class Bias in Turnout, 1964–1988: The Voters Remain the Same." *American Political Science Review* 86(3): 725–36.

———. 1992b. "Individual and Systemic Influences on Turnout: Who Votes?" *Journal of Politics* 54(3): 718–40.

Leighley, Jan E., and Arnold Vedlitz. 1999. "Race, Ethnicity, and Political Participation: Competing Models and Contrasting Expectations." *Journal of Politics* 61(4): 1092–1114.

Lien, Pei-Te, M. Margaret Conway, and Janelle Wong. 2004. *The Politics of Asian Americans*. New York: Routledge.

Lindblom, Charles. 1977. *Politics and Markets: The World's Political Economic Systems*. New York: Basic Books.

Lipset, Seymour Martin, and William Schneider. 1983. *The Confidence Gap: Business, Labor, and Government in the Public Mind*. New York: Macmillan.

Lipsky, Michael. 1968. "Protest as a Political Resource." *American Political Science Review* 62(4): 1144–58.

Lowi, Theodore. 1969. *The End of Liberalism: Ideology, Policy, and the Crisis of Public Authority*. New York: W. W. Norton.

———. 1971. *The Politics of Disorder*. New York: W. W. Norton.

Mansbridge, Jane J. 1986. *Why We Lost the ERA*. Chicago: University of Chicago Press.

Manza, Jeff, Fay Lomax Cook, and Benjamin Page, eds. 2002. *Navigating Public Opinion: Polls, Policy, and the Future of American Democracy*. New York: Oxford University Press.

McAdam, Doug. 1982. *Political Process and the Development of Black Insurgency, 1930–1970*. Chicago: University of Chicago Press.

McCarthy, John, and Mayer Zald. 1977. "Resource Mobilization and Social Movements: A Partial Theory." *American Journal of Sociology* 82(6): 1212–41.

McCarty, Nolan, Keith T. Poole, and Howard Rosenthal. 1997. *Income Redistribution and the Realignment of American Politics*. Washington, D.C.: AEI Press.

McClosky, Herbert, and John R. Zaller. 1984. *The American Ethos: Public Attitudes Toward Capitalism and Democracy*. Cambridge, Mass.: Harvard University Press.

McConnell, Grant. 1966. *Private Power and American Democracy*. New York: Alfred A. Knopf.

McDonald, Michael, and Samuel Popkin. 2001. "The Myth of the Vanishing Voter." *American Political Science Review* 95(4): 963–74.

McFarland, Andrew. 1992. "Interest Groups and The Policymaking Process:

Sources of Countervailing Power in America." In *The Politics of Interests*, edited by Mark P. Petracca. Boulder, Colo.: Westview Press.

McGerr, Michael. 1986. *The Decline of Popular Politics: The American North, 1865–1928*. New York: Oxford University Press.

Mehrtens, F. John, III. 2004. "Three Worlds of Public Opinion? Values, Variation, and the Effect on Social Policy." *International Journal of Public Opinion Research* 16(2): 115–43.

Meltzer, Allan H., and Scott F. Richard. 1981. "A Rational Theory of the Size of Government." *The Journal of Political Economy* 89(5): 914–27.

Meyer, David S. 2000. "Social Movements: Creating Communities of Change." In *Feminist Approaches to Social Movements, Community, and Power*, vol. 1: *Conscious Acts and the Politics of Social Change*, edited by Robin L. Teske and Mary Ann Tetreault. Columbia: University of South Carolina Press.

Meyer, David, Nancy Whittier, and Belinda Robnett, eds. 2002. *Social Movements: Identity, Culture, and the State*. Oxford: Oxford University Press.

Milbrath, Lester W., and M. L. Goel. 1977. *Political Participation: How and Why Do People Get Involved in Politics?* 2nd ed. Chicago: Rand McNally.

Minkoff, Debra C. 1995. *Organizing for Equality*. New Brunswick, N.J.: Rutgers University Press.

Morgan, Robin, ed. 1970. *Sisterhood Is Powerful*. Vintage; New York: Random House.

Morris, Aldon. 1984. *The Origins of the Civil Rights Movement: Black Communities Organizing for Change*. New York: Free Press.

Morris, Aldon, and Carol McClurg Mueller, eds. 1992. *Frontiers of Social Movement Theory*. New Haven, Conn.: Yale University Press.

National Telecommunications and Information Administration. 1997. "Falling Through the Net II: New Data on the Digital Divide." Available at: http://www.ntia.doc.gov/ntiahome/net2/falling.html (accessed April 19, 2005).

Nie, Norman, Jane Junn, and Kenneth Stehlik-Barry. 1996. *Education and Democratic Citizenship in America*. Chicago: University of Chicago Press.

Norris, Pippa. 2001. *Digital Divide: Civic Information, Information Poverty, and the Internet Worldwide*. Cambridge: Cambridge University Press.

Olson, Mancur, Jr. 1965. *The Logic of Collective Action: Public Goods and the Theory of Groups*. Cambridge, Mass.: Harvard University Press.

Osberg, Lars, and Timothy Smeeding. 2003. An International Comparison of Preferences for Leveling. Working Paper. New York: Russell Sage Foundation.

Page, Benjamin I. 2000. "Is Social Security Reform Ready for the American Public?" In *Social Security and Medicare: Individual vs. Collective Risk and Responsibility*, edited by Sheila Burke, Eric Kingson, and Uwe Reinhardt. Washington, D.C.: National Academy of Social Insurance.

——. 2001. "Public Support for Medicare Coverage of Younger Age Groups." Paper presented at the annual meeting of the American Public Health Association. Atlanta (October 21–25).

Page, Benjamin I., and Robert Y. Shapiro. 1992. *The Rational Public: Fifty Years of Trends in American's Policy Preferences*. Chicago: University of Chicago Press.

Page, Benjamin I., Robert Y. Shapiro, and Glenn R. Dempsey. 1987. "What Moves Public Opinion?" *American Political Science Review* 81(1): 23–43.

Page, Benjamin I., and James R. Simmons. 2000. *What Government Can Do: Dealing with Poverty and Inequality*. Chicago: University of Chicago Press.

Piven, Frances Fox, and Richard Cloward. 1971. *Regulating the Poor*. New York: Vintage Books.

——. 1977. *Poor People's Movements*. New York: Vintage Books.

Powell, G. Bingham. 1986. "American Voter Turnout in Comparative Perspective." *American Political Science Review* 80(1): 17–43.

Presser, Stanley, and Michael Traugott. 1992. "Little White Lies and Social Science Models: Correlated Response Errors in a Panel Study of Voting." *Public Opinion Quarterly* 56(1): 77–86.

Putnam, Robert D. 2000. *Bowling Alone: The Collapse and Revival of American Community*. New York: Simon & Schuster.

Radcliff, Benjamin, and Patricia Davis. 2000. "Labor Organization and Electoral Participation in Industrial Democracies." *American Journal of Political Science* 44(1): 132–41.

Robnett, Belinda. 1997. *How Long? How Long? African-American Women in the Struggle for Civil Rights*. New York: Oxford University Press.

Rosenstone, Steven J., and John Mark Hansen. 1993. *Mobilization, Participation, and Democracy in America*. New York: Macmillan.

Rusk, Jerrold G. 1970. "The Effect of Australian Ballot Reform on Split Ticket Voting: 1876–1908." *American Political Science Review* 64(4): 1220–38.

Saloma, John S. III. 1984. *Ominous Politics: The New Conservative Labyrinth*. New York: Hill and Wang.

Schattschneider, E. E. 1960. *The Semi-Sovereign People: A Realist's View of Democracy in America*. New York: Holt, Rinehart and Winston.

Schier, Steven E. 2000. *By Invitation Only: The Rise of Exclusive Politics in the United States*. Pittsburgh: University of Pittsburgh Press.

Schlozman, Kay Lehman. 2002. "Citizen Participation in America: What Do We Know? Why Do We Care?" In *Political Science: The State of the Discipline*, edited by Ira Katznelson and Helen V. Milner. New York: W. W. Norton.

Schlozman, Kay Lehman, Henry E. Brady, Sidney Verba, and Jennifer Erkulwater. 2001. "Growing Up, Settling Down, and Becoming Active: Political Participation over the Life Cycle." Paper presented at the annual meeting of the Midwest Political Science Association. Chicago (April 19–22).

Schlozman, Kay Lehman, and John T. Tierney. 1986. *Organized Interests and American Democracy*. New York: Harper and Row.

Schlozman, Kay Lehman, and Sidney Verba. 1987. "Sending a Message–Getting a Reply: Presidential Elections and Democratic Accountability." In *Elections in America*, edited by Kay Lehman Schlozman. Winchester, Mass.: Allen and Unwin.

Schuman, Howard, Charlotte Steeh, and Lawrence Bobo. 1985. *Racial Attitudes in America: Trends and Interpretations*. Cambridge, Mass.: Harvard University Press.

Scott, Anne Firor, and Andrew MacKay Scott. 1975. *One Half the People*. Urbana: University of Illinois Press.

Sears, David O. 1988. "Symbolic Racism." In *Eliminating Racism: Profiles in Controversy*, edited by Phylis Katz and Dalmas A. Taylor. New York: Plenum.

Sears, David O., Jim Sidanius, and Lawrence Bobo. 2000. *Racialized Politics: The Debate about Racism in America*. Chicago: University of Chicago Press.

Shafer, Byron E., and William J. M. Claggett. 1995. *The Two Majorities: The Issue Context of American Politics*. Baltimore: Johns Hopkins University Press.

Shields, Todd G., and Robert K. Goidel. 1997. "Participation Rates, Socioeconomic Class Biases, and Congressional Elections: A Cross Validation." *American Journal of Political Science* 41(2): 683–91.

———. 2000. "Who Contributes? Checkbook Participation, Class Biases, and the Impact of Legal Reforms, 1952–1994." *American Politics Quarterly* 28(1): 216–33.

Silbey, Joel H. 1991. *The American Political Nation 1838–1893*. Stanford, Calif.: Stanford University Press.

Silver, Brian D., Barbara A. Anderson, and Paul R. Abramson. 1986. "Who Over-reports Voting?" *American Political Science Review* 80(2): 612–24.

Sitkoff, Harvard. 1981. *The Struggle for Black Equality*. New York: Hill and Wang.

Skocpol, Theda. 2003. *Diminished Democracy: From Membership to Management in American Civic Life*. Norman: University of Oklahoma Press.

———. 2004a. "Civic Transformations and Inequality in the Contemporary United States." In *Social Inequality*, edited by Kathryn M. Neckerman. New York: Russell Sage Foundation.

———. 2004b. "Voice and Inequality: The Transformation of American Civic Democracy." *Perspectives on Politics* 2(1): 3–20.

Sniderman, Paul M., and Thomas Piazza. 1993. *The Scar of Race*. Cambridge, Mass.: Harvard University Press.

Snow, David, and Robert Benford. 1988. "Ideology, Frame Resonance and Participant Mobilization." *International Social Movement Research* 1: 197–217.

Snow, David, E. Burke Rochford, Jr., Steven K. Worden, and Robert Benford. 1986. "Frame Alignment Processes, Micromobilization, and Movement Participation." *American Sociological Review* 51(4): 464–81.

Stefancic, Jean, and Richard Delgado. 1996. *No Mercy: How Conservative Think Tanks and Foundations Changed America's Social Agenda*. Philadelphia: Temple University Press.

Stonecash, Jeffrey M. 2000. *Class and Party in American Politics.* Boulder, Colo.: Westview Press.

Strate, John M., Charles J. Parrish, Charles D. Elder, and Coit Ford III. 1989. "Life Span Civic Development and Voting Participation." *American Political Science Review* 83(2): 443–64.

Swenson, Peter A. 2002. *Capitalists Against Markets: The Making of Labor Markets and Welfare States in the United States and Sweden.* New York: Oxford University Press.

Tarrow, Sidney. 1998a. *Power in Movement*, 2nd ed. Cambridge: Cambridge University Press.

——. 1998b. "'The Very Excess of Democracy': State Building and Contentious Politics in America." In *Social Movements and American Political Institutions*, edited by Anne N. Costain and Andrew S. McFarland. Lanham, Md.: Rowman and Littlefield.

Teixeira, Ruy A. 1992. *The Disappearing American Voter.* Washington, D.C.: Brookings Institution.

Tilly, Charles. 1978. *From Mobilization to Revolution.* Reading, Mass.: Addison-Wesley.

Traugott, Michael W., and Katosh, John P. 1979. "Response Validity in Surveys of Voting Behavior." *Public Opinion Quarterly* 43(3): 359–77.

Truman, David B. 1971. *The Governmental Process: Political Interests and Public Opinion*, 2nd ed. New York: Alfred A. Knopf.

Verba, Sidney, Henry Brady, and Kay Lehman Schlozman. 2004. "Why No Confiscation in America?: Political Participation, Political Parties, and the Median Voter Theorem." Paper presented at the annual meeting of the American Political Science Association. Chicago (September 3).

Verba, Sidney, and Norman H. Nie. 1972. *Participation in America.* New York: Harper and Row.

Verba, Sidney, Norman Nie, and Jae-on Kim. 1979. *Participation and Political Equality: A Seven Nation Comparison.* New York: Cambridge University Press.

Verba, Sidney, and Gary R. Orren. 1985. *Inequality in America: The View from the Top.* Cambridge, Mass.: Harvard University Press.

Verba, Sidney, Kay Lehman Schlozman, and Henry Brady. 1995. *Voice and Equality: Civic Voluntarism in American Politics.* Cambridge, Mass.: Harvard University Press.

Vogel, David. 1989. *Fluctuating Fortunes: The Power of Business in America.* New York: Basic Books.

Walker, Jack. 1991. *Mobilizing Interest Groups in America: Patrons, Professions, and Social Movements.* Ann Arbor: University of Michigan Press.

Wattenberg, Martin P. 1991. *The Rise of Candidate-Centered Politics.* Cambridge, Mass.: Harvard University Press.

Weakliem, David L., Robert Andersen, and Anthony F. Heath. 2003. "The Direct-

ing Power? A Comparative Study of Public Opinion and Income Distribution."
Storrs, Conn.: Department of Sociology, University of Connecticut.

West, Darell M., and Burdett A. Loomis. 1998. *The Sound of Money: How Political Interests Get What They Want.* New York: W. W. Norton.

Wilcox, Clyde. 2003. "Individual Donors in the Presidential Nomination Process." Unpublished manuscript.

Wilson, James Q. 1960. *The Amateur Democrat.* Chicago: University of Chicago Press.

———. 1973. *Political Organizations.* New York: Basic Books.

Wolfinger, Raymond, and Steven Rosenstone. 1980. *Who Votes?* New Haven, Conn.: Yale University Press.

Wuthnow, Robert. 2002. "The United States: Bridging the Privileged and Marginalized?" In *Democracies in Flux,* edited by Robert D. Putnam. New York: Oxford University Press.

Chapter Three | Inequality and American Governance

Larry M. Bartels
Hugh Heclo
Rodney E. Hero
Lawrence R. Jacobs

WHAT GOVERNMENT officials hear influences what they do. The processes of American governance—from the activities of interest groups and political parties to the often Byzantine operations of lawmakers—are readily penetrated by the strong, clear, and frequent political voices of privileged and highly active citizens. Differences in the abilities of individual citizens and groups to set the policy agenda, frame debates, and adapt to institutional processes prompts governing institutions to respond unevenly to the concerns and preferences of American citizens. Yet the governing process is not simply a mechanical cash register that tabulates the unequal political voices of the advantaged and organized. Entrenched institutional norms, patterns of behavior, and collective conceptions of purposes and goals interact with the struggle for political power among rival individuals and government bodies to prevent any single group or set of ideas from consistently steering government decisionmaking in one direction.

The most persistent impact of stratified political participation is to reinforce the enduring bias of the American political process toward "deadlock and delay"—as the framers of the U.S. constitution and James Madison intended (Burns 1963). The recent growth in economic inequality appears to be increasing the power of individuals and groups who have a stake in doing little or nothing about substantially counteracting disparities based on income and wealth.

American government is characterized by a level of individualization and lack of authoritative lines of control that makes it particularly ill suited to respond to a broad, aggregate phenomenon such as economic inequality by consistently enacting effective remedial policies. The American political process is geared toward particularistic, piecemeal issues rather than the big picture. Politicians and government may respond to the rising income and wealth of a small proportion of citizens in a thousand little (and not so little) ways, but they are not likely to consistently do so in one big way. Even if officeholders were generally motivated to enact egalitarian tax and spending policies to stem the rising tide of economic inequality, their efforts to significantly change these policies would likely run into the kind of collective action problems that have stalled efforts on environmental protection, heath care, and homeland security.

The bias in the American political process toward inaction and responding to pressure from well-organized particularistic groups has created multiple and competing centers of influence and a corresponding patchwork of contradictory and incomplete economic and social welfare policies. One of the most demonstrable developments in the United States over the past half century has been the expansion of civil and political rights and, specifically, equality of opportunity in the economic realm and procedural equality in the political realm. Historically entrenched racial, ethnic, and gender discrimination has been challenged and the presence of previously underrepresented groups in the policymaking process has modestly expanded as a result. The ostensible aims of equity have been shaped, however, by the entrenched bias in the American political process to produce social rights for concrete and discrete groups such as seniors or the poor. The broader claims for establishing universal social rights and delivering substantive political and economic equality to all citizens lacked the intense support of powerful encompassing groups and institutional allies and clashed with the trajectory of American political development toward ensuring equality of opportunity more than equality of results. The consequence is that rising economic inequality has neither expanded nor reduced political inequality, nor even produced a dramatic redirection of overall government policy in the egalitarian or antiegalitarian direction. The pitched political battles over the past several decades and partisan cycles of frustrations and mobilizations have fueled the polarization of the Democratic and Republican parties and intimidated even the Democratic Party from energetically promoting the kind of egalitarian programs that some of its activists favor.

This chapter—which is divided into four parts—is based on a review of existing research on American governing institutions, political organizations, and the making of public policy. Our review was undertaken with an eye to identifying continuity and change in who makes government policy, how, and to what effect. In particular, we examined research on whether and how political influences on government policy reflects enduring disparities in political voice and has changed as economic inequality has risen and long entrenched racial, ethnic, and gender inequalities have been challenged.

We begin by acknowledging limitations on our efforts to evaluate the potential impact of unequal power in the making of public policy. The second section describes the broad institutional context of policymaking in the United States, including the complexities of the legislative process, federalism, and the nature of party politics. The third section outlines the role of interest groups and the impact of money in elections and in the policymaking process. The last section examines biases in political representation, with particular emphasis on whether patterns of unequal influence have altered in recent decades either with changing patterns of economic inequality or with expansions of civil and political rights.

CHALLENGES IN EVALUATING INEQUALITY IN AMERICAN GOVERNMENT

Our review of research that investigates the potential impacts of rising economic inequality and skewed political participation on the process of governing has faced two daunting challenges—a limited body of research and complex questions of causality.

Inequality is Understudied

Although the openness of the American governing process has attracted the critical scrutiny of political observers since the framing of the U.S. constitution in the late eighteenth century, contemporary political scientists who study political institutions and the governing process have generally not focused on studying this question with notable exceptions (for example, Mayhew 1991). There are two reasons that the current generation of American political scientists has generally failed to produce a substantial body of research motivated by a burning concern over the impact of unequal political voice and economic inequality on a democratic governing process. First, the increased theoretical and empirical sophistication of research on the governing process has coincided with a kind of hyperspecialization. It is not uncommon for students of Congress, for instance, to specialize in the House of Representatives, leaving research on the Senate to specialists on this chamber. Scholars retreat into specialized communities where self-enclosed debates are disconnected from broader research questions. One consequence of this growing specialization is that the impact on the governing process of political behavior and public opinion—separate scholarly enclaves themselves—is often neglected or understudied. A two step professional fragmentation has resulted—the carving of research on unequal voice as one field as distinct from the study of institutions, and then further compartmentalizing these fields into discrete sub-fields. Hyperspecialization has produced research that has expanded our understanding in particular areas but also makes efforts at synthesis—such as ours—quite difficult. In effect, we have pieces of the puzzle but are not sure if and how they fit together.

Second, the hyperspecialization of political science has generated a series of theoretical expectations and empirical generalizations that have avoided what are seen as inappropriate or distracting normative questions about the extent and nature of democratic governance. We fully appreciate that theoretically informed and empirically rigorous studies have dramatically expanded our understanding of distinct aspects of the national governing process including the internal dynamics of the legislative, executive, and judicial branches and specific aspects of their interactions. For instance, sophisticated research has been conducted on the interaction of presidents and Congress in passing legislation and scholars have developed theories and methodologies to investigate the processes by which the speaker of the House of Representatives refers bills to one or more committees as well as the significance of imperfect information for legislative organization and behavior. These and other bodies of research on the governing process have been impressive and professionally recognized but they have also generally avoided—with a few notable exceptions—an explicit, sustained, and critical consideration of larger questions about the nature of American democracy.

The result is that the contemporary political science profession has not maintained the tradition of investigating inequality and American democracy established by earlier generations of scholarly leaders including Woodrow Wilson, Charles Merriam, Pendleton Herring, E. E. Schattschneider, V. O. Key, Robert Dahl, and others. Although the APSA presidential address of Charles E. Lindblom highlighted this tendency in 1981 and scholars have documented it (Seidelman 1984), the subsequent response by scholars of American politics and policymaking institutions has been meager. The lack of a large and thoughtful body of research that links unequal political voice to the governing process has inevitably restricted our efforts at synthesis.

Wrestling with Causal Ambiguity

The second challenge to studying the connections of unequal political voice and rising economic inequality to the governing process is a series of conceptual and methodological hurdles that complicate efforts to establish causality. Four interrelated problems have plagued the efforts of political scientists attempting to analyze the relationships among economic and social conditions, political participation, and policy influence.

First is the *conversion problem*. Leading scholars have long warned about the error of confusing the possible bases of power (economic resources, military might, specialized knowledge, etc.) with the exercise of power (Simon 1953; Dahl 1963). While the disparity of resources available to some and not others can serve as an indicator of potential power, political scientists have to recognize that there is no self-evident conversion rate between nonpolitical resources and political power. Studying the ambiguities of skill, interest, and chance by which potential power is converted into realized power over policy outcomes requires a very fine-grained analytic reconstruction of events, something that few researchers have accomplished.

A second difficulty is the *nondecision problem*. Even where careful accounts are constructed, there remains the vexing problem of power over important decisions that were not made.[1] Power in repose, so to speak, can exercise its less empirically verifiable influence over what is not on the policy agenda, what options are off the bargaining table, and so on. For example, growing economic inequality since the mid-1970s appears to have been associated temporally with lessened, not greater, attention in policy debates to the principle of progressivity in federal income taxation (compared with the post–World War II generation when economic inequalities were narrower). Is this because concentrated economic power has translated into political power to keep progressivity off the policy agenda? The failure to enact national health insurance in the United States is an unusually salient illustration of entrenched interests preferring the status quo to change—a public decision on behalf of nonaction (Morone and Jacobs, 2005).

The third problem is one of *connecting inputs to outcomes*. The actual outcomes produced by government decisions on complicated matters of public policy—such as federal tax policy or social welfare policy—are usually the result of immensely long, tangled causal chains. The connection of these outcomes to any background assessments of political power is tenuous and often counterintuitive. The Earned Income Tax Credit (EITC) shows that changing the "black box" configures and reconfigures the connections between inputs and policy outcomes in ways that are difficult to trace or to predict. It was created, institutionalized, and rapidly expanded under dramatically shifting partisan and ideological developments (from the Reagan Revolution of the 1980s to the Clinton administrations) as well as under the presumed stern hand of conditional party government that is hostile to redistributive policy (Thorndike and Ventry 2002).

Finally, there is the *problem of observation*. Research on some of the most important questions in American politics—such as the influence of money on the governing process—relies on analyzing concrete, observable patterns of influence: namely, situations in which the efforts of distinct individuals and organizations (whether interest groups or congressional leaders or party caucuses) explain the behavior of others (such as individual members of Congress). Contemporary political scientists have generally neglected a second approach that relies on functional and structural analysis of the political system to explain patterns of behavior for which there may not be concrete and observable connections (for example, Easton 1965; O'Connor 1973). This approach focuses on identifying the imperatives for the continued maintenance of the political order and then reasons backwards to identify critical functions of government and systemwide incentives that constrain individual actors. Although there is no consistent evidence that campaign contributions are related to the votes of members of Congress (controlling for party and ideology), a structural and functional analysis may valuably highlight predispositions of members to align their views with important contributors before they run for office.

In short, any effort to search for connections between skewed political participation and policy outcomes are beset by daunting questions of causality, prompting us to proceed with humility. The political dynamics in complex and multilevel causal chains are far richer than can be captured by an assumed clash of egalitarian versus antiegalitarian interests over government policy on taxes and spending. The play of ideas, offsetting interests, institutional biases, and electoral calculations seem designed to scramble any neat patterns of conversion and nondecision regarding potential power and actual outcomes in tax policy.[2] Effects of growing economic inequality on governance are not likely to emerge as a few big, demonstrable causal statements but as a multitude of indirect influences and inferences.

POLITICAL PARTIES, POLARIZATION, AND INEQUALITY

A common critique of American political institutions is that their fragmentation, decentralized structures, weak authoritative lines of control, and multiple veto points position the organized and politically vocal to block policies that threaten their intense preferences and to push through targeted decisions that favor their particularistic interests.[3] American political scientists have commonly argued that the cure for these ills of the political system would be found in stronger, more unified and "responsible" political parties. Indeed, the most influential previous task force of the American Political Science Association argued vigorously half a century ago for movement "Toward a More Responsible Two-Party System" (American Political Science Association 1950).

In the past three decades, political parties have emerged as an increasingly coherent and significant force, both in the electorate and in the halls of government—much as the advocates of "responsible parties" hoped they would. Somewhat surprisingly, however, the increasing unity of each political party and their growing bifurcation within government has reinforced rather than counteracted existing institutional tendencies (especially within Congress) toward deadlock on comprehensive policy and disproportional influence for the well-organized and vocal on more targeted policy. In particular, the increasing polarization of the parties in the electorate and in Congress seems to be fueling two developments in national legislative politics that reinforce political inequality—conditional party government in Congress that often stymies comprehensive policy responses to rising economic inequality and increased partisan segmentation of beneficiaries of government policy.

The Resurgence of Political Parties in the Electorate

One of the most-analyzed developments in modern American politics is the "decline of parties" in the 1960s and early 1970s (for example, Broder 1971; Abramson 1976; Wattenberg 1998). Evidence of decline appeared in each of the three arenas monitored by scholars of party politics—parties as organizations, parties in government, and parties in the electorate. In the organizational realm, the last of the traditional party machines that dominated many American cities through the first half of the twentieth century seemed to be disappearing (Mayhew 1986). Politicians seeking office relied increasingly on their own efforts (and those of professional campaign consultants, pollsters, and television ad producers) to secure a "personal vote" (Cain, Ferejohn, and Fiorina 1987; Kelley 1956). In government, party unity and party-line voting in Congress declined significantly through the 1960s, while Republican presidents (first Eisenhower, then Nixon) appeared to accept and entrench their Democratic predecessors' ambitious domestic policy initiatives. Meanwhile, partisan loyalties in the electorate weakened markedly, with the proportion of "strong" party identifiers in National Election Study (NES) surveys declining by almost one-third between 1964 and 1972 (from more than 35 percent to about 25 percent) and the proportion of "independents" increasing correspondingly. As Fiorina summarized the thrust of scholarly interpretations, "parties were deteriorating, decomposing, and disappearing. The country had entered a period of electoral disaggregation, an era of dealignment" (2002, 94).

But just as political scientists began to conclude that "organized political parties may be an anachronism" (Niemi and Weisberg 1976, 414), the electorate became more attentive to political parties. The proportion of "strong" party identifiers in the electorate increased substantially after 1976, while the proportion of "independents" declined; at the same time, the strength of the relationship between partisanship and voting behavior also increased markedly, reaching levels by the late 1990s well in excess of those prevailing in the 1950s (Miller 1991; Bartels 2000). And citizens increasingly saw important differences between the parties, recognized their relative ideological positions, and preferred one party to the other in both overall ratings and open-ended comments (Hetherington 2001).

These trends continued in 2004. Exit poll data from the 2004 presidential election show a continued high level of consistency between partisanship and voting behavior, with 93 percent of Republicans supporting Bush and 89 percent of Democrats casting their ballots for Kerry.

A Shifting Landscape   If these signs of party resurgence do not bespeak a return to the status quo ante, they nevertheless reflect an important shift in the American political landscape. While many citizens remain disengaged from the parties—and, for that matter, from the political process more generally—those who are interested and attentive have increasingly been choosing up sides, producing an electoral landscape that is more partisan and more ideological than at any point in the past half-century. The precise causal connections between partisanship and ideology are a matter of some scholarly dispute at the mass level, as they are at the elite level (Fiorina 2002; Miller 2000; Bartels 2002; and Krehbiel 1993). Nevertheless, party competition seems more vibrant, and potentially more consequential, than at any time in recent memory.

A particularly important development for our purposes is that mass partisanship has become increasingly correlated with income over the past half-century (McCarty, Poole, and Rosenthal 2003). As the parties in Congress have polarized on economic issues (Poole and Rosenthal 1984; McCarty, Poole, and Rosenthal 1997), the public has followed suit, with the rich gravitating increasingly to the Republican Party and the poor aligning more reliably with the Democratic Party. Thus, for example, NES respondents in the top income quintile were only a little more likely than those in the bottom income quintile to identify as Republicans in 1956 and 1960, but more than twice as likely as those in the bottom income quintile to identify as Republicans in 1992 and 1996 (McCarty, Poole, and Rosenthal 2003, 3–4). The result is a class cleavage in partisanship and voting behavior that is modest by European standards but considerably sharper than in the recent American past.

Political parties are bifurcating along not only class lines but also racial lines, which in some cases has complicated class alliances. The Civil

Rights legislation of the 1960s sparked an exodus of white voters in the South from the Democratic to the Republican Party. After the 1960s, the Democrats became more likely than Republicans to support government action to aid minorities, and racial policy became a key distinguishing feature separating the two parties (Carmines and Stimson 1989; Poole and Rosenthal 1997). Race contributed to the polarization of the political parties, complicating efforts to redress entrenched inequalities between the races in terms of life opportunities and conditions.

Congressional Polarization and "Conditional Party Government"

The emergence since the 1970s of "conditional party government"—characterized by the steady increase in party unity and party-line voting in Congress—has further complicated the already treacherous arena of redistributive politics and reduced the potential for mitigating economic and political inequalities among more diffuse publics. Compared to the enfeebled legislative parties that existed during the golden age of the committee process, parties reasserted themselves in the 1970s as a decisive force in congressional organization (Aldrich and Rhode 1998, 2000, 2001; Cox and McCubbins 1993; Kiewiet and McCubbins 1991; Rohde 1991; Sinclair 1995). The core organizational change was the reduction in the autonomy and control of standing committees regarding the content of legislation and its flow to the floor as well as the selection of its chairs based on seniority. In place of committee dominance, party caucuses and leaders assumed greater power over the composition of committees (including its chairs) and the full range of legislative business (particularly in the House where committees are more crucial than the more loosely structured Senate). Legislative parties have been found to exert particular influence on the policymaking agenda (Sinclair 1995; Taylor 1998), committee behavior (Maltzman 1998), and, especially, roll call voting. The emergence of legislative parties as the primary political muscle was reflected in significant changes in campaign contribution patterns: PACs disproportionately funneled contributions not only to members who sit on committees with jurisdiction over issues of importance to them (Hall and Wayman 1990; Romer and Snyder 1994; Grier and Munger 1991, 1993) but also to members of the majority party and its leaders (Taylor 2003; Cox and Magar 1999; Rudolph 1999).

Conditional party government arises from two significant developments. First, the Democratic and, especially, Republican parties became more ideologically homogenous. The proportion of members who had regularly crossed the aisle to work with members of the opposite party (such as conservative southern Democrats like the powerful chair of the Ways and Means Committee, Wilbur Mills, and the liberal northern Republican Jacob Javits) declined and were replaced in each party by more ideologically extreme politicians who offered unwavering support for their party's core philosophy (McCarty, Poole, and Rosenthal 1997; Bond and Fleisher 1990; Fleisher and Bond 1996). It is telling that the Republican surge in 1994 hurt moderate Democrats more than extreme liberals who fared much better. The homogenization of intraparty preferences is evident in a number of trends. Most roll call votes on the floor of the House and Senate no longer divided each party as they did from 1945 to 1976. There was also a significant decline since the mid-1970s in the proportion of close floor votes in Congress where more than 10 percent of each party disagreed with a majority of their party. Finally, the ideological position of each party's members moved closer together. Analysis of the distance between the votes of members of the same party in the House and Senate shows that there was less division within each party by the end of the twentieth century than at any time since 1947 (Poole and Rosenthal 1997, 1984; McCarty, Poole, and Rosenthal 1997).

Second, both political parties moved further from each other and became increasingly polarized. The bold lines in figures 3.1 and 3.2 show the distance separating the average Democrat from the average Republican in the House and the Senate, respectively, on a liberal-conservative scale (Poole and Rosenthal 1997; McCarty, Poole, and Rosenthal, forthcoming). The separate plots for Democrats and Republicans at the bottom of each figure show the average ideological distance between members of the same party. Both figures show that interparty ideological distances have increased markedly since the early 1970s while intraparty ideological heterogeneity has decreased. The result is that roll call votes in Congress are more frequently divided between liberals and conservatives in the 1990s than at any time since 1947 when President Harry Truman faced a contentious Republican-dominated Congress. As Democrats and Republicans became more ideologically homogeneous and polarized, political parties decisively influenced roll call voting and, more generally, provided the organizational glue that the committee system had previously supplied (Cox and Poole 2002).

The partisan realignment in the South due to the Civil Rights movement contributed to the polarization. The steady increase in the identification of white southerners with the Republican Party produced a decline in the number of conservative southern Democrats in Congress (improving the legislative unity of the Democratic Party) and an increase in the number of Republicans at a time when the rising population of the South boosted the region's representation in the House. The gradual transfor-

Figure 3.1   Average Ideological Distance in the House

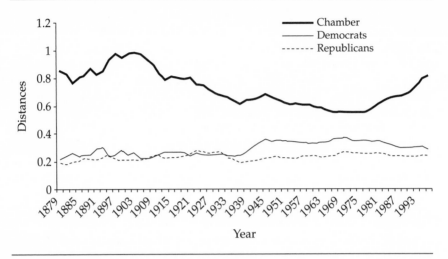

Source: McCarty, Poole, and Rosenthal (forthcoming).

Figure 3.2   Average Ideological Distance in the Senate

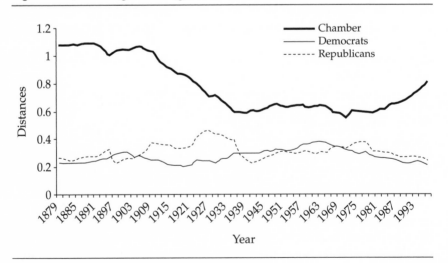

Source: McCarty, Poole, and Rosenthal (forthcoming).

mation of southern politics coincided with the historic trend in Congress toward more conservative Republicans, proportionately more liberal Democrats, and fewer moderates. The result is that political parties are fiercely polarized over policies that explicitly aim to reverse racial differences in economic and political resources.

The degree of party unity and party-line voting in Congress would seem to meet the requirements for "responsible party government" called for by E. E. Schattschneider and the American Political Science Task Force he chaired (Schattschneider 1942, 1960; American Political Science Association 1950), notwithstanding the persistent potential for gridlock in a complex, fragmented political system (Krehbiel 1998). Progressive observers of mid-century American politics hoped that a "responsible" party system would usher in policy changes favorable to broad publics and the less well off by making it possible for voters to choose between cohesive party teams offering distinct platforms and then be empowered to implement those platforms once elected. Recent American politics does not indicate, however, that party government—or at least the conditional form in the U.S. Congress—inherently favors progressive policy change.

Indeed, some research suggests that changes in partisan polarization in Congress and changes in economic inequality have gone hand in hand. Figure 3.3 (reproduced from McCarty, Poole, and Rosenthal, forthcoming) plots the level of economic inequality since 1947 (measured by the Gini coefficient) against the level of political polarization (measured by the average distance between the parties in the House of Representatives on a liberal-conservative continuum). In terms of timing, at least, the growing polarization of political elites has been closely related to rising economic inequality during the past three decades. The explanation for this relationship is not clear, and suggests the need for careful investigation of the political sources (and consequences) of rising economic inequality.

Partisan Differences in Redistributive Policies

Previous research on the significance of political parties for democratic governance has tended to focus on the process or nature of party competition rather than on the policy content or distributional consequences of which political party controls the reins of government. More recent research on the policy effects of party competition suggests that which party controls government matters, with Democrats (until recently) pursuing policies that redistribute economic resources from the rich to the poor and Republicans moving in the opposite direction. In other words, the interaction of party control and political polarization may be an important factor in rising economic inequality or, more precisely, in the ineffectiveness of

Figure 3.3   Income Inequality and Political Polorization

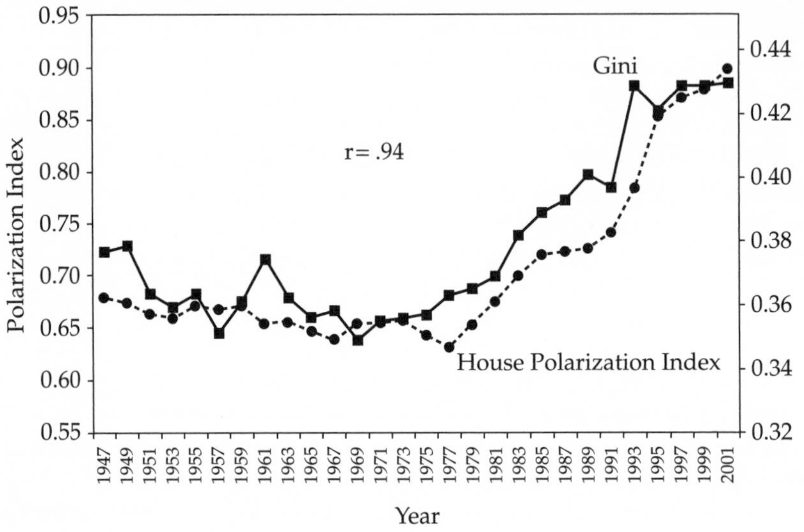

Source: McCarty, Poole, and Rosenthal (forthcoming).
Note: Polarization, Computation of Average DW-NOMINATE distance between Republicans and Democrats by authors. There is one data point for each two-year Congress. The Gini index value is for the first year of the Congress. For example, the first data point is polarization for the 80th House, 1947–49 and the Gini value for 1947.

government in offsetting economic disparities that are generated by structural changes in the economy.

The Process Approach   The process approach to parties and inequality has origins in V. O. Key's famous argument in *Southern Politics in State and Nation* that well-organized party competition (defined as stable, programmatically coherent, and "factional[ly] responsible") facilitates the political participation and influence of the economically disadvantaged. For Key, "over the long run the have-nots lose in a disorganized politics (Key 1949, 307)." Key's "have not" hypothesis was inspired by his close study of the one-party politics of the South in the Jim Crow era, which suggested that the southern states with the most stable, cohesive factional structures had more genuine competition between "ins" and "outs," a greater "sense of corporate responsibility" among elected officials, less "favoritism and graft" in the conduct of government business, and more "power to discipline wild-eyed men" on the explosive issue of race—all factors contributing, in Key's view, to rational public consideration of the "crucial issues" of "taxation and expenditure." By comparison, less stable factional structures only sporadically facilitated "the old Populist battle of the poor, white farmer against the plantation regions," while the states with the most "discontinuous and kaleidoscopic" factional structures were marked by "issueless politics" lacking even "a semblance of factional responsibility," placing "a high premium on demagogic qualities of personality," and providing "great negative power to those with a few dollars to invest in legislative candidates." The implication Key drew from these observations was that stable, organized factional competition (which he thought of as approximating, under the peculiar historical conditions of the one-party South, "the role assigned elsewhere to political parties") is necessary, if not sufficient, to provide an "institutionalized mechanism for the expression of lower-bracket viewpoints" (Key 1949, 298–310).

Although Key appeared to abandon his hypothesized link of the "have nots" with organized party competition and students of parties have not generated much systematic empirical support for it,[4] the process account evolved from studying the structure of party competition to examining the closeness of the electoral division between Democrats and Republicans as measured by vote shares or seats in the state legislature. Early analyses of this sort found little impact of party competition on state policy outcomes (for example, Lockard 1959; Dye 1966; Winters 1976). The results of more recent studies are also mixed, but suggest, if anything, that an even partisan division between Democrats and Republicans may produce policy outcomes generally considered harmful to the political interests of "have-nots." For example, some research has found inconsistent but generally negative effects of party competition on the size of state governments (Rogers and Rogers 2000), while other research has found that evenly divided state legislatures produced lower taxes and lower levels of workers' compensation benefits (although the former result disappeared when the analysis included the ideology of the state electorate as a control variable) (Besley and Case 2003).

The Policy Approach   The critical missing piece of the process account was a consistent examination of the policy consequences of which party controls the reins of government. The policy approach to party competition helps to explain the tilt against egalitarianism in American governance.

A particularly important study of policy effects of party competition reported that the class basis of party competition rather than the closeness of party competition affects the political fortunes of the economically disadvantaged (as measured by the generosity of state welfare benefits) (Jennings 1979). Analysis of data from eight states showed that the six with class-based party systems from the New Deal through the 1960s (Connecticut, Louisiana, Massachusetts, Michigan, Minnesota, and Wisconsin) spent more on welfare than the two that did not (Indiana and Virginia). This study also found that the states with class-based party systems spent more on welfare when Democrats controlled state politics than when Republicans were in charge, suggesting that class-based politics is especially good for "have-nots" when their side wins. A broader analysis produced further empirical support for the latter effect, but not for the former effect: on average, states characterized by a class-based "New Deal" cleavage structure did not provide more generous welfare benefits than southern or "post-New Deal" states; but Democratic control did have a strong positive effect on welfare spending in the "New Deal" states, while partisan control had little or no impact in Southern or "post-New Deal" states (Brown 1995).

There is now a substantial body of research that establishes the political importance of which party controls the reins of government at any given time. Notwithstanding the popular perception that there's not a dime's worth of difference between Democrats and Republicans (as George Wallace used to say)—and notwithstanding a strong emphasis on the moderating effects of electoral competition in formal theories of majoritarian politics (Downs 1957)—political scientists have documented significant effects of partisan control on policymaking in a variety of realms.

Some of this research is based on comparisons across states and parallels the research on the effects of party competition. For example, studies have found partisan differences in state revenues and expenditures (Rogers and Rogers 2000), in taxes and spending patterns (though not in overall spending) (Besley and Case 2003), in state taxes as a share of gross state product (Knight 2000), and in Medicaid spending (Grogan 1994).[5] Related work demonstrated that welfare benefits were more generous in states with higher turnout rates among low-income voters, whether measured in absolute or relative terms (Hill, Leighley, and Hinton-Andersson 1995; Husted and Kenny 1997).

Analyses of partisan effects at the national level have been constrained by the obvious limitations of data imposed in the study of one political system rather than fifty. Notwithstanding those limitations, partisan control generally seems to be even more important at the national level than at the state level. For example, studies of state tax policy have documented only small partisan effects, presumably due to the political constraints imposed by federal tax policies and state constitutions (Lowery 1987; Morgan 1994). By comparison, studies of federal tax policy have found strong partisan effects on the progressivity of nominal or "symbolic" tax rates, albeit more modest effects on the progressivity of effective tax rates (Page 1983; Allen and Campbell 1994).

Post–World War II   A much more comprehensive study of the American political economy from the late 1940s through the early 1980s found significant partisan differences in a variety of important macroeconomic policies and outcomes, including monetary and fiscal policy (both more expansive under Democratic presidents), unemployment (lower under Democrats), real output (higher under Democrats), and income inequality (lower under Democrats) (Hibbs 1987; Hibbs and Dennis 1988).

Partisan differences in income growth patterns continued through the Clinton years. Lower- and middle-income families experienced substantial, statistically significant differences in their economic fortunes under Democratic as compared to Republican presidents from 1948 to 2001 (Bartels 2003). The less well off did slightly better than the affluent under Democratic presidents, producing a slight net decline in economic inequality. By contrast, the affluent did considerably better than the less affluent under Republican administrations, producing a notable net rise in income inequality. The average real pre-tax income growth rate in the second half of the 1900s for less affluent families at the 20th percentile of the income distribution was 2.6 percent under Democratic presidents, but only 0.6 percent under Republican presidents. Middle-class family incomes grew about twice as fast under Democrats (2.4 percent versus 0.9 percent at the fortieth percentile; 2.5 percent versus 1.3 percent at the sixtieth percentile), while the most affluent families at the ninety-fifth percentile of the income distribution fared equally well under both parties (with an average real income growth rate of 2.1 percent).

Obviously, substantial partisan differences in income growth patterns by income class have substantial implications for prevailing levels of economic inequality. Simulations suggest that steady application of Democratic income growth patterns throughout the past half-century would have entirely counteracted the dramatic increase in economic inequality experienced over this period, while steady application of Republican growth patterns would have caused inequality to increase almost 80 percent faster than it actually did (Bartels 2003).

For the post–World War II period as a whole, partisan differences in income growth rates seem to be traceable to the corresponding partisan differences in macroeconomic outcomes.[6] For example, the average unemployment rate from 1948 to 2001 was 30 percent higher under Republican presidents than under Democrats, while the average rate of real GDP growth was 30 percent lower; controlling for these differences accounted exactly for the observed partisan differences in lower- and middle-class income growth patterns. However, there is also some evidence suggesting that partisan differences in macroeconomic outcomes may have diminished in recent years, while partisan differences in tax and transfer policies have become relatively more important—due, for example, to the expansion of the Earned Income Tax Credit under Bill Clinton or tax cuts for the wealthy under George W. Bush (Bartels 2003).

Finally, large-scale historical analysis of "the macro polity" underscores the impact of political parties on the broad course of American public policy (Erikson, MacKuen, and Stimson 2002). Partisan control of government was by far the most important determinant of policy outputs in a complex analysis relating economic conditions, liberal or conservative shifts in "public mood," partisan loyalties in the electorate, presidential approval, election outcomes, and policymaking in the White House, Congress, and the Supreme Court. For example, the estimated effect on White House policy activity of replacing a Republican president with a Democrat was more than three times larger than the estimated direct effect of moving from the most conservative public mood on record (in 1952) to the most liberal public mood on record (in 1961). The estimated effects of partisan control on congressional policy activity were even larger (Erikson, MacKuen, and Stimson 2002, 204, 305, 308, 310). Although this macro analysis did not stress these findings, it is hard to interpret its findings without being mightily impressed by how substantially the course of public policy alters with changes in partisan control of the reins of government.

The Limits of Conditional Party Government

The current configuration of the American party system features a highly competitive balance between Republicans and Democrats in the electorate, in Congress, and in the Electoral College. But the intense competition has not produced a convergence at the midpoint of public opinion.[7] Rather, the parties are now more ideological, more cohesive, and more distinct in their supporting coalitions than at any time in recent memory. While a large segment of the public remains politically disengaged, attentive citizens have increasingly responded to these developments by choosing up sides, adopting more or less consistent packages of policy positions and partisan loyalties. The unusually high levels of voter turnout and partisan voting in 2004 may be significant indications of this heightened political consciousness.

The implications of increasing economic and ideological polarization of the parties and their supporting coalitions for the pursuit of egalitarian policies appear to depend primarily on the outcome of the partisan struggle for political dominance. For most of the twentieth century, the "have-nots" have benefited when the Democratic Party has won. Until recently, Democrats have consistently used their control over the reins of government to pursue high employment, high taxes, and other policies that generally redistributed economic resources from the rich to the poor. When Republicans have governed they have fairly consistently done the opposite.

Conditional Party Government makes it possible, at least in principle, to overcome the Madisonian system that deadlocks efforts to enact comprehensive policy and, in particular, to pursue concerted action on wide-ranging egalitarian initiatives. Indeed, the election in 1992 that brought Bill Clinton to the White House and Democratic control of both legislative chambers made it possible to formulate and introduce comprehensive health reform that would help lower income Americans, though of course the Madisonian system contributed to its demise.

But three factors have mitigated the potential of conditional party government to open the way for consistent egalitarian policies. First, the progressive preoccupation with encouraging party competition and Madison's fears that majorities would use democratic government to confiscate wealth both overlooked the fact that voters might choose a political party opposed to egalitarian policies. As it happens, the Republican Party has enjoyed greater leverage over both lawmaking branches in the past four decades than in the middle third of the twentieth century. The 2002 and 2004 elections have solidified Republican control over Congress and the White House, making egalitarian policy change increasingly unlikely in the short term. Second, divided government has positioned a disciplined contemporary Republican Party to capitalize on the Madisonian tools of deadlock to stymie egalitarian policies. The Republican Congress checked Clinton's policies, obstructing the president's efforts to enact health care reform and forcing the President to accept, for instance, significantly more draconian welfare reform legislation than he had originally proposed.

Third, the contemporary Democratic Party is ideologically further from Republicans than in decades but appears to have moved in a conservative direction. Even during Clinton's first two years in office when Democrats controlled Congress, he did not pursue a consistently egalitarian policy and his partisans never even voted on his top domestic priority—health care reform. The relative timidity of the contemporary Democratic Party reflects its dependence on raising campaign funds from the more affluent as well as strategic caution as it faces nearly unified Republican attacks for wastefulness and mismanagement, as concisely summarized in the charges of "tax and spend Democrats." The inability of the Democratic Party to regularly recruit a sizable group of moderate or liberal Republicans has both reduced its potential to form coalitions to support the kind of egalitarian policies enacted during the New Deal and Great Society legislation and stripped away valuable political cover against sweeping attacks on the Party's reputation. Fears of attacks from Republicans and the search for allies in a shrinking pool of cross-over Republicans have produced cautiousness among contemporary Democrats about proposing redistributive legislation.

In short, conditional party government has not ushered in redistributive government policies because they face fierce and unified Republican opposition, and strategically calibrated defensiveness by Democrats.

The Narrowcasting of Distributional Politics

The first major bias in the political process against the disadvantaged is that conditional party government in Congress "delays and deadlocks" comprehensive policy responses to rising economic inequality. The second main bias is that the well-organized and most vocal disproportionately receive piecemeal, particularistic policies.

Distributional politics and, specifically, the allocation of discretionary government expenditures to concentrated groups have a long and well-known tradition in American government. New developments over the past several decades have produced finer targeting of benefits to increasingly narrow groups.

By the 1970s, distributional politics or, in more earthy terms, "pork barrel" politics was well known as a process geared toward helping incumbents of both political parties in Congress. The call to "bring home the bacon" represented an institutional commitment to aiding incumbents by delivering benefits to congressional districts that would be clearly traceable to specific members of Congress and offer tangible evidence of the members' effectiveness in fighting for their constituents. A line of research reported that members of Congress had changed their institutional routines toward the non-partisan and non-controversial process of distributing particularized benefits to woo constituents (Fiorina 1989; Mayhew 1974; Ferejohn 1974). The bipartisan commitment to winning reelection and helping incumbents gave rise to the famed "triple alliance" or "iron triangles" of American politics in which sub-units within the legislative branch (committees and subcommittees) and the executive branch (agencies) worked with peak interest groups. Rather than interest groups and congressional committees competing and thereby counteracting each other as pluralist theory predicted, members of Congress abided by the norms of cooperation and mutual non-interference and allowed a substantial part of government decisions to fall under the control of narrow, semi-autonomous elites working within discrete policy areas (McConnell 1966; Lowi 1969). The committee system served as the focal point for the construction of logrolling coalitions.

Reforms of the Democratic and Republican Party nomination process, which enhanced the influence of party activists and campaign contributors, as well as shifts in the electorate (especially, the growing ideological homogenization of many congressional districts) generated incentives for targeting the distribution of pork in two directions after the 1970s. First, the power of political parties and their leaders increased, and the political incentives within Congress shifted toward disproportionately expanding the incumbency advantage of members of the majority party and away from a logrolling process aimed at helping members of both parties. With members increasingly convinced that pork produced votes (Alvarez and Saving 1997; Levitt and Snyder 1997), the majority party kept the lion's share of pork for their members to advantage their members. Research has found that the districts of majority party members has been disproportionately favored in the legislative distribution of defense dollars (Carsey and Rundquist 1999), transportation funding (Lee 2000), appropriation earmarks for higher education institutions (Balla et al. 2002), and federal grants generally (Levitt and Snyder 1995). The study of higher education demonstrated that the majority party made a shrewd strategic decision: even as the majority party disproportionately funneled funds to the districts of their members, it also "inoculated" itself against charges of wastefulness by legislators from the minority party by distributing some (albeit fewer) resources to them (Balla et al. 2002).

Second, the favoritism toward districts of majority party members was intensified by the efforts of members themselves to differentially funnel federal discretionary spending *within* their district. Evidence since the mid-1980s suggests that members calculated that the effectiveness of pork to enhance their prospects of reelection could be maximized by targeting federal money toward specific geographic areas within their districts that voted at higher rates (Martin 2003). Findings of politicians rewarding their supporters confirm V. O. Key's observation that "politicians and officials are under no compulsion to pay much heed to classes and groups of citizens that do not vote" (Key 1949, 527).[8]

The intensified targeting of discretionary federal funds expands inequalities in political and economic resources. Bias in political voice, which our colleagues document in a separate review, joins together with bias in political influence. Martin suggests that "unequal participation leads to unequal representation:" "If members of Congress allocate resources based on participation, then inequalities in representation are further exacerbated." Moreover, skewing resource allocation to selective participation "shifts scarce federal allocations away from those areas in society that need it most—based on concentrations of social problems—toward those areas that participate the most" (Martin 2003, 123).

In short, the distributive politics that have always favored well-organized particularistic groups have become more selective, while the politics of redistributing resources for the benefit of racially and economically disadvantaged groups now faces unified Republican Party opposition and defensive Democratic Party strategizing.

Continuing Opportunities for Addressing Political Inequality in Legislative Politics

Despite the persistent biases of the political process against Americans who lack a substantial political voice, the legislative process is not closed to pressures from voters for addressing economic, racial, ethnic, and gender inequalities. The main check on legislators is that they are held accountable on Election Day. Research continues to find that roll call votes by members affect the decisions of voters. In particular, decisions by members to vote with the extreme (liberal or conservative) wings of their respective parties decrease their share of the vote and decrease the probability of retaining office for members in both marginal and safe seats, controlling for the ideology of the district (Erikson and Wright 1989, 1997; Canes-Wrone, Brady, and Cogan 2002).

INTEREST GROUPS AND MONEY

Interest groups form and maintain themselves to exert influence and advantage their members in the competition for scarce public resources. Although interest groups can be a vehicle for transmitting the views of a wide spectrum of American society, their purpose is not equality, but to serve as a vehicle for differentiation. Campaign contributions are a favorite tool of interest groups and individuals. The impact of money and the contributors who wield it is significant but defies the simplistic cartoon version of corrupt government officials literally "selling" their vote. The effect of campaign contributions is to empower the best organized and most affluent with a powerful weapon for blocking egalitarian legislation and promoting particularistic policies that favor them. We begin by outlining the role of interest groups in American politics and then turn to identify the ways that money influences American elections and governance.

Interest Groups and Public Policy

Interest groups are now a widely accepted part of America's system of government. But students of politics in the eighteenth and nineteenth centuries used such unflattering terms as "factions," "vested interests," and "influence peddlers" to describe what they considered as aberrations and corruptions of self-government in a republic. During the twentieth century, political scientists learned to see such groups as normal features of political behavior in modern government. Leading political scientists have strongly disagreed about their democratic value (Schattschneider 1960; Truman 1951), but today scholars and the public have come to regard interest groups as legitimate actors in the highly complex mix of forces that combine to produce today's policymaking processes.

At the same time, one constant in political science research is that interest groups tend to reinforce rather than challenge preexisting inequalities in American society and government. The bias toward maintaining the status quo emerges as a theme in a number of ways. Many political scientists have focused on the disparity in resources (finances, human capital, organizational capacity, etc.) that transform economic inequalities into unequal political clout for discrete groups.[9] Others have focused on the advantages entailed in holding certain strategic socioeconomic positions, such as the leverage of granting or withholding business confidence for investment (Lindblom 1977). Still others have focused on the cooperative alliances of interest groups with members of Congress and subunits in the bureaucracy to form "iron triangles" that control narrow slices of government policy, quietly locking out other organized or unorganized interests (Lowi 1969; McConnell 1966).

Whatever the angle of vision, the general picture portrays the power of moneyed interests and the well-organized to thwart any major distributive policies (for example, see Page and Simmons 2000; Ferguson 1995). Of course, there are exceptions such as the organizations on behalf of African Americans, the poor, or consumers that challenged existing structures of inequality (Berry 1999). Political scientists have found such cases interesting to study, however, precisely because they are so exceptional.

Looking for Influence, Not Equality?   By its very nature, the interest group system exists to achieve selective influence, not equality. The legal norm of equal justice under law and the electoral norm of one person/one vote have no counterpart in the realm of interest groups. The regime of organized groups espouses no standard for "equal protection of interests", or "one person–one lobbyist." This inherent difference from legal and political norms of equality means that the legitimacy of interest groups per se coexists with an inescapable public distrust of the unlevel playing field represented by interest group politics. Not surprisingly, many Americans suspect that not much will be done to redress economic grievances if those who dominate the economic marketplace also dominate the political marketplace.

While economic inequality grew in the last quarter of the twentieth century, there were also important changes occurring simultaneously in the
world of American interest groups. The separate research review of *Political Voice* summarized important changes in what might be thought of as
interest group demographics. First, the sheer size of the interest group
community grew considerably after the 1960s. Second, and more importantly, the types of interests represented in the total advocacy and lobbyist
population broadened to include many of those formerly outside or only
marginally represented by politically active groups. Examples since the
1960s include minorities, consumers, the disabled, women, gays, environ-
mentalists, and "public interest" groups more generally. Third, while the
organized power of labor unions declined in this period, many professional associations, corporations and other business organizations became
politically active in their own right. Rather than relying solely on traditional trade associations or hiring part-time lobbyists, many more business interests found it worthwhile to establish a permanent and active
presence in Washington to deal with the new policy challenges posed by
environmental, consumer and other groups.

Demographic changes in the American interest group community have
generally left the overall distribution of political influence in the halls of
government less equal. (Chapter 2 provides a fuller discussion of changes
in the interest group community.) The impact of interest groups on American government is illustrated by health policy, a long-standing focus of
interest group scholars (Eckstein 1958, 1960; Morone and Jacobs 2005).
American government decisions on health policy have remained under
the dominant influence of groups with the greatest economic and organizational muscle (Marmor 1983; Gordon 2003). The same calculus of privilege holds within the subset of interest groups supposedly speaking for
the vulnerable, such as workers and the aged. Research shows that organized labor has mainly used its influence to expand private sector solutions favorable to its control over companies' employee benefit funds
rather than to fully invest in the fight for national health insurance
(Gottschalk 2000). Likewise, it was the vocal organization of more wealthy
seniors that forced repeal of the one-year old Medicare Catastrophic Coverage Act in 1989, even though 60 percent of beneficiaries would have received benefits in excess of costs (Himmelfarb 1995). On the larger political stage, an aroused public opinion and Democratic political victory in
1992 generated President Clinton's plan for comprehensive health reform,
but the fragmentation of its supporters and coalescence of better-funded
corporate interest groups and political action committees along with
steadfast Republican leadership in Congress did much to ensure its defeat
(Skocpol 1996).

On the other hand, the common perceptions of moneyed interests directly pressuring officials or dictating policy over the objections of voters are too simplistic. They may not be entirely untrue, but they are so incomplete as to falsify the deeper reality. Research on health policy shows, for instance, that interest group influence has varied with conditions in the larger political system, rising in periods of deadlocked party politics and public apathy about health policy and falling in the wake of critical elections and an aroused public opinion (Jacobs 1993). Although the American Medical Association was successful in defeating federal health policy initiatives for many decades, it and other groups could not prevent passage of Medicare in 1965 (Starr 1982; Oberlander 2003).

The simple stereotype of interest groups is also misleading because it misses significant changes in how interest groups have learned to function under modern political circumstances. Effective pressure groups have turned from strong arm tactics to the distribution of information, the formulation of credible explanations to offer constituents, and the development of sophisticated public communication strategies. In the post-1960s world of proliferating lobbying organizations, watchdog groups, and non-stop political reporting, savvy interest groups have learned the value of injecting their influence into the deep tissue of policymaking. This does not mean civic engagement by ordinary citizens in large membership associations. Rather, it means a growing emphasis in recent decades on mobilizing professional resources for expertly managed advocacy. Even interest groups that focus on redistributive issues or broader "public interest" claims have found it useful to shift from mobilizing large memberships to public relations strategies run by professional advocates who target appeals to more affluent and educated supporters (Skocpol 1999, 2003). With so many voices saying so many things in so many media venues, the premium for exerting influence lies in an ability to cut through the noise.

"Buying" Policy, Not Politicians?   Research shows that contemporary interest groups use their economic advantages not to buy officials, but to buy means to orchestrate the public and private conversations that constitute policymaking. The growing presence in Washington of advocacy think tanks and "educational" initiatives on behalf of specific interest groups are only the most obvious expressions of this trend.

In the early 1960s, for example, one of the most thorough research studies of interest groups ever conducted found a relatively straightforward picture of business group lobbying on trade policy. A limited number of competing groups provided valuable information and expertise to government officials (Bauer, Pool, and Dexter 1963). More recent case studies present a rather different picture that extends beyond direct lobbying. Now financially powerful interest groups work to use the communications process to focus political attention on persuasive narratives that define problems and solutions in ways that advance their stakes (West and Loomis 1998). At the same time, professional advocacy groups have developed sophisticated new abilities to tightly target points of political leverage and orchestrate the appearance of "grassroots" pressure. For example, consulting companies such as Legislative Demographic Services are hired to match data provided by clients (mainly Fortune 500 companies, major associations and industries) with individual legislator's voting records and committee positions on issues, information which can then be used to mobilize employees, suppliers and others to influence politicians in their districts. For instance, the repeal of the estate tax—a tax paid by at most only 2 percent of the wealthiest taxpayers—was scripted as a populist cause. Its repeal in 2001 occurred with broad popular and bipartisan support after a decade-long campaign by a coalition of interest groups and political entrepreneurs (Birney and Shapiro 2003).

Of course, well-financed, professionally managed interest coalitions are not always as successful as they were in the 1994 defeat of the Clinton Health Plan or the 2001 repeal of the "death tax" (a term carefully chosen after test marketing). However, even if mere "access" to policymakers is the goal, obtaining a hearing is not some sort of neutral achievement. It is a significant contour line marking out the uneven political playing field. Continued access can build the relationships that allow scarcely noticed, pinpoint policy favors (a change in statutory language here, a line in a regulatory provision there) that are immensely important to a given group. Moreover, given limitations of time and attention, access for some also generally entails a crowding out of others. The mirror image of access is the silences that are created as those with entrée press in to obtain a hearing.

The deeper involvement of interest groups in the public policy conversation of government offers particular advantage to pressure groups with the deep pockets necessary to sustain sophisticated efforts at professional advocacy. This development in the political marketplace harmonizes well with the growing economic inequality in the economic marketplace. Under contemporary political circumstances, it may be easier to achieve an upward redistribution from the "have-nots" to the "haves" than the reverse.

Money in the American Political System

In an era when the financing of ever more expensive election campaigns breaks a new record with nearly every election cycle, money clearly plays an important role in American politics. In the 2004 election cycle, presidential and congressional candidates raised over $2 billion. Surpassing even the record-setting figures of the 2000 presidential contest, President Bush, Senator John Kerry, and the other candidates closed in on a tidy $1 billion, having raised $862,997,556 according to not yet finalized tallies (Center for Responsive Politics 2005).

The influx of vast sums of money into American politics has sparked dire warnings about corruption and a steady stream of journalistic accounts with sky-is-falling titles like "Selling Out: How Big Corporate Money Buys Elections, Rams through Legislation and Betrays our Democracy" or "The Best Congress Money Can Buy" (Green 2002; Stern 1988; Drew 1983; but see Mann 2003). These accounts of corruption tell a simple story of money literally buying votes in Congress and the president's signature or veto. In this telling, political equality is fiction, sold to the highest bidder.

Research regarding the impact of money on elections and governing refutes the crudest popular impressions of rampant corruption, though they do point to subtle but quite significant influences. Indeed, some scholars have tried to temper the shrill alarms about the growing amount of money in the electoral process by showing that the costs have remained relatively constant over time when adjusted for inflation, the size of the economy, the growth in national income, or the costs of media buys. Others describe the money flowing into American politics as a "good deal" given the stakes (Overacker 1932; Ansolabehere, Gerber, and Snyder 2001; Ansolabehere, de Figueiredo, and Snyder 2003; Mann and Corrado 2002; Tullock 1972).[10] Nonetheless, the absolute and relative amount of money devoted to campaigns can be quite significant in high-stake elections, targeted races, and elections to particular offices (Mann 2003; Magleby 2002). Moreover, the average cost of a successful challenge to a House incumbent increased between 1976 and 2000 at a rate far higher than the growth of the national income (Mann 2003). Sorauf argues that campaign funding has become something akin to a destabilizing international arms race, characterized by "overkill" that has both parties constantly "scrambling for more weapons" and unable to realistically evaluate their needs (Sorauf 1988, 1992, 1999).

Money has two basic impacts—it can influence elections and it can affect the behavior of elected representatives.[11]

The Impact of Money on Election Outcomes

The most powerful effect of money on elections is on the selection and competitiveness of challengers. The costs of running a modern campaign erect a steep hurdle for challengers, creating a substantial advantage for the incumbent. The incumbent advantage in raising campaign funds and dependence on contributors who do support them reinforces the predisposition of the political process to favor deadlock on broad egalitarian policy directions and narrow-gauge responsiveness to particularistic groups.

Research shows that challengers are increasingly unable to keep up with incumbents or with spiraling campaign costs. Weak competitiveness in election to the U.S. House results from the "increasing costs of campaigns and the decreasing ability of House challengers to raise campaign funds" (Abramowitz 1991, 53). The average incumbent in 1988 spent more than 300 percent more than the average incumbent in 1974, while average challenger spending increased only 25 percent in the same period. The effects of these differences are further magnified by increases in the costs of advertising, consultants, and other campaign services.

The "financial handicap" that challengers face starts out quite high and then grows with each day of the campaign. Incumbents raise far more money than their opponents at every point in the campaign and are much better able to counter well-financed challengers. As one set of researchers noted, "challengers start out behind and incumbents are able to mobilize the resources to make sure they stay there" (Krasno, Green, and Cowden 1994, 472–73). Although scholars have engaged in a lively debate over how to measure and analyze the decisions of incumbents to spend campaign funds, there is agreement that they generally enjoy a substantial advantage over challengers.[12] A major part of the incumbency advantage in fund raising stems from the dramatic increases in campaign contributions by PACs (Abramowitz 1991). For instance, analysis of AFL-CIO spending in the 1996 elections on "voter education" campaigns was found to be "highly effective against the freshmen [Republicans] they targeted, but not against more senior Republicans" (Jacobson 1999, 193).

Faced with the large campaign war chest that incumbents can amass, potential challengers may not even enter the race (Goidel and Gross 1994; Hersch and McDougall 1994). Even challengers with a distinguished record to run on may be discouraged by the "daunting expense of a serious campaign and a belief that incumbents can raise much more money if they need to do so" (Mann 2003, 76). Research has shown that House incumbents with large war chests do deter quality challengers (Goldenberg, Traugott, and Baumgartner 1986; Box-Steffensmeier 1996), though some studies have not found this deterrent effect for House races (Krasno and Green 1988) or Senate contests (Squire 1991; Goodliffe 2001; Epstein and Zemsky 1995).

Challengers who can clear the financial hurdle pose a threat to incumbents. One of the most consistent research findings is that increased spending by challengers produces a greater share of the vote and more competitive races because it enables them to increase their name recognition and get their message out.[13] This puts enormous power in the hands of contributors to determine the pool of potential officeholders. To win a seat in national office, the incumbent and the challenger usually have to win the support of funders before they go before voters. The effect can be to discourage certain kinds of challengers who, for instance, promote egalitarian policies that would redistribute resources from affluent campaign contributors.

Although campaign finance winnows down the field of challengers to a set amenable to contributors, the caricatures of big money buying elections are, as we have said, crude and inaccurate. If challengers can raise the funds to meet the entry fee, campaign spending appears to contribute to expanding voters' knowledge of candidates and their affective connections with candidates (especially challengers in House races), though it has no notable effect on voters' trust, efficacy, involvement, or attention (Coleman and Manna 2000). Spending by the challenger improves the ability of advantaged and disadvantaged groups to accurately recall the challenger's name and identify their ideology and policy positions on services and spending (Coleman 2001). These findings help to explain why increased spending by challengers is associated with a greater share of the vote. Expenditures by incumbents (who already enjoy name recognition and visibility), on the other hand, do not produce similar improvements in name recall or ideological placement, though they do increase the ability of all voters to identify the policy positions of officeholders. When challenger spending matches incumbent spending, however, these effects dissipate.

The Influence of Money on Elected Representatives

The most vivid pictures of money in American politics are fictional or videotaped recordings (as in the Abscam sting of members of Congress) of government officials stuffing their pockets with money in exchange for their votes. Indeed, a large body of research has equated the influence of money with the "buying" of congressional votes. Case studies have shown large, statistically significant associations between contributions and roll call votes on diverse issues: labor contributions have been associated with support for minimum wage legislation in 1972 (Silberman and Durden 1976), and contributions from the American Trucking Association have been related to support for trucking deregulation (Frendreis and Waterman 1985). In addition, statistically significant relationships between contributions and representatives' votes have been found in the discrete issue areas of labor legislation (Wilhite and Theilmann 1987), a cargo preference bill (Chappell 1981), dairy price supports (Welch 1982), auto emissions standards, defense appropriations, and truck weight limits (Chappell 1982); and the debt limit, windfall profits tax, and price controls (Kau and Rubin 1982).

Despite these results, the balance of research does not reveal consistent and persuasive evidence that campaign contributions and PAC money cause floor votes. As one comprehensive review of research concludes, "overall, PAC contributions show relatively few effects on voting behavior [in Congress]" (Ansolabehere, de Figueiredo, and Snyder 2003, 114). Past research that claimed to find a connection between campaign contributions and congressional voting has been extensively critiqued on three grounds: its findings were not generalizeable beyond one case (Grenzke 1989); it failed to distinguish the tendency of contributors to back already supportive legislators rather than to fund "swing" members (Bailey 2003; Hall and Wayman 1990; Kau and Rubin 1982; Chappell 1982; Jacobson 1980; Welch 1982); and it did not control for competing influences on legislators' roll call votes, including their party affiliation, their own beliefs and ideology, and the preferences of their constituents (Ansolabehere, de Figueiredo, and Snyder 2003; Grenzke 1989).

Although money may not consistently "buy" the votes of members of Congress, campaign contributions by interest groups, PACs, and individuals are a kind of "entrance fee" to gain access or a hearing with lawmakers (Heard 1956; Alexander 1972; Hearndon 1982; Gopoian 1984; Kroszner and Stratmann 1998; Austen-Smith 1995). Some research demonstrates that contributions "buy" an interest group time with congressional staff: a contribution of $6,400 "buys," on average, twenty-five minutes of access to the office of a member of Congress and $72,300 is rewarded with an hour-long meeting (Langbein 1986).

Committee deliberations are one place where members of Congress reward contributors (Hall and Wayman 1990; Evans 1996). PACs use contributions to motivate members to increase their commitment of time, staff, and political capital to promoting their concerns in the committee process, where they face less public scrutiny and can afford to be more sympathetic. A critical purpose, then, of contributing to a member's reelection is to influence "not simply the *direction* of legislators' preferences but the *vigor* with which those preferences are promoted in the decision-making process" (Hall and Wayman 1990, 802).

Moneyed interests do exert, then, a substantial influence on policymaking by using their contributions to mobilize legislators already predisposed to support them to increase their levels of participation at the committee level. The ability to make contributions, which is largely restricted to the affluent or well organized, creates an unequal playing field in the halls of Congress. Money does "buy" something—privileged access for contributors and the special attention of members who reward them with vigorous help in minding their business in the committee process.

In short, interest groups and money are tools wielded disproportionately by a small segment of American citizens to enact policies that concentrate benefits on them and to block egalitarian policies that would impose onerous costs on them.

POLITICAL REPRESENTATION

One of the most basic principles of democracy is popular sovereignty and the expectation that the decisions of government should, as a general rule, parallel the preferences of citizens. Vibrant debates regarding the importance of government leaders possessing the discretion to act and, on occasion, to exert independence from public opinion in solving urgent problems or crises are, of course, long standing (Burke 1949; Dahl 1989). Nonetheless, the normative underpinning of democratic government and the practical reality of political equality is that the decisions of government should normally reflect the policy preferences of its citizens (Pitkin 1967). In some respects, this is the most basic standard for evaluating American democracy.

An enduring body of research has investigated the extent and nature of popular sovereignty by studying the relationship of mass opinion and elite action in the American political system. Although past research suggests that policy responds to public opinion, more recent analysis indicates that the government has become less responsive than it was several decades ago and that it is particularly attentive to the views of the affluent and business leaders. Evidence that politicians are disconnected from citizens is consistent with the broad findings previously reported that the American governing process tends to cater to the organized and vocal and to block egalitarian policies that are supported by the broad public.

Empirical Studies of Political Representation

Representation is a complex, multifaceted phenomenon with a long history in both democratic theory and political practice (Pitkin 1967). However, systematic empirical research on representation only emerged in the past half century or so, with the advent of public opinion surveys making it possible to quantify popular preferences and relate them to the observed behavior of public officials or to the actual outcomes of democratic policymaking. Work along these lines has tended to ignore many of the complexities of the relationship between democratic masses and elites; for example, symbolic representation, trust, leadership, misperception, political manipulation, and inequalities within the mass public all figure much less prominently in systematic statistical analyses than in qualitative studies of representation (Fenno 1978; Bianco 1994; Page and Shapiro 1992, chap. 9; Jacobs and Shapiro 2000). Notwithstanding these limitations, political scientists have generated a good deal of evidence regarding the extent of consistency and congruence between mass opinion and elite action in the American political system—a simple but important measure of popular sovereignty in the liberal populist interpretation of democracy.

The most influential study of political representation in the scholarly field of American politics is undoubtedly Warren Miller and Donald Stokes's (1963) path-breaking article on "Constituency Influence in Congress," in which they investigated political representation in terms of the dyadic relationship between members of Congress and their constituents. In particular, Miller and Stokes married a survey of constituents' political opinions in 116 congressional districts with a parallel survey of incumbent members of Congress and challengers in the 1958 congressional elections in those districts, and with information about the roll call votes cast by the incumbent representatives on the floor of Congress. They assessed the accuracy of representatives' perceptions of constituency opinion, the strength of the relationship between constituents' opinions and incumbent representatives' policy views, and the impact of both perceived constituency opinion and representatives' views on roll call votes. They found that votes on civil rights issues were strongly correlated both with fairly accurate perceptions of constituency attitudes (as would be expected under the instructed-delegate model of representation) and with representatives' racial attitudes. In the domain of social welfare issues, roll call votes were correlated with constituency opinions primarily because representatives shared the views of their constituents, not because they accurately recognized and responded to those views. In the domain of foreign policy, there was virtually no correlation between constituency opinions and roll call votes.

Subsequent analyses have found positive relationships between constituency opinion and representatives' behavior, even though they improved upon Miller and Stokes's original work and used quite different bodies of evidence, statistical methods, and policy areas. Some studies reanalyzed Miller and Stokes's data, making allowances for measurement error in constituency opinion (due to the very small samples of constituents in each congressional district in Miller and Stokes's survey) (Achen 1978; Erikson 1978) and attending to the potential pitfalls of comparing correlation coefficients across policy domains (Achen 1977). Additional work applied structural equation models to Miller and Stokes's data in order to probe the interrelationship of constituency opinion and

House members' own policy views (Hill and Hurley 1999). Some analysis relied on National Election Study (NES) surveys from 1956 through 1972 to examine the temporal consistency of the relationship between constituents' opinions and their representatives' roll call votes (Stone 1982). Other scholars used subsequent NES surveys that were specifically designed to provide larger and more representative samples of opinion in congressional districts or entire states (Powell 1982; Page et al. 1984; Shapiro et al. 1990; Bartels 1991a). Part of this reanalysis broke into the black box of political decisionmaking (Jacobs 1993; Sobel 2001). For instance, one study found that policy attitudes reported in polls commissioned by John Kennedy were correlated with his public policy statements (Jacobs and Shapiro 1994; Jacobs 1993, conclusion).

Aggregate Public Opinion and Public Policy

Part of the reanalysis of the Miller and Stokes's classic study shifted the focus of analysis from a dyadic representation between individual members of Congress and their constituents to systemic or collective representation—the relationship between aggregate public opinion and the collective decisions of government or one of its separate institutions such as Congress (Weissberg 1978; see for discussion of this tradition Manza, Cook, and Page 2002). It was argued that a strong correlation across districts between constituents' views and their representatives' roll call votes was neither necessary nor sufficient to produce responsiveness by the government as a whole to the will of the people. Unfortunately, the cross-sectional research design that Miller and Stokes and the many other scholars who have followed in their footsteps used is ill suited to shed light on systemic representation. Effective analyses of aggregate responsiveness require variation in actual policy outcomes in a collection of comparable political units, across a considerable variety of issues, or in a single political system over a substantial period of time.

One research strategy for improving the analysis of systemic representation was to expand the variation in policy outcomes by shifting the analysis from the national level to the state level.[14] One pioneering approach compared public opinion in American states to a broad measure of "state policy liberalism." (The measure of "state policy liberalism" was based on the presence of laws regarding consumer protection, criminal justice, and legalized gambling; state spending for education, Medicaid, and welfare; ratification of the federal Equal Rights Amendment; and state tax progressivity [Erikson, Wright, and McIver 1989, 1993].) This approach found a very strong (.82) correlation between the ideological views of each state's citizens (as captured in public opinion polls) and the ideological flavor of its public policies. This correlation is partly, though by no means entirely, attributable to the fact that more liberal states elected more liberal legislators. (It may also be partly attributable to long-term feedback effects of state policy on public opinion; the authors reported but did not remark on the fact that state policies in 1990 were even more strongly correlated with state policies in 1940 than with contemporary public opinion, whereas public opinion itself was much more unstable.)

While research has exploited cross-sectional variation in opinion and policy across the American states, another approach exploited temporal variation in national public opinion and policy across a wide range of political issues (Page and Shapiro 1983). This approach gathered data on the American public's policy preferences from hundreds of publicly available opinion polls conducted between 1935 and 1979, isolating 357 instances of significant aggregate opinion change in successive polls employing identical policy questions over periods ranging from one month to several years. In each case, this research looked for evidence of congruent or incongruent shifts in corresponding policies over a period beginning at the time of the first poll and ending one year after the second poll. It found evidence of congruent policy changes in 153 cases (43 percent), evidence of incongruent policy change in only 78 cases (22 percent), and no evidence (or uncertain evidence) of policy change in 126 cases (35 percent). Moreover, many of the instances of no change reflected situations in which policy already corresponded with opinion (for example, abolition of the draft), and many of the instances of incongruent change reflected small or unstable shifts in opinion, imperfect measures of policy change, or misspecification of appropriate time lags. This work concluded that "(especially when opinion changes are large and sustained, and issues are salient) . . . opinion changes are important causes of policy change" (Page and Shapiro 1983, 188–89).

The research team of James A. Stimson, Michael B. MacKuen, and Robert S. Erikson analyzed much of the same data in a rather different way to reach conclusions broadly consistent with the early analysis of congruent change in public opinion and policy (Stimson, MacKuen, and Erikson 1995; Erikson, MacKuen, and Stimson 2002). They constructed a summary measure of annual "policy mood" from survey data on domestic policy preferences dating back to the 1950s (Stimson 1999), then related liberal or conservative shifts in "policy mood" to election outcomes and to policy-making activities in the White House, Congress, and the Supreme Court. They suggested that both direct responsiveness by incumbent officials and electoral replacement contributed to producing a strong connection between shifts in public mood and shifts in policy activity by the president

and the House of Representatives. The Senate, too, responded significantly to shifts in public mood, but only through electoral replacement,
while the Supreme Court responded less strongly and less quickly. They
concluded that the American political system "combines both short- and
long-term considerations through both rational anticipation and compositional change to produce a strong and resilient link between public and
policy" (Erikson, MacKuen, and Stimson 2002, 321).

Erikson, MacKuen, and Stimson's ambitious broad-brush analysis appears to be limited in three respects. First, their global measures of public
opinion and public policy may lump together a wide range of specific (domestic) policy issues that tend to move in tandem. Research on public
support for specific policies and on changes in these preferences over time
demonstrates that the public consistently draws reasonable distinctions—
based on available information—between different government programs
(Page and Shapiro 1992; Zaller 1992; Best 1999; Cook 1979). In addition,
there may be important differences in political responsiveness across specific policy domains. Research on defense policy, where aggregate public
opinion has been sufficiently well-measured (and sufficiently variable) to
facilitate time-series analyses of policy responsiveness, finds evidence of
government responsiveness (Ostrom and Marra 1986; Hartley and Russett
1992; Wlezien 1996). Specifically, Pentagon budgets since the 1960s have
been significantly influenced by public preferences for more or less defense spending. Analysis of the Reagan defense buildup of the early 1980s
indicated that individual legislators' support for larger defense appropriations was strongly related to public support in their own districts for increased defense spending, and that the aggregate magnitude of the spending increase was almost entirely accounted for by the aggregate public
demand for more defense spending (Bartels 1991a).

Although these findings indicate government responsiveness in individual policy areas, concerns remain. Benjamin Page recently took stock of
this area of research and concluded that the use of global measures of public opinion and policy "greatly restricts the domain and range of variation
in the independent and dependent variables" to the point that the results
do "not necessarily tell us much about . . . public opinion and policymaking" (Page 2002, 329).

A second possible limitation is that global analysis of public opinion
and policy (as well as other studies of political representation in this tradition) omits critical independent variables that may influence both opinion and policy (Jacobs and Page 2005; Page 2002; Jacobs 1993, conclusion).
The danger is that strong statistical findings of association may be spuri-
ous: public opinion and policy may both be influenced by other important

omitted factors—namely, business mobilization, campaign contributors and interest groups, party activists, and other factors discussed earlier or in the research review on *Political Voice.*

A third potential limitation is that public opinion is not autonomous. Rather, public opinion is influenced by a host of factors including information (some of which is controlled by government officials) and the efforts of interest groups and politicians to frame arguments in self-serving ways (Zaller 1992; Jacobs and Shapiro 2000; Page 2002). The challenge is to establish that close statistical associations of opinion and policy are not merely the result of political elites deceiving the public to support their desired policies.

Trends in Political Responsiveness

Although research on dyadic and systemic representation has generally found that decided government policy or the positions of elected officials is consistent or congruent with public opinion, two growing bodies of analysis show much less elite-public connection than previously assumed or that may have existed. One line of analysis reports that policy has become less responsive to public opinion since the 1970s; another finds that government responsiveness is highly skewed toward the more affluent, with little attention to the preferences of lower income groups.

As we have seen, most studies of representation have focused on the relationship between constituents' opinions and legislators' behaviors at a single point in time or on the relationship between aggregate opinion and shifts in policy from year to year. Neither of these research designs is well suited to monitoring changes over time in the responsiveness of the American government to the policy preferences of the public—in the former case because there is no temporal variation, and in the latter case because annual time-series are too short to be usefully subdivided. Even repeated studies of representation focusing on different periods may not facilitate confident inferences about changing responsiveness due to changes in the nature of the available data or of the methods used to analyze those data.[15]

In a few cases, however, political scientists have produced more systematic comparisons of responsiveness in different time periods. One body of work examined the correspondence between public opinion and changes in public policy across a wide range of issues in two periods, from 1960 to 1979 and from 1980 to 1993 (Monroe 1998). In the earlier period, it found that government policies were consistent with the policy preferences of a majority of the public 63 percent of the time; in the latter period policy was congruent with majority opinion only 55 percent of the time. A separate team of researchers likewise reported the results of a "preliminary study" suggesting "a noticeable decline in correspondence" between public opinion and policy changes in the areas of welfare, crime, social security, and health care, from 67 percent congruence in President Reagan's second term to 40 percent in the elder President Bush's administration and 36 percent during President Clinton's first term (Jacobs and Shapiro 2000, 4).

Congressional responsiveness to district opinion has been measured less directly but over a much longer period of time, from 1874 to 1996 (Ansolabehere, Snyder, and Stewart 2001). This approach related the ideological stances of incumbent members of Congress (and of challengers who were subsequently elected) as reflected in roll call votes on the floor of Congress to district opinion as reflected in presidential election outcomes in each congressional district. Over most of the period covered by their analysis, the roll call votes cast by members of Congress were virtually unrelated to presidential voting patterns in the districts those members represented. A positive relationship emerged in the middle of the twentieth century and peaked in about 1970, but subsequently declined markedly, especially for Republican members of Congress.

These disparate findings of declines in congressional responsiveness after 1970 and in aggregate policy responsiveness seem plausibly consistent.[16] However, another analysis of congressional responsiveness suggests a rather different temporal pattern for a period before the early 1970s (Stone 1982). This work used district-level breakdowns of data on social welfare policy preferences from NES surveys to calculate the correlation between constituency opinion and the roll call votes cast by members of Congress in various years from 1956 through 1972. It found that the correlation between roll call votes and overall district opinion was generally low throughout this period, and that it declined fairly steadily from .36 in 1956 to .09 in 1968 before rebounding to .23 in 1972. (The correlation between roll call votes and the opinions of constituents from the congressman's own party was somewhat higher throughout this period, increasing from .43 in 1956 to .59 in 1960 and 1964 before declining gradually to .33 in 1972.)

These discrepant results—congressional responsiveness reaching a low point in 1968 in one analysis while a separate study found it reaching a historical high point at almost exactly the same time—may be attributable to unrepresentative samples of district opinion (since most of the NES surveys employed in the analysis of congressional responsiveness used metropolitan statistical areas rather than congressional districts as sampling units) or to the difficulty of comparing correlation coefficients from different populations. Further investigation of these issues is clearly warranted. In the meantime, however, we believe there is good reason to worry that the American political system has, indeed, become significantly less responsive than it once was to aggregate public opinion regarding important issues of public policy.

Inequalities in Political Responsiveness

Unfortunately, political scientists have done surprisingly little to investigate the extent of actual inequalities in government responsiveness to public opinion—that is, whether distinct segments of the country exert more influence than others. Studies of public opinion and public policy have almost invariably treated constituents in an undifferentiated way, using simple averages of opinions in a given district or at a given point in time to account for representatives' policy choices. The research we have summarized here, rich as it is, provides rather little purchase on the fundamental issue of political equality.

A few analysts have attempted to provide direct comparisons of the political influence of ordinary citizens and political elites. One found that elite opinion (as measured by the mail and phone calls reported in a survey of congressional offices) was more important than mass opinion (as measured by district-level survey data) in accounting for House members' support of President Reagan's policy agenda in the early 1980s (West 1988). Another study similarly found that elite ideology (as measured by a survey of state convention delegates and county party chairs) was more important than mass ideology (as measured by state-level survey data) in accounting for the roll call votes of U.S. senators in the early 1980s (Wright 1989). (The views of independents in the mass public received some weight, but the views of ordinary Republicans and Democrats received little or none.)

Analysis of state policymaking that allowed for reciprocal influence between the views of political elites and ordinary citizens within each state discovered that public opinion had rather little direct impact on state policy, but strongly influenced the ideologies of political elites, especially within each political party.[17] Since the ideologies of political elites in turn strongly shaped the ideological content of state policy, public opinion had an important indirect effect on policy. However, this representative relationship is complicated by the fact that public opinion was also strongly influenced *by* the ideologies of political elites, rather than being an essentially independent driving force in the political system.

The relative influence of the general public, business leaders, labor leaders, and policy experts on the opinions of government officials regarding various aspects of U.S. foreign policy has also been analyzed (Jacobs and Page 2005). Using data from a series of eight parallel surveys of citizens, elites, and government officials conducted for the Chicago Coun-

Figure 3.4   Influences on Foreign Policy Preferences of All
Government Officials

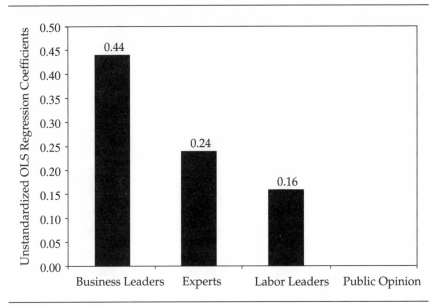

Source: Jacobs and Page (2005, table 2).
Note: The dependent variable is the percentage of government officials who took a given position; the independent variables are the percentages of members of each of the listed groups who took that position. The coefficient for public opinion was not significantly different from zero at the $p < .10$ level. The remaining coefficients are significant at the $p < .01$ level. The analysis controlled for the previous positions of government officials (not shown). See article for more details.

cil on Foreign Relations between 1974 and 2002, this research found that the views of policy experts and, especially, business leaders have a significant impact on the views of government officials, but that the views of ordinary citizens had very little discernible impact. (Modest positive effects of public opinion appeared on economic issues and on issues that were highly salient.) Figure 3.4 illustrates a consistent pattern of statistically significant effects on government officials: the policy stands of foreign policy decisionmakers are most influenced by business leaders, with the general public exerting no significant effect. Foreign policy "experts" from academia and think tanks appear to play a role, but additional analysis suggests that experts themselves are influenced by other elites (including business).

While systematic comparisons of the influence of elites and ordinary citizens are unhappily rare, there is even less work to survey on disparities

Figure 3.5   Congressional Responsiveness to Income Classes (Senate W-NOMINATE Scores, 1989–1994)

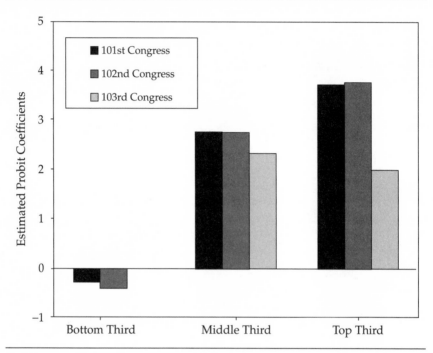

Source: Bartels (2005).

in political influence *within* the mass public. One unpublished study relates the roll call votes cast by U.S. senators in the late 1980s and early 1990s to the policy views of their constituents in much the same way as in Miller and Stokes's pioneering article, but allowing for the possibility of differential responsiveness to the views of rich and poor constituents (Bartels 2005). This analysis suggests that income-weighted preferences were much more influential than simple averages of state opinion, especially for Republican senators. Indeed, the related analysis summarized in figure 3.5 suggests that constituents in the bottom third of the income distribution had *no* discernible impact on their senators' general voting patterns across three congresses. Similar disparities appear in specific salient roll call votes on the minimum wage, civil rights, government spending, and abortion. These discrepancies in influence were partly, but by no means entirely, attributable to differences in political participation between the rich and the poor. According to this research, senators are consistently much more responsive to the views of affluent constituents than to the views of the poor.

An even more recent (and very preliminary) unpublished analysis extends the analysis of changes in public opinion and changes in policy by investigating the possibility of unequal responsiveness to the policy preferences of rich and poor citizens (Gilens 2003a).[18] This recent study used data from 755 survey questions from 1992 through 1999 in which national samples of the public were asked about proposed changes in U.S. national policy. In a two-step procedure, it estimated the (possibly nonlinear) relationship between income and policy preferences for each of these 755 questions, then related the (imputed) preferences of survey respondents at various income levels separately to actual changes (if any) in corresponding public policy. Its findings suggest that a 10 percentage point increase in support for policy change among citizens at the ninetieth percentile of the income distribution was associated with a 4.8 percentage point increase in the likelihood of a corresponding policy change, whereas the same public demand for policy change among citizens at the tenth percentile of the income distribution produced only a 2 percentage point increase in the likelihood of a corresponding policy shift. For the 300 policy questions on which the imputed preferences of rich and poor citizens differed by 10 percentage points or more the disparities in apparent influence were even more stark, with a 10 percentage point shift in opinion among the rich associated with a 7.6 percentage point difference in the likelihood of policy change, but a 10 percentage point shift in opinion among the poor associated with only a 0.5 percentage point difference in the likelihood of policy change. This analysis of national opinion and policy (along with the analysis of legislative representation) suggest that the American political system is a great deal more responsive to the preferences of the rich than to the preferences of the poor.

Federalism and Policy Responsiveness

The latitude enjoyed by states in the American system of federalism has been lauded for creating "laboratories of experimentation" and yet the diversity across the states also reinforces and perhaps expands political and economic inequality in two related ways: it accommodates the existing disparities in political voice and influence, and it fragments the authority and administrative capacity of government that could be used to offset political and economic inequalities by establishing uniform national standards.

The federal structure of the U.S. political system—its separation of powers among the three branches of government and between the national and state governments—was in large part intended to segment policy by dividing authority horizontally and vertically. By "reserving" many of the most important powers of government to state (and local) governments, the federal structure allows and ultimately all but guarantees there will be substantial differences in the governing structures and domestic policies across many of the subnational governments. The effect is to accept and accommodate economic and political inequalities within the separate states rather than challenge these disparities by establishing national uniform standards.

Race and gender relations are major exceptions to the pattern of deference to states. The Civil Rights movement led to the establishment and enforcement of national laws that forbid formal, de jure, racial, and gender discrimination.

The national government continues, though, to defer, in important respects, to states on a range of policies that affect economic and social standing. The reform of welfare in 1996, for instance, expanded the discretion of states to make decisions about eligibility, work requirements, time limits and family caps. The effect of shifting responsibilities from the federal to state levels was to weaken the influence that poor people and their advocates had previously wielded at the national level under the Aid to Families with Dependent Children program (Winston 2002).

The kind of national uniform standards that were established in the aftermath of the Civil Rights movement have not been applied, for instance, on health care policy. Research shows that there are large differences in the nature, timing, and effectiveness of state regulation efforts. A comparative case study of California and New York suggests that their distinctive political processes produced divergent approaches to controlling Medicaid costs and widening access to medical care for the poor: California officials extended the most generous Medicaid benefits of all fifty states, while New York's Medicaid program was twice the cost, dominated by interest groups, and offered less access (Sparer 1996).

The first process by which federalism reinforces political and economic inequality is by accepting rather than challenging the existing status quo within the states. The second is that federalism dissipates and disperses the authority and administrative capacity of the national government, which could be used (as in the area of civil rights) for mitigating severe economic and political disparities.

Indeed, the watering down of the national government's authority and capacity was a deliberate strategy pursued by the framers of the U.S. constitution. In particular, the constitution's framers identified federalism as an institutional arrangement that would check the national government and "exten[d] the sphere" of political interactions to aid in controlling po-

litical factions and in undermining the formation of majoritarian movements that would use the national government as a cudgel against "minorities"—especially, the owners of land and wealth. E. E. Schattschneider
(1960) worried that the framers' handiwork had, indeed, been quite effective in restraining the "scope of conflict" and tamping down the formation
of a broad public movement that would use the national government to
redistribute economic and political resources across the country.

The three decade old effort to devolve responsibility on economic and
social welfare policy from the national government to state governments
has (with a few exceptions) not emphasized equality as a primary policy
goal. The Johnson administration's War on Poverty engendered what was
referred to as "creative federalism," with an emphasis on national government directives, in pursuing certain egalitarian goals. But the New Federalism of the Nixon administration and its later incarnations in the Reagan
administration's policies and the Welfare Reform legislation of 1996 were
part of a "devolution revolution" that delegated authority and control to
the states, curtailing the national government's responsibilities and capacities. As the national government has pulled back, it is in less of a position
to set a national standard for the basic floor of economic well-being. Some
fear—perhaps mistakenly—that the new federalism invites states to "race
to the bottom" for fear of becoming "welfare magnets" (Peterson 1981).

Although the general drift of intergovernmental relations is toward the
states, there are notable cases of expanded national government responsibility. Fear of terrorism spawned legislation under presidents Clinton and
Bush to expand the powers of national law enforcement officials at the
Federal Bureau of Investigation, Justice Department, and elsewhere. The
No Child Left Behind Act imposes extensive directives on state and local
governments, though it has not been funded at the expected levels. Perhaps the most notable feature of these new initiatives is that they avoid the
redistribution of economic resources.

Inequality and Popular Sovereignty

Political scientists have produced substantial evidence of meaningful connections between the policy preferences of the American public and the
actions of their elected representatives. Those connections appear in cross-
sectional analyses of individual legislators' roll call votes, in cross-sectional
analyses of state policymaking, in time-series analyses of government
spending in (at least some) specific policy domains, and in broader historical analyses relating liberal or conservative shifts in government policy to
shifts in the ideological mood of the public.

Despite the impressive quantity of these analyses and a fair degree of consistency in their results, they are limited in important ways. In most cases they provide no meaningful metric for comparing preferences and policies. The consequence is that they shed rather little light on complaints that the political system responds consistently but too weakly to shifts in public opinion due to institutional fragmentation and gridlock.

They also shed virtually no light on claims of consistent ideological biases in policymaking. This omission is particularly troubling given the broader tendency in American politics toward deadlock—the Madisonian system of governance offers numerous veto points to obstruct comprehensive egalitarian policy that would address rising economic inequality.

In addition, the research on public opinion and policy has seldom paid serious attention to the possibility of reciprocal influences of policy on opinion, or more generally to the possibility that public opinion is systematically misinformed or manipulated by political elites (Jacobs and Shapiro 2000).

Moreover, government responsiveness to public opinion is unlikely to be fixed over time but rather to vary in reactions to the dynamics of changing political coalitions, election results, and institutional conditions.[19] The findings of a small but growing number of recent studies of a decline in government responsiveness since the 1970s coincides with important political developments, which were examined above and in the separate research review on *Political Voice*. The growing importance of campaign contributions and polarization of the political parties during this period help to explain a significant change in the incentives of national politicians toward tailoring policy to reflect the policy goals of their intense supporters even if it means compromising the views of the more diffuse general public.

Perhaps most importantly for our purposes here, studies relating public opinion and public policy have seldom dug below the level of aggregate opinion in a congressional district, a state, or the nation as a whole to examine *whose* preferences impact the course of public policy and how much influence they exert. The research that has been conducted has found substantial disparities in apparent influence between political activists and ordinary people, between business leaders and the public, and between well-off citizens and their less-well-off counterparts. These disparities go to the heart of any assessment of inequality and American democracy, and they raise fundamental problems for a political system grounded on the normative ideal of political equality.

Evidence that government officials are less responsive to public opinion than commonly assumed or only selectively responsive to the affluent raises a practical puzzle: how could politicians regularly win reelection if they were defying voters? The answer is that the policy decisions of government officials are, often by design, difficult for voters to monitor

(Arnold 1990) and, as we suggested earlier, contributors and party activists have intense preferences that they vigorously press on government officials. In addition, voters often cast their vote based on a personal bond, creating strong incentives for officeholders and candidates to rest their appeal to voters on non-policy considerations such as personal attributes and image.[20]

THE CONTINUING STRUGGLE FOR RACIAL EQUALITY

One of the great stories of the past century in the United States has been the reduction of overt discrimination that once excluded millions of Americans from the core of political, economic, and social life. Women gained the right to vote and the right to run for office alongside men. Popular struggles by ordinary African Americans culminated in the Civil Rights Act of 1964, which outlawed racial discrimination in public accommodations, prohibited federal funding of educational institutions if they discriminated, and forbade racial and gender discrimination by employers and unions. Another landmark was the Voting Rights Act of 1965, which cleared the way for all African Americans to vote.

Despite landmark legislation and major Supreme Court decisions in dismantling overt discrimination and expanding rights to equal treatment and fair process, the United States still has substantial de facto political inequality along racial lines. The ongoing debates on achieving racial equality in American politics and public life have interacted with rising economic inequality in ways that have intensified the existing biases in American government toward deadlock on egalitarian issues and accommodation of the organized and vocal. Rising economic inequality undermines the substantive conditions for racial minorities to capitalize on newly won procedural rights; conversely, the debate on race distracts policy efforts and public discussion from comprehensive policies to redistribute resources that would help establish the substantive conditions for the equal exercise of formal rights. The result is that inequality is often discussed in racial and often procedural terms, rather than substantive and economic terms even as racial differences in the political process and in policy outcomes remain.

The latest chapters in America's long struggle for racial equality in democratic life has been characterized by two somewhat conflicting developments. First, there has been some progress in reducing long-entrenched political inequality and increasing (in some cases) the election of racial, ethnic, or gender groups. Second, political equality has not been achieved in terms of either descriptive representation (that is, the racial, ethnic, and gender characteristics of the individuals elected to government institutions) or substantive representation (that is, the outcomes produced by government bodies). Indeed, the sometimes separate agendas to achieve descriptive and substantive representation may work at cross purposes or, at times, collide. It is clear that race continues to be a significant factor in American politics, accentuated at times by growing economic inequality: widening economic disparities undercut, in certain respects, the procedural victories of minorities.

Much of the research in American politics, and therefore our discussion, focuses on legislatures and, specifically, on how and whether minority interests are represented in legislatures.[21] Although our discussion concentrates on race, there has been some research on the representation of women in U.S. legislatures in terms of both the substantive issues that are voted upon and the structure and procedures of debate and deliberation (Kathlene 1994, 1995; Swers 1998; Mansbridge 1999; Phillips 1995).

Tension Between Descriptive and Substantive Representation

Efforts to expand the number of racial and ethnic minorities in national and state legislative bodies (that is, "descriptive representation") may be antagonistic to the struggle for substantive representation to enact policies that would reduce economic inequality and by extension lift the economic and living conditions of the minority community (Wilson 1987). The promoters of racial redistricting expected it to protect minorities from the tyranny of the majority and to ensure that minorities had a voice in determining the policies that affect them.

A critical tool for expanding the representation of minorities in legislatures was to redraw districts to make blacks and ethnic minorities a majority of the electorate (what is known as "majority-minority" districts). "Descriptive representation" and redistricting to elect more minorities to office may, however, undercut "substantive representation" in two ways. First, racial redistricting may "dilute" the presence of minority voters in surrounding districts and produce a net drop in legislators who would join coalitions to enact policies that advanced the interests of minorities. There may be more people of color in legislatures and less overall political support for legislation that advances the interests of the minority community.[22]

Second, racial redistricting may prime race as the principal political identity and spark political conflict that deflects attention from economic and material interests. Research shows that that African Americans more strongly favor the goal of increasing minority representation than the principle of color blindness in congressional redistricting (Tate 2003). On the other hand, efforts to restrict and mobilize African Americans run the risk of provoking a political backlash from whites. Focusing on racialized policies ignites racial reactions including prejudice among whites (Kinder and Mendelberg 1995). One study demonstrated, for instance, that as the size of the black population increased in Louisiana parishes ("counties"), whites were more likely to join the Republican Party (Giles and Hertz 1994; Glaser 1994). In states where black voter turnout has been relatively higher, there has been less spending on social policies, which implies a "backlash" effect.[23] Moreover, increases in the proportion of racial and ethnic minority officeholders appear to produce more powerful interest groups to counter elected officials (without a commensurate rise in interest groups that directly represented minority interests) (Hero 1998; Thomas and Hrebenar 1999).

Although racial redistricting has been controversial and may have complicated efforts to enact substantive policy to help minorities, it is important not to lose sight of the larger context of race relations in America that helps explain both the origins of efforts to promote descriptive representation and the enduring obstacles to descriptive and substantive representation.

"Majority-minority" districts were not created in a vacuum; they are the historic product of persistent opposition to political equality. After the passage of the historic Voting Rights Act of 1965, southern states (especially Mississippi) implemented new electoral strategies to minimize black electoral success during the 1960s and 1970s (Parker 1991). The concept of majority-minority districts was developed as a concrete strategy of legal defense organizations and civil rights attorneys to counter this ongoing opposition to implementing the Voting Rights Act. The tension, then, between descriptive and substantive representation that we live with today is an institutional legacy of the enduring opposition and ambivalence to creating political equality on racial and ethnic grounds.

Moreover, the controversy over descriptive representation results from the demands and concerns of white Americans as much as black Americans. Research shows that white constituents place more importance than black constituents on descriptive representation and are more likely to contact congressional representatives who share their racial identity (Gay 2002). In addition, the battle over majority-minority districts is only one of several fronts on which race and elections are being contested (Schmidt 1989). Indeed, the tools of direct democracy—namely, the initiative, referendum and recall—have been wielded to strike down civil rights.[24]

It seems particularly telling that after all the attention given to race and representation and to challenging to overt racial, ethnic, and gender discrimination, minorities continue to be underrepresented. The presence of racial and ethnic minorities in governing institutions has increased but remains below their percentages in the general population. Women also remain underrepresented in Congress despite improvements—they constitute 14 percent of the House, 13 percent of the Senate, and 22 percent of state legislatures (though this varies considerably from state to state).[25] A series of interlocking factors converge to restrict the extent and impact of representation of minority groups.

• The institutional rules of elections and governing bodies depress advances for minority groups. The election of minorities is discouraged by their residential segregation and the residential dispersion of whites (who rarely vote for minority candidates) in at-large elections. In addition, the huge majorities of white legislators make it improbable for modest increases in the number of minority officeholders alone to move the position of the median legislator toward greater responsiveness to the concerns of minorities. What minimal growth in minority representation that does occur is checked by the separation of powers and the bifurcation of legislative chambers in Congress and in most states.

• Rather than facilitating the political participation of all diffuse and disadvantaged groups (Schattschneider 1960), political parties tend to "capture" blacks and other minority groups and provide little in return in their rush to appeal to the median voter (Frymer 1999).

• Racial divisions may be so entrenched that they determine party cleavage and resist revision. In particular, the racial composition of states generates three enduring types of party cleavages: racially defined southern party divisions, the New Deal cleavages in which race was submerged by economic conflicts, and the post–New Deal divisions characterized by conflict over both race and class (Brown 1995).

• The mass media reinforce negative stereotypes by associating the poor with blacks more than is justified by actual demographic data (Gilens 2003b).

• The large upsurge in immigration in the 1990s has fueled concerns about national sovereignty and cultural and economic nationalism. It has fanned underlying fears and perceptions of threat toward racial and ethnic groups and may have complicated efforts to build broad political coalitions.

In short, descriptive representation has expanded the presence of minorities in government institutions but the improvement and impact has been limited and may have deterred egalitarian policies that would help minorities. At best, minority legislators have reached a position to block or modify policies they find objectionable, a notable accomplishment though somewhat short of more lofty expectations.

The Synergy of Descriptive and Substantive Representation

Despite the constraints on what has been achieved through expanded representation of minorities in government institutions, descriptive representation and substantive representation are not mutually exclusive but may reinforce each other. Greater descriptive representation does influence policy substance in significant ways.

The mobilization and empowerment of the southern black electorate has prompted long-serving white southern Democratic members of the U.S. House to change their roll call voting and become more liberal (Whitby and Gilliam 1991; Whitby 1985). Moreover, the race and gender of state legislators influence their conduct and the issues they put on the agenda and promote (Bratton and Haynie 1999). Constituency service was taken more seriously by female and black city council members than their male and white counterparts (Thomas 1990). Analysis of state senate roll call voting in Louisiana, Georgia, and Alabama in 1979 through 1981 found that white senators are not as responsive to black constituents as black senators are (Herring 1990). (There are, however, proportionately fewer black legislators.)

Latino members of the U.S. House had distinct, more "liberal," patterns on a set of roll call votes that were most relevant to Latino concerns (Hero and Tolbert 1995). These votes resulted more from their constituency's socioeconomic profile (that is, levels of poverty and urbanization) than the ethnic traits of the constituents or ethnic background of the representatives themselves.

Similarly, electing (or appointing) representatives from historically excluded groups to city government has been found to expand substantive representation. Studies of minority political incorporation in ten San Francisco Bay Area cities and the Bradley regime in Los Angeles show that expanded political representation of African Americans and Latinos produced broad coalitions with white liberal allies that expanded the delivery of services and goods to minorities (Browning, Marshall, and Tabb 1984; Sonenshein 1993).

The Civil Rights movement and passage of the Voting Rights Act produced some landmark programs that improved the living conditions of Americans who are minorities as well as those who are not. Changes in health policy illustrate how the expanded political representation of minorities influenced substantive representation. The prohibition against

racial discrimination in the Voting Rights Act (especially Title VI) precipitated a transformation in medical treatment when Medicare and Medicaid
were implemented following their passage in 1965. One history of this
period reported: "More than a thousand acute-care hospitals, ignoring the
trepidation of board members, physicians, and patients, within a few
months broke down the wall that had racially divided their staffs and patients since their founding in order to become Medicare providers on July
1, 1966" (Smith 1999, 200–1, 316–17). The impressive result was that black
and white use of physicians and hospital use converged. Although racial
inequities in health policy remain, expanded political equality led to a remarkably quick change in health policy and medical practice.

CONCLUSION

The framers of the U.S. constitution feared that majorities of the landless
would use their equal rights as citizens to exercise government power for
the purpose of redistributing economic resources. Their strategy to dis-
rupt and discourage majoritarian movements was, in part, to disperse
government power to ensure that it was not wielded by a single person or
government body and to instill personal motives for the temporary occu-
pants of government positions to check the broad and comprehensive exercise of power. The result is a political process that has operated, as designed, to deter and hinder the concerted exercise of power to pursue "big
ideas" that would reshuffle social, economic, and political relations. A side
result is that the dispersal of authority opened up multiple points of access
into government bodies (Bentley 1908). The actual practice of political participation and American governance has both fulfilled the aspirations of
America's institution builders to obstruct the active exercise of government authority for redistributive purposes and introduced unintended
dynamics—namely, the exploitation of porous and decentralized institutions by the organized and vocal.

The American constitutional system has helped to create one of the
most enduring puzzles of representative government: the embrace of
equality (fervently, at times) and yet a seeming complacency in accepting
wide inequalities in economic and political resources. In the realm of public life, political rights are guaranteed to all citizens but political participation continues to be stratified. All adult citizens enjoy equal rights to vote,
join organizations, lobby lawmakers, and pursue other avenues for expressing their interests and concerns but the actual exercise of these rights
is skewed toward those with higher levels of income, education, and other
advantageous social and economic attributes.

The tendency of Americans to embrace equality of opportunity while
tolerating inequality in outcomes, as de Tocqueville famously observed in

the early nineteenth century, certainly helps to explain the puzzle of equality in principle and inequality in practice. The process of American governance has also contributed to sustaining this odd dualism by institutionalizing inclusion rather than exclusion and the dispersal rather than concentration of government authority. The American process of governance has ample points of access; it is the organized and vocal that rush through the avenues of access in order to promote policies that deliver targeted benefits and to block comprehensive policies that redistribute resources and power at their expense. Indeed, these peculiar features of the American political process account for why it does not readily avail itself to deductive analysis that reasons backwards from inequalities in influence and outcomes to identify the broad and consistent deployment of government authority that produced it. The doors to the halls of government are open but its Byzantine highways and byways amplify and reinforce the unequal voice of citizens—both the silences and the loud and consistent chorus of the few.

Economic inequality and its sharp increase over the past three decades has not remade or transformed American institutions as much as it has reinforced already existing tendencies. The dispersal of government authority and multiple points of access facilitate the continued institutional patterns of deadlocking egalitarian policies and producing selective benefits for the organized and vocal. The long-standing bias toward inert government institutions on redistributive issues and selective action on particularistic benefits stand out because the living conditions of Americans changed, not because of a makeover of government institutions. Giving money to political campaigns is one of the few areas where the growing concentration of income and wealth appears to have directly expanded political inequality—increasing the advantage of the affluent to use their check books to express their views, to narrow the pool of viable candidates for elected office, and to win access to government officials.

The continuing tension of American governance is that political rights are guaranteed to all citizens and stand as a living testament to democratic equality, even as those rights are exercised disproportionately by the most advantaged to obstruct and discourage government responsiveness to majoritarian concerns. As the next chapter shows, the consequences of government policies both perpetuate existing inequalities and give birth to new ones.

In addition to the comments of our colleagues on the Task Force that helped guide our work, we have benefited from the advice and comments of Sarah Binder (Brookings Institution and George Washington University), Forrest

Maltzman (George Washington University), Jon Oberlander (University of North Carolina at Chapel Hill), and Dara Strolovich (University of Minnesota). We also thank Michael Illuzzi (University of Minnesota), Hilary Kennedy (George Mason University), and Jonathan Ladd (Princeton University) for able research assistance. Finally, we are especially grateful to Christopher Karpowitz (Princeton University), who researched and drafted an initial review of the literature on money in the American political system.

NOTES

1. In political science, the classic case is Dahl's (1961) effort to reconstruct the exercise of power over policy decisions in New Haven. The critical reaction to this work includes McCoy and Playford (1967), Bachrach and Baratz (1962), and Gaventa (1980).
2. For examples, see Davidson (1988) and Beam, Conlan, and Wrightson (1990).
3. The classic analyses include Wilson (1885), McConnell (1966), Lowi (1969), and Skowronek (1982).
4. Some of the factors that may have contributed to Key's abandonment of the "have not" hypothesis may include the evolution of southern state politics in unexpected ways and the expansion of Key's own scholarly focus to one-party systems in nonsouthern states (Key 1956; Mayhew 1988).
5. See Besley and Case (2003) for a comprehensive review of these and other relevant studies.
6. The macroeconomic outcomes were identified by Hibbs (1987).
7. The prediction of convergence is most closely associated with Downs (1957).
8. The political consequences of unequal political participation have been dismissed on the grounds that the preferences of voters and non-voters are similar (Highton and Wolfinger 2001; Wolfinger and Rosenstone 1980). Recent research has challenged this view on two grounds. First, it neglects the strategic reactions of political elites (Martin 2003). Second, it falsely assumes that survey instruments provide a neutral mechanism for providing comparable evidence regarding the policy preferences of voters and nonvoters. It turns out that current opinion survey instruments do not provide an accurate measure of the policy preferences of nonvoters (Berinsky, 2002). A similar critique is offered in the separate research review on *Political Voice*.
9. A classic account is Dahl (1961).
10. See also Mann (2001, 2003) for a brief history of political science work on the cost of elections.
11. Contributors may not see as mutually exclusive the strategies of influencing election outcome (Type 1 in Wright's [1985] terms) and influencing elected officials (Type II). An organized interest or political action committee (PAC) may choose to pursue one strategy rather than the other or may pursue both.

There is some evidence that the choice of strategy is influenced by the goals and organizational structure of the interest group (Wright 1985).

12. Extensive debate was sparked by Gary Jacobson's (1980) finding of a negative relationship between incumbent spending and votes and his explanation that officeholders increase their campaign spending only when running against well-funded, high-quality challengers (also see Krasno, Green, and Cowden 1994). A number of methodological critiques have been made focusing on measuring candidate expenditures on direct communications with voters rather than total expenditures (Ansolabehere and Gerber 1994; also see Goldenberg and Traugott 1984) and on the difficulty of separating out the simultaneous effects of reactive spending decisions of incumbents, the propensity of quality challengers to run against weaker candidates, the ability of high quality challengers to raise money, and other factors (Green and Krasno 1988, 1990; Goidel and Gross 1994; Thomas 1989; Kenny and McBurnett 1994; Gerber 1998; also see Bartels 1991b, and Jacobson 1990). Research on state-level legislative elections suggests a complex range of influences on campaign spending and the votes it is associated with including the media market and the cost of media buys, the strength of party organization, the length of the campaign, though it also emphasizes incumbency as critical (Gierzynski and Breaux 1996).

13. Candidate expenditures are associated with increased vote share in elections for congress (Jacobson 1978, 1980; Green and Krasno 1988; Abramowitz 1988, 1989; Squire 1989; Thomas 1989), state legislatures (Breaux and Gierzynski 1991; Abramowitz 1991; Caldeira and Patterson 1982; Gierzynski and Breaux 1991, 1993; Giles and Pritchard 1985; Glantz, Abramowitz, and Burkart 1976), and governorships (Jewell 1984; Morehouse 1990).

14. Other comparative state research has examined the relationship between political participation and government policymaking (Hill and Leighley, 1992, 1994, and 1996).

15. For example, compare Erikson and Wright (1989, 1997).

16. Research by Ansolabehere, Snyder, and Stewart (2001), Monroe (1998), and Jacobs and Shapiro (2000) use different methodologies but appear to be identifying a common underlying tendency toward declining government responsiveness over time.

17. Specifically, Hill and Hinton-Andersson (1995) extended Erikson, Wright, and McIver's (1993) state-level analysis.

18. Gilens (2003a) builds on Page and Shapiro's (1983) study of policy responsiveness in much the same way that Bartels's paper extends Miller and Stokes's study of congressional representation

19. See Jacobs (1993, conclusion) for a discussion of the "conditional relevance" of public opinion and the political and institutional barriers that prevent government policy from being an "epiphenomenon" of public opinion.

20. Fenno (1978) provides a classic analysis of the nonpolicy appeals that members of Congress make to their constituents. Druckman, Jacobs, and Ostermeier (2004) demonstrate "image responsiveness"—the responsiveness of President Nixon to private White House polling regarding his personality traits.

21. We do not discuss two additional questions. The first is the normative question, "how *should* representation be provided within a majority rule system?" The second is the legal question, "how *can* representation be provided" (Canon 2002).

22. For example, Cameron, Epstein, and O'Halloran (1996), but see Lublin (1997).

23. Radcliff and Saiz (1995); but see Radcliff and Saiz (1998).

24. There is a debate over whether civil rights are being challenged using the tools of direct democracy frequently (Gamble 1997) or infrequently (Hajnal, Gerber, and Louch 2002; but see Bowler, Donovan, and Tolbert 1998).

25. See Swers (1998) for a review.

REFERENCES

Abramowitz, Alan I. 1988. "Explaining Senate Election Outcomes." *American Political Science Review* 82(2): 385–403.

———. 1989. "Campaign Spending in U.S. Senate Elections." *Legislative Studies Quarterly* 14(4): 487–507.

———. 1991. "Incumbency, Campaign Spending, and the Decline of Competition in U.S. Elections." *Journal of Politics* 53(1): 34–56.

Abramson, Paul R. 1976. "Generational Change and the Decline of Party Identification in America: 1952–1974." *American Political Science Review* 70(2): 469–78.

Achen, Christopher H. 1977. "Measuring Representation: Perils of the Correlation Coefficient." *American Journal of Political Science* 21(4): 805–15.

———. 1978. "Measuring Representation." *American Journal of Political Science* 22(3): 475–510.

Aldrich, John, and David Rhode. 1998. "Measuring Conditional Party Government." Paper presented to the Midwest Political Science Association. Chicago (April 23–25).

———. 2000. "The Republican Revolution and the House Appropriations Committee." *Journal of Politics* 62(1): 1–33.

———. 2001. "The Logic of Congressional Party Government: Revising the Electoral Connection." In *Congress Reconsidered*, 7th ed., edited by Lawrence Dodd and Bruce Oppenheimer. Washington, D.C.: CQ Press.

Alexander, Herbert E. 1972. *Money in Politics*. Washington, D.C.: Public Affairs Press.

Allen, Michael Patrick, and John L. Campbell. 1994. "State Revenue Extraction from Different Income Groups: Variations in Tax Progressivity in the United States, 1916 to 1986." *American Sociological Review* 59(2): 169–96.

Alvarez, Michael and Jason Saving. 1997. "Deficits, Democrats, and Distributive Benefits: Congressional Elections and the Pork Barrel in the 1980s." *Political Research Quarterly* 50(4): 809–31.

American Political Science Association. Committee on Political Parties. 1950. "Toward a More Responsible Two-Party System." *American Political Science Review* 44(3, part 2): supplement.

Ansolabehere, Stephen, and Alan Gerber. 1994. "The Mismeasure of Campaign Spending: Evidence from the 1990 U.S. House Elections." *Journal of Politics* 56(4): 1106–18.

Ansolabehere, Stephen, John M. de Figueiredo, and James M. Snyder. 2003. "Why Is There So Little Money in U.S. Politics?" *Journal of Economic Perspectives* 17(1): 105–30.

Ansolabehere, Stephen, Alan Gerber, and James M. Snyder Jr. 2001. "Corruption and the Growth of Campaign Spending." In *A User's Guide to Campaign Finance Reform*, edited by Gerald C. Lubenow. Lanham, Md.: Rowman and Littlefield.

Ansolabehere, Stephen, James M. Snyder Jr., and Charles Stewart III. 2001. "Candidate Positioning in U.S. House Elections." *American Journal of Political Science* 45(1): 136–59.

Arnold, R. Douglas. 1990. *The Logic of Congressional Action*. New Haven, Conn.: Yale University Press.

Austen-Smith, David. 1995. "Campaign Contributions and Access." *American Political Science Review* 89(3): 566–81.

Bachrach, Peter, and Morton S. Baratz. 1962. "The Two Faces of Power." *American Political Science Review* 56(4): 947–52.

Bailey, Michael. 2003. "The Democratic Folly of BCRA." Unpublished manuscript, Georgetown University.

Balla, Steven, Eric Lawrence, Forrest Maltzman, and Lee Sigelman. 2002. "Partisanship, Blame Avoidance, and the Distribution of Legislative Pork." *American Journal of Political Science* 46(3): 515–25.

Bartels, Larry M. 1991a. "Constituency Opinion and Congressional Policy Making: The Reagan Defense Buildup." *American Political Science Review* 85(2): 457–74.

———. 1991b. "Instrumental and 'Quasi-Instrumental' Variables." *American Journal of Political Science* 35(3): 777–800.

———. 2000. "Partisanship and Voting Behavior, 1952–1996." *American Journal of Political Science* 44(1): 35–50.

———. 2002. "Beyond the Running Tally: Partisan Bias in Political Perceptions." *Political Behavior* 24(2): 117–50.

———. 2003. "Partisan Politics and the U.S. Income Distribution." Paper presented at the Russell Sage Foundation Conference on Social Dimensions of Inequality. Washington, D.C. (May 29–30).

———. 2005. "Economic Inequality and Political Representation." Revised paper originally presented at the Annual Meeting of the American Political Science Association. Boston (August 2002).

Bauer, Raymond A., Ithiel de Sola Pool, and Lewis Anthony Dexter. 1963. *American Business and Public Policy: The Politics of Foreign Trade*. New York: Atherton Press.

Beam, David R., Timothy J. Conlan, and Margaret T. Wrightson. 1990. "Solving the Riddle of Tax Reform: Party Competition and the Politics of Ideas." *Political Science Quarterly* 105(2): 193–217.

Bentley, Arthur. 1908. *The Process of Government: A Study of Social Pressures*. Chicago: University of Chicago Press.

Berinsky, Adam J. 2002. "Silent Voices: Social Welfare Policy Opinions and Political Equality in America." *American Journal of Political Science* 46(2): 276–87.

Berry, Jeffrey. 1999. *The New Liberalism: The Rising Power of Citizen Groups*. Washington, D.C.: Brookings Institution.

Besley, Timothy, and Anne Case. 2003. "Political Institutions and Policy Choices: Evidence from the United States." *Journal of Economic Literature* 41(1): 7–73.

Best, Samuel. 1999. "The Sampling Problem in Studying Public Mood: An Alternative Solution." *Journal of Politics* 61(3): 721–40.

Bianco, William T. 1994. *Trust: Representatives and Constituents*. Ann Arbor: University of Michigan Press.

Birney, Mayling, and Ian Shapiro. 2003. "Death and Taxes: The Estate Tax Repeal and American Democracy." Paper presented at the Princeton University Conference on Inequality and American Democracy. Princeton, N.J. (November 7–8).

Bond, Jon R., and Richard Fleisher. 1990. *The President in the Legislative Arena*. Chicago: University of Chicago Press.

Bowler, Shaun, Todd Donovan, and Caroline Tolbert, eds. 1998. *Citizens as Legislators: Direct Democracy in the United States*. Columbus: Ohio State University Press.

Box-Steffensmeier, Janet M. 1996. "A Dynamic Analysis of the Role of War Chests in Campaign Strategy." *American Journal of Political Science* 40(2): 352–71.

Bratton, Kathleen, and Kerry Haynie. 1999. "Agenda Setting and Legislative Success in State Legislatures: The Effects of Gender and Race." *Journal of Politics* 61(3): 658–79.

Breaux, David A., and Anthony Gierzynski. 1991. "'It's Money that Matters': Campaign Expenditures and State Legislative Primaries." *Legislative Studies Quarterly* 16(3): 429–43.

Broder, David S. 1971. *The Party's Over: The Failure of Politics in America*. New York: Harper & Row.

Brown, Robert. 1995. "Party Cleavages and Welfare Effort in the American States," *American Political Science Review* 89(1): 23–33.

Browning, Rufus P., Dale Rogers Marshall, and David H. Tabb. 1984. *Protest is Not Enough: The Struggle of Blacks and Hispanics for Equality in Urban Politics*. Berkeley: University of California Press.

Burke, Edmund. 1949. "Speech to the Electors of Bristol." In *Burke's Politics, Selected Writings and Speeches*, edited by Ross Hoffmann and Paul Levack. New York: Alfred A. Knopf.

Burns, James MacGregor. 1963. *The Deadlock of Democracy: Four-Party Politics in America*. Englewood Cliffs, N.J.: Prentice-Hall.

Cain, Bruce, John Ferejohn, and Morris Fiorina. 1987. *The Personal Vote: Constituency Service and Electoral Independence*. Cambridge, Mass.: Harvard University Press.

Caldeira, Gregory A., and Samuel C. Patterson. 1982. "Bringing Home the Votes: Electoral Outcomes in State Legislative Races." *Political Behavior* 4(1): 33–67.

Cameron, Charles, David Epstein, and Sharyn O'Halloran. 1996. "Do Majority-Minority Districts Maximize Substantive Black Representation in Congress?" *American Political Science Review* 90(4): 794–812.

Canes-Wrone, Brandice, David Brady, and John Cogan. 2002. "Out of Step, Out of Office: Electoral Accountability and House Members' Voting." *American Political Science Review* 96(1): 127–40.

Canon, David. 2002. "The Representation of Racial Interests in the U.S. Congress." Paper presented at University of Notre Dame Conference on The Politics of Democratic Inclusion. South Bend, Ind. (October 17–19).

Carmines, Edward G., and James Stimson. 1989. *Race and the Transformation of American Politics*. Princeton, N.J.: Princeton University Press.

Carsey, Thomas, and Barry Rundquist. 1999. "Party and Committee in Distributive Politics: Evidence from Defense Spending." *Journal of Politics* 61(4): 1156–69.

Center for Responsive Politics. 2005. "2004 Election Overview." Available at: http://www.opensecrets.org/overview/stats.asp?Cycle=2004 (accessed April 20, 2005).

Chappell, Henry W., Jr. 1981. "Campaign Contributions and Voting on the Cargo Preference Bill: A Comparison of Simultaneous Models." *Public Choice* 36(2): 301–12.

———. 1982. "Campaign Contributions and Congressional Voting: A Simultaneous Probit-Tobit Model." *Review of Economics and Statistics* 62(1): 77–83.

Coleman, John J. 2001. "The Distribution of Campaign Spending Benefits across Groups." *Journal of Politics* 63(3): 916–43.

Coleman, John J., and Paul F. Manna. 2000. "Congressional Campaign Spending and the Quality of Democracy." *Journal of Politics* 62(3): 757–89.

Cook, Fay Lomax. 1979. *Who Should be Helped? Public Support for Social Services*. Beverly Hills, Calif.: Sage Publications.

Cox, Gary, and Eric Magar. 1999. "How Much is Majority Status in the U.S. Congress Worth?" *American Political Science Review* 93(2): 299–309.

Cox, Gary, and Mathew McCubbins. 1993. *Legislative Leviathan: Party Government in the House*. Berkeley: University of California Press.

Cox, Gary, and Keith Poole. 2002. "On Measuring Partisanship in Roll-Call Voting:

The U.S. House of Representatives, 1877–1999." *American Journal of Political Science* 46(3): 477–89.

Dahl, Robert A. 1963. *Modern Political Analysis.* Englewood Cliffs, N.J.: Prentice-Hall.

———. 1961. *Who Governs? Democracy and Power in an American City.* New Haven, Conn.: Yale University Press.

———. 1989. *Democracy and Its Critics.* New Haven, Conn.: Yale University Press.

Davidson, Roger. 1988. "The New Centralization on Capital Hill." *Review of Politics* 50(3): 345–63.

Downs, Anthony. 1957. *An Economic Theory of Democracy.* New York: Harper & Row.

Drew, Elizabeth. 1983. *Politics and Money: The New Road to Corruption.* New York: Macmillan.

Druckman, James N., Lawrence R. Jacobs, and Eric Ostermeier. 2004. "Candidate Strategies to Prime Issues and Image." *Journal of Politics* 66(4): 1180–1202.

Dye, Thomas. 1966. *Politics, Economics, and the Public: Policy Outcomes in the American States.* Chicago: Rand McNally.

Easton, David. 1965. *A Systems Analysis of Political Life.* New York: John Wiley & Sons.

Eckstein, Harry. 1958. *The English Health Service: Its Origins, Structure, and Achievements.* Cambridge, Mass.: Harvard University Press.

———. 1960. *Pressure Group Politics: The case of the British Medical Association.* London: Allen and Unwin.

Epstein, David, and Peter Zemsky. 1995. "Money Talks: Deterring Quality Challengers in Congressional Elections." *American Political Science Review* 89(2): 295–308.

Erikson, Robert S. 1978. "Constituency Opinion and Congressional Behavior: A Reexamination of the Miller-Stokes Data." *American Journal of Political Science* 22(3): 511–35.

Erikson, Robert S., Michael B. MacKuen, and James A. Stimson. 2002. *The Macro Polity.* New York: Cambridge University Press.

Erikson, Robert S., and Gerald C. Wright Jr. 1989. "Voters, Candidates, and Issues in Congressional Elections." In *Congress Reconsidered,* 4th ed., edited by Lawrence C. Dodd and Bruce I. Oppenheimer. Washington, D.C.: CQ Press.

———. 1997. "Voters, Candidates, and Issues in Congressional Elections." In *Congress Reconsidered,* 6th ed., edited by Lawrence C. Dodd and Bruce I. Oppenheimer. Washington, D.C.: CQ Press.

Erikson, Robert S., Gerald C. Wright Jr., and John P. McIver. 1989. "Political Parties, Public Opinion, and State Policy in the United States." *American Political Science Review* 83(3): 728–50.

———. 1993. *Statehouse Democracy: Public Opinion and Policy in the American States.* New York: Cambridge University Press.

Evans, Diana. 1996. "Before the Roll Call: Interest Group Lobbying and Public Policy Outcomes in House Committees." *Political Research Quarterly* 49(2): 287–304.

Fenno, Richard F. 1978. *Homestyle: House Members in Their Districts.* Boston, Mass.: Little, Brown.

Ferejohn, John. 1974. *Pork Barrel Politics.* Stanford, Calif.: Stanford University Press.

Ferguson, Thomas. 1995. *Golden Rule: The Investment Theory of Party Competition and the Logic of Money-Driven Political Systems.* Chicago: University of Chicago Press.

Fiorina, Morris P. 1989. *Congress: Keystone of the Washington Establishment,* 2nd ed. New Haven, Conn.: Yale University Press.

———. 2002. "Parties and Partisanship: A 40-Year Retrospective." *Political Behavior* 24(2): 93–115.

Fleisher, Richard, and Jon R. Bond. 1996. "The President in a More Partisan Legislative Arena." *Political Research Quarterly* 49(4): 729–48.

Frendreis, John, and Richard Waterman. 1985. "PAC Contributions and Legislative Behavior: Senate Voting on Trucking Deregulation." *Social Science Quarterly* 66(2): 401–12.

Frymer, Paul. 1999. *Uneasy Alliances: Race and Party Competition in America.* Princeton, N.J.: Princeton University Press.

Gamble, Barbara. 1997. "Putting Civil Rights to a Popular Vote." *American Journal of Political Science* 41(1): 245–69.

Gaventa, John. 1980. *Power and Powerlessness: Quiescence and Rebellion in an Appalachian Valley.* Urbana: University of Illinois Press.

Gay, Claudine. 2002. "Spirals of Trust? The Effect of Descriptive Representation on the Relationship Between Citizens and their Government." *American Journal of Political Science* 46(October): 717–33.

Gerber, Alan. 1998. "Estimating the Effect of Campaign Spending on Senate Election Outcomes Using Instrumental Variables." *American Political Science Review* 92(2): 401–11.

Gierzynski, Anthony, and David Breaux. 1991. "Money and Votes in State Legislative Elections." *Legislative Studies Quarterly* 16(2): 203–17.

———. 1993. "Money and the Party Vote in State House Elections." *Legislative Studies Quarterly* 18(4): 515–33.

———. 1996. "Legislative Elections and the Importance of Money." *Legislative Studies Quarterly* 21(3): 337–57.

Gilens, Martin. 2003a. "Public Opinion and Democratic Responsiveness: Who Gets What They Want from Government?" Paper presented at the Princeton University Conference on Inequality and American Democracy. Princeton, N.J. (November 7–8).

———. 2003b. "How the Poor Became Black: The Racialization of American Poverty in the Mass Media." In *Race and the Politics of Welfare Reform,* edited by Sanford F. Schram, Joe Soss, and Richard C. Fording. Ann Arbor: University of Michigan Press.

Giles, Michael W., and Kaenan Hertz. 1994. "Racial Threat and Partisan Identification." *American Political Science Review* 88(2): 317–26.

Giles, Michael W., and Anita Pritchard. 1985. "Campaign Expenditures and Legislative Elections in Florida." *Legislative Studies Quarterly* 10(1): 71–88.

Glantz, Stanton A., Alan I. Abramowitz, and Michael P. Burkart. 1976. "Election Outcomes: Whose Money Matters?" *Journal of Politics* 38(4): 1033–41.

Glaser, James M. 1994. "Back to the Black Belt: Racial Environment and White Racial Attitudes in the South" *Journal of Politics* 56(1): 21–41.

Goidel, Robert K., and Donald A. Gross. 1994. "A Systems Approach to Campaign Finance in U.S. House Elections." *American Politics Quarterly* 22(2): 125–53.

Goldenberg, Edie N., and Michael W. Traugott. 1984. *Campaigning for Congress.* Washington, D.C.: CQ Press.

Goldenberg, Edie N., Michael W. Traugott, and Frank R. Baumgartner. 1986. "Preemptive and Reactive Spending in U.S. House Races." *Political Behavior* 8(1): 3–20.

Goodliffe, Jay. 2001. "The Effect of War Chests on Challenger Entry in U.S. House Elections." *American Journal of Political Science* 45(4): 830–44.

Gopoian, J. David. 1984. "What Makes PACs Tick? An Analysis of the Allocation Patterns of Economic Interest Groups." *American Journal of Political Science* 28(2): 259–81.

Gordon, Colin. 2003. *Dead on Arrival: The Politics of Health Care in Twentieth-Century America.* Princeton, N.J.: Princeton University Press.

Gottschalk, Marie. 2000. *The Shadow Welfare State: Labor, Business, and the Politics of Health Care in the United States.* Ithaca, N.Y.: Cornell University Press.

Green, Donald Philip, and Jonathan S. Krasno. 1988. "Salvation for the Spendthrift Incumbent: Reestimating the Effects of Campaign Spending in House Elections." *American Journal of Political Science* 32(4): 884–907.

——. 1990. "Rebuttal to Jacobson's 'New Evidence for Old Arguments.'" *American Journal of Political Science* 34(2): 363–72.

Green, Mark. 2002. *How Big Corporate Money Buys Elections, Rams through Legislation, and Betrays Our Democracy.* New York: HarperCollins.

Grenzke, Janet. 1989. "PACs and the Congressional Supermarket: The Currency is Complex." *American Journal of Political Science* 33(1): 1–24.

Grier, Kevin, and Michael Munger. 1991. "Committee Assignments, Constituent Preferences, and Campaign Contributions to House Incumbents." *Economic Inquiry* 29(1): 24–43.

——. 1993. "Comparing Interest Group PAC Contributions to House and Senate Incumbents, 1980–1986." *Journal of Politics* 55(3): 615–43.

Grogan, Coleen M. 1994. "Political-Economic Factors Influencing State Medicaid Policy." *Political Research Quarterly* 47(3): 589–623.

Hajnal, Zoltan L., Elisabeth R. Gerber, and Hugh Louch. 2002. "Minorities and Direct Legislation: Evidence from California Ballot Proposition Elections." *Journal of Politics* 64(1): 154–77.

Hall, Richard, and Frank Wayman. 1990. "Buying Time: Moneyed Interests and the Mobilization of Bias in Congressional Committees." *American Political Science Review* 84(3): 797–820.

Hartley, Thomas, and Bruce Russett. 1992. "Public Opinion and the Common Defense: Who Governs Military Spending in the United States?" *American Political Science Review* 86(4): 905–15.

Heard, Alexander. 1956. *Money and Politics*. Public Affairs Pamphlet No. 242. New York: Public Affairs Committee.

Hearndon, James F. 1982. "Access, Record and Competition as Influences on Interest Group Contributions to Congressional Campaigns." *Journal of Politics* 44(4): 996–1019.

Hero, Rodney E. 1998. *Faces of Inequality: Social Diversity in American Politics*. New York: Oxford University Press.

Hero, Rodney E., and Caroline J. Tolbert. 1995. "Latinos and Substantive Representation in the U.S. House of Representatives: Direct, Indirect, or Non-existent?" *American Journal of Political Science* 39(3): 640–52.

Herring, Mary. 1990. "Legislative Responsiveness to Black Constituents in Three Deep South States." *Journal of Politics* 52(3): 740–58.

Hersch, Philip L., and Gerald S. McDougall. 1994. "Campaign War Chests as a Barrier to Entry in Congressional Races." *Economic Inquiry* 32(4): 630–41.

Hetherington, Marc J. 2001. "Resurgent Mass Partisanship: The Role of Elite Polarization." *American Political Science Review* 95(3): 619–31.

Hibbs, Douglas A., Jr. 1987. *The American Political Economy: Macroeconomics and Electoral Politics*. Cambridge, Mass.: Harvard University Press.

Hibbs, Douglas A., Jr., and Christopher Dennis. 1988. "Income Distribution in the United States." *American Political Science Review* 82(2): 467–90.

Highton, Benjamin and Raymond Wolfinger. 2001. "The Political Implications of Higher Turnout." *British Journal of Political Science* 31(1): 179–223.

Hill, Kim Quaile, and Angela Hinton-Andersson. 1995. "Pathways of Representation: A Causal Analysis of Public Opinion-Policy Linkages." *American Journal of Political Science* 39(4): 924–35.

Hill, Kim Quaile, and Patricia A. Hurley. 1999. "Dyadic Representation Reappraised." *American Journal of Political Science* 43(1): 109–37.

Hill, Kim Quaile, and Jan E. Leighley. 1992. "The Policy Consequences of Class Bias in State Electorates." *American Journal of Political Science* 36(2): 351–65.

——. 1994. "Mobilizing Institutions and Class Representation in U.S. State Electorates" *Political Research Quarterly* 47(1): 137–50.

——. 1996. "Political Parties and Class Mobilization in Contemporary United States Elections" *American Journal of Political Science* 40(3): 787–804.

Hill, Kim Quaile, Jan E. Leighley and Angela Hinton-Andersson. 1995. "Lower-Class Mobilization and Policy Linkage in the U.S. States" *American Journal of Political Science* 39(1): 75–86.

Himmelfarb, Richard. 1995. *Catastrophic Politics: The Rise and Fall of the Medicare Catastrophic Coverage Act of 1988.* University Park: Pennsylvania State University Press.

Husted, Thomas A., and Lawrence W. Kenny. 1997. "The Effect of the Expansion of the Voting Franchise on the Size of Government." *Journal of Political Economy* 105(1): 54–82.

Jacobs, Lawrence R. 1993. *The Health of Nations: Public Opinion and the Making of Health Policy in the U.S. and Britain.* Ithaca, N.Y.: Cornell University Press.

Jacobs, Lawrence R., and Benjamin I. Page. 2005. "Who Influences U.S. Foreign Policy?" *American Political Science Review* 99(1): 107–24.

Jacobs, Lawrence R., and Robert Y. Shapiro. 1994. "Issues, Candidate Image and Priming: The Use of Private Polls in Kennedy's 1960 Presidential Campaign." *American Political Science Review* 88(3): 527–40.

———. 2000. *Politicians Don't Pander: Political Manipulation and the Loss of Democratic Responsiveness.* Chicago: University of Chicago Press.

Jacobson, Gary C. 1978. "The Effects of Campaign Spending in Congressional Elections." *The American Political Science Review* 72(2): 469–91.

———. 1980. *Money in Congressional Elections.* New Haven, Conn.: Yale University Press.

———. 1990. "The Effects of Campaign Spending in House Elections: New Evidence for Old Arguments." *American Journal of Political Science* 34(2): 334–62.

———. 1999. "The Effect of the AFL-CIO's 'Voter Education' Campaigns on the 1996 House Elections." *Journal of Politics* 61(1): 185–94.

Jennings, Edward T., Jr. 1979. "Competition, Constituencies, and Welfare Policies in American States." *American Political Science Review* 73(2): 414–29.

Jewell, Malcolm. 1984. *Parties and Primaries: Nominating State Governors.* New York: Praeger.

Kathlene, Lyn. 1994. "Power and Influence in State Legislative Policymaking: The Interaction of Gender and Position in Committee Hearing Debates." *American Political Science Review* 88(3): 560–76

———. 1995. "Alternative Views of Crime: Legislative Policymaking in Gendered Terms" *Journal of* Politics 57(3): 696–723.

Kau, James B., and Paul H. Rubin. 1982. *Congressmen, Constituents, and Contributors: Determinants of Roll Call Voting in the House of Representatives.* Boston, Mass.: Martinus Nijhoff.

Kelley, Stanley, Jr. 1956. *Professional Public Relations and Political Power.* Baltimore: Johns Hopkins University Press.

Kenny, Christopher, and Michael McBurnett. 1994. "An Individual-Level Multiequation Model of Expenditure Effects in Contested House Elections." *American Political Science Review* 88(3): 699–707.

Key, V.O., Jr. 1949. *Southern Politics in State and Nation.* New York: Alfred A. Knopf.

——. 1956. *American State Politics: An Introduction.* New York: Alfred A. Knopf.

Kiewiet, Roderick, and Mathew McCubbins. 1991. *The Logic of Delegation: Congressional Parties and the Appropriations Process.* Chicago: University of Chicago Press.

Kinder, Donald R., and Tali Mendelberg. 1995. "Cracks in the American Apartheid: The Political Impact of Prejudice among Desegregated Whites." *Journal of Politics* 57(2): 402–24.

Knight, Brian. 2000. "Supermajority Voting Requirements for Tax Increases: Evidence from the States." *Journal of Public Economics* 76(1): 41–67.

Krasno, Jonathan S., and Donald Philip Green. 1988. "Preempting Quality Challengers in House Elections." *Journal of Politics* 50(4): 920–36.

Krasno, Jonathan S., Donald P. Green, and Jonathan A. Cowden. 1994. "The Dynamics of Campaign Fundraising in House Elections." *Journal of Politics* 56(2): 459–74.

Krehbiel, Keith. 1993. "Where's the Party?" *British Journal of Political Science* 23(2): 235–66.

——. 1998. *Pivotal Politics: A Theory of U.S. Lawmaking.* Chicago: University of Chicago Press.

Kroszner, Randall S., and Thomas Stratmann. 1998. "Interest Group Competition and the Organization of Congress: Theory and Evidence from Financial Services Political Action Committees." *American Economic Review* 88(5): 1163–87.

Langbein, Laura. 1986. "Money and Access: Some Empirical Evidence." *Journal of Politics* 48(4): 1052–62.

Lee, Frances. 2000. "Senate Representation and Coalition Building in Distributive Politics." *American Political Science Review* 94(1): 59–72.

Levitt, Steven, and James Snyder. 1995. "Political Parties and the Distribution of Federal Outlays." *American Journal of Political Science* 39(4): 958–80.

——. 1997. "The Impact of Federal Spending on House Election Outcomes." *Journal of Political Economy* 105(1): 30–53.

Lindblom, Charles. 1977. *Politics and Markets: The World's Political Economic Systems.* New York: Basic Books.

Lockard, Duane. 1959. *New England State Politics.* Chicago: Henry Regnery.

Lowery, David. 1987. "The Distribution of Tax Burdens in the American States: The Determinants of Fiscal Incidence." *Western Political Quarterly* 40(1): 137–58.

Lowi, Theodore. 1969. *The End of Liberalism: Ideology, Policy, and the Crisis of Public Authority.* New York: W. W. Norton.

Lublin, David. 1997. *The Paradox of Representation.* Princeton, N.J.: Princeton University Press.

Magleby, David B., ed. 2002. *Financing the 2000 Election*. Washington, D.C.: Brookings Institution.

Maltzman, Forrest. 1998. "Maintaining Congressional Committees: Sources of Member Support." *Legislative Studies Quarterly* 23(2): 197–218.

Mann, Thomas E. 2001. "Political Money and Party Finance." *International Encyclopedia of the Social and Behavioral Sciences* 3(11): 681–84.

———. 2003. "Linking Knowledge and Action: Political Science and Campaign Finance Reform." *Perspectives on Politics* 1(1): 69–83.

Mann, Thomas E., and Anthony Corrado. 2002. "The Flow of Money in Federal Elections." In *The New Campaign Finance Sourcebook*. Brookings Institutions Online Materials.

Mansbridge, Jane J. 1999. "Should Blacks Represent Blacks and Women Represent Women? A Contingent Yes." *Journal of Politics* 61(3): 628–57.

Manza, Jeff, Fay Lomax Cook, and Benjamin Page, eds. 2002. *Navigating Public Opinion: Polls, Policy, and the Future of American Democracy*. New York: Oxford University Press.

Marmor, Theodore R. 1983. *Political Analysis and American Medical Care*. Cambridge, Mass.: Cambridge University Press.

Martin, Paul. 2003. "Voting's Reward: Voter Turnout, Attentive Publics, and Congressional Allocation of Federal Money." *American Journal of Political Science* 47(1): 110–27.

Mayhew, David R. 1974. *Congress: The Electoral Connection*. New Haven, Conn.: Yale University Press.

———. 1986. *Placing Parties in American Politics: Organization, Electoral Settings, and Government Activity in the Twentieth Century*. Princeton, N.J.: Princeton University Press.

———. 1988. "Why Did V.O. Key Draw Back from His 'Have-Nots' Claim?" In *V.O. Key, Jr. and The Study of American Politics*, edited by Milton C. Cummings Jr. Washington, D.C.: American Political Science Association.

———. 1991. *Divided We Govern: Party Control, Lawmaking, and Investigations, 1946–1990*. New Haven, Conn.: Yale University Press.

McCarty, Nolan, Keith T. Poole, and Howard Rosenthal. 1997. *Income Redistribution and the Realignment of American Politics*. Washington, D.C.: AEI Press.

———. 2003. "Political Polarization and Income Inequality." Paper presented at the Russell Sage Foundation Conference on Politics and Inequality. New York (January).

———. Forthcoming. *Polarized America: The Dance of Ideology and Unequal Riches*. Cambridge, Mass.: MIT Press.

McConnell, Grant. 1966. *Private Power and American Democracy*. New York: Knopf.

McCoy, Charles A., and John Playford, eds. 1967. *Apolitical Politics: A Critique of Behavioralism*. New York: Thomas Crowell.

Miller, Warren E. 1991. "Party Identification, Realignment, and Party Voting: Back to the Basics." *American Political Science Review* 85(2): 557–68.

———. 2000. "Temporal Order and Causal Inference." *Political Analysis* 8(2): 119–40.

Miller, Warren E., and Donald Stokes. 1963. "Constituency Influence in Congress." *American Political Science Review* 57(1): 45–56.

Monroe, Alan D. 1998. "Public Opinion and Public Policy 1980–1993." *Public Opinion Quarterly* 62(1): 6–28.

Morone, James, and Lawrence Jacobs, eds. 2005. *Healthy, Wealthy, and Fair: Health Care and the Good Society*. New York: Oxford University Press.

Morehouse, Sarah M. 1990. "Money Versus Party Effort: Nominating for Governor." *American Journal of Political Science* 34(3): 706–24.

Morgan, David R. 1994. "Tax Equity in the American States—A Multivariate Analysis." *Social Science Quarterly* 75(3): 510–23.

Niemi, Richard G., and Herbert F. Weisberg. 1976. "Are Parties Becoming Irrelevant?" In *Controversies in American Voting Behavior*, edited by Richard G. Niemi and Herbert F. Weisberg. San Francisco: W. H. Freeman.

Oberlander, Jonathan. 2003. *The Political Life of Medicare*. Chicago: University of Chicago Press.

O'Connor, James. 1973. *The Fiscal Crisis of the State*. New York: St. Martin's Press.

Ostrom, Charles W., Jr., and Robin F. Marra. 1986. "U.S. Defense Spending and the Soviet Estimate." *American Political Science Review* 80(3): 819–42.

Overacker, Louise. 1932. *Money in Elections*. New York: Macmillan.

Page, Benjamin I. 1983. *Who Gets What from Government*. Berkeley: University of California Press.

———. 2002. "The Semi-Sovereign Public." In *Navigating Public Opinion: Polls, Policy, and the Future of American Democracy*, edited by Jeff Manza, Fay Lomax Cook, and Benjamin Page. New York: Oxford University Press.

Page, Benjamin I., and Robert Y. Shapiro. 1983. "Effects of Public Opinion on Policy." *American Political Science Review* 77(1): 175–90.

———. 1992. *The Rational Public: Fifty Years of Trends in American's Policy Preferences*. Chicago: University of Chicago Press.

Page, Benjamin I., Robert Y. Shapiro, Paul W. Gronke, and Robert M. Rosenberg. 1984. "Constituency, Party, and Representation in Congress." *Public Opinion Quarterly* 48(4): 741–56.

Page, Benjamin I., and James R. Simmons. 2000. *What Government Can Do: Dealing with Poverty and Inequality*. Chicago: University of Chicago Press.

Parker, Frank R. 1991. *Black Votes Count*. Chapel Hill: University of North Carolina Press.

Peterson, Paul. 1981. *City Limits*. Chicago: University of Chicago Press.

Phillips, Anne. 1995. *The Politics of Presence*. Oxford: Oxford University Press.

Pitkin, Hanna. 1967. *The Concept of Representation*. Berkeley: University of California Press.

Poole, Keith T., and Howard Rosenthal. 1984. "The Polarization of American Politics." *Journal of Politics* 46(4): 1061–79.

———. 1997. *Congress: A Political-Economic History of Roll Call Voting*. New York: Oxford University Press.

Powell, Linda W. 1982. "Issue Representation in Congress." *Journal of Politics* 44(3): 658–78.

Radcliff, Benjamin, and Martin Saiz. 1995. "Race, Turnout, and Public Policy in the American States." *Political Research Quarterly* 48(4): 775–94.

———. 1998. "Labor Organization and Public Policy in the American States." *Journal of Politics* 60(1): 113–25

Rogers, Diane Lim, and John H. Rogers. 2000. "Political Competition and State Government Size: Do Tighter Elections Produce Looser Budgets?" *Public Choice* 105(1): 1–21.

Rohde, David. 1991. *Parties and Leaders in the Post-Reform House*. Chicago: University of Chicago Press.

Romer, Thomas, and James Snyder. 1994. "An Experimental Investigation of the Dynamics of PAC Contributions." *American Journal of Political Science* 38(3): 745–69.

Rudolph, Tomas. 1999. "Corporate and Labor PAC Contributions in House Elections: Measuring the Effects of Majority Party Status." *Journal of Politics* 61(1): 195–206.

Schattschneider, Elmer Eric. 1942. *Party Government*. New York: Holt, Rinehart and Winston.

———. 1960. *The Semi-Sovereign People: A Realist's View of Democracy in America*. New York: Holt, Rinehart and Winston.

Schmidt, David. 1989. *Citizen Lawmakers: The Ballot Initiative Revolution*. Philadelphia: Temple University Press.

Seidelman, Raymond. 1984. *Disenchanted Realists: Political Science and the American Crisis, 1884–1984*, with the assistance of Edward J. Harpham. Albany: State University of New York Press.

Shapiro, Catherine R., David W. Brady, Richard A. Brody, and John A Ferejohn. 1990. "Linking Constituency Opinion and Senate Voting Scores: A Hybrid Explanation." *Legislative Studies Quarterly* 15(4): 599–621.

Silberman, Jonathan, and Garey C. Durden. 1976. "Determining Legislative Preferences on the Minimum Wage: An Economic Approach." *Journal of Political Economy* 84: 317–29.

Simon, Herbert. 1953. "Notes on the Observation and Measurement of Power." *Journal of Politics* 15(3): 500–16.

Sinclair, Barbara. 1995. *Legislators, Leaders, and Lawmaking: The U.S. House of Representatives in the Postreform Era*. Baltimore: Johns Hopkins University Press.

Skocpol, Theda. 1996. *Boomerang: Clinton's Health Security Effort at the Turn Against Government in U.S. Politics*. New York: W. W. Norton.

———. 1999. "Advocates without Members: The Recent Transformation of American Civic Life." In *Civic Engagement in American Democracy,* edited by Theda Skocpol and Morris P. Fiorina. Washington, D.C.: Brookings Institution.

———. 2003. *Diminished Democracy: From Membership to Management in American Civic Life.* Norman: University of Oklahoma Press.

Skowronek, Stephen. 1982. *Building a New American State: The Expansion of National Administrative Capacities, 1877–1920.* New York: Cambridge University Press.

Smith, David B. 1999. *Health Care Divided: Race and Healing a Nation.* Ann Arbor: University of Michigan Press.

Sobel, Richard. 2001. *The Impact of Public Opinion on U.S. Foreign Policy Since Vietnam.* New York: Oxford University Press.

Sonenshein, Raphael. 1993. *Politics in Black and White: Race and Power in Los Angeles.* Princeton, N.J.: Princeton University Press.

Sorauf, Frank. 1988. *Money in American Elections.* Glenview, Ill.: Scott, Foresman.

———. 1992. *Inside Campaign Finance: Myths and Realities.* New Haven, Conn.: Yale University Press.

———. 1999. "What *Buckley* Wrought." In *If* Buckley *Fell: A First Amendment Blueprint for Regulating Money in Politics,* edited by E. Joshua Rosenkranz. New York: Century Foundation Press.

Sparer, Michael S. 1996. *Medicaid and the Limits of State Health Reform.* Philadelphia: Temple University Press.

Squire, Peverill. 1989. "Challengers in U.S. Senate Elections." *Legislative Studies Quarterly* 14(4): 531–47.

———. 1991. "Preemptive Fundraising and Challenger Profile in Senate Elections." *Journal of Politics* 53(4): 1150–64.

Starr, Paul. 1982. *The Social Transformation of American Medicine.* New York: Basic Books.

Stern, Philip M. 1988. *The Best Congress Money Can Buy.* New York: Pantheon.

Stimson, James A. 1999. *Public Opinion in America: Moods, Cycles, and Swings,* 2nd ed. Boulder, Colo.: Westview Press.

Stimson, James A., Michael B. MacKuen, and Robert S. Erikson. 1995. "Dynamic Representation." *American Political Science Review* 89(3): 543–65.

Stone, Walter J. 1982. "Electoral Change and Policy Representation in Congress: Domestic Welfare Issues from 1956–1972." *British Journal of Political Science* 12(1): 95–116.

Swers, Michele. 1998. "Are Congresswomen More Likely to Vote for Women's Issues Bills than Their Male Colleagues?" *Legislative Studies Quarterly* 23(3): 435–48.

Tate, Katherine. 2003. "Black Opinion on the Legitimacy of Racial Redistricting and Minority-Majority Districts. *American Political Science Review* 97(1): 45–56.

Taylor, Andrew. 1998. "Domestic Agenda Setting, 1947–1994." *Legislative Studies Quarterly* 23(2): 373–97.

———. 2003. "Conditional Party Government and Campaign Contributions: Insights from the Tobacco and Alcoholic Beverage Industries." *American Journal of Political Science* 47(3): 293–304.

Thomas, Clive, and Ronald J. Hrebenar. 1999. "Interest Groups in the States." In *Politics in the American States: A Comparative Analysis*, 7th ed., edited by Virginia Gray, Russell L. Hanson, and Herbert Jacob. Washington, D.C.: CQ Press.

Thomas, Robert D. 1990. "National-Local Relations and the City's Dilemma." *Annals of the American Academy of Political and Social Science* 509(May): 106–17. American Federalism: The Third Century.

Thomas, Scott J. 1989. "Do Incumbent Campaign Expenditures Matter?" *Journal of Politics* 51(4): 965–76.

Thorndike, Joseph J., and Dennis J. Ventry Jr. , eds. 2002. *Tax Justice: The Ongoing Debate*. Washington, D.C.: Urban Institute Press.

Truman, David B. 1951. *The Governmental Process: Political Interests and Public Opinion*. New York: Alfred A. Knopf.

Tullock, Gordon. 1972. "The Purchase of Politicians." *Western Economic Journal* 10(3): 354–55.

Wattenberg, Martin P. 1998. *The Decline of American Political Parties, 1952–1996*. Cambridge, Mass.: Harvard University Press.

Weissberg, Robert. 1978. "Collective vs. Dynamic Representation in Congress." *American Political Science Review* 72(2): 535–47.

Welch, William P. 1982. "Campaign Contributions and Legislative Voting: Milk Money and Dairy Price Supports." *Western Political Quarterly* 35(4): 478–95.

West, Darrell M. 1988. "Activists and Economic Policymaking in Congress." *American Journal of Political Science* 32(3): 662–80.

West, Darrell M., and Burdett A. Loomis. 1998. *The Sound of Money: How Political Interests Get What They Want*. New York: W. W. Norton.

Whitby, Kenny. 1985. "Effects of the Interaction Between Race and Urbanization on Votes of Southern Congressmen." *Legislative Studies Quarterly* 10(4): 505–17.

Whitby, Kenny, and Franklin Gilliam. 1991. "A Longitudinal Analysis of Competing Explanations for the Transformation of Southern Congressional Politics." *Journal of Politics* 53(2): 504–18.

Wilhite, Allan, and John Theilmann. 1987. "Labor PAC Contributions and Labor Legislation: A Simultaneous Logit Approach." *Public Choice* 53(3): 267–76.

Wilson, William J. 1987. *The Truly Disadvantaged: The Inner City, The Underclass, and Public Policy*. Chicago: University of Chicago Press.

Wilson, Woodrow. 1885. *Congressional Government*. Boston: Houghton, Mifflin.

Winston, Pamela. 2002. *Welfare Policymaking in the States*. Washington, D.C.: Georgetown University Press.

Winters, Richard. 1976. "Party Control and Policy Change." *American Journal of Political Science* 20(4): 597–636.

Wlezien, Christopher. 1996. "Dynamics of Representation: The Case of US Spending on Defense." *British Journal of Political Science* 26(1): 81–103.

Wolfinger, Raymond, and Steven Rosenstone. 1980. *Who Votes?* New Haven, Conn.: Yale University Press.

Wright, John R. 1985. "PACs, Contributions, and Roll Calls: An Organizational Perspective." *American Political Science Review* 79(2): 400–14.

———. 1989. "PAC Contributions, Lobbying, and Representation." *Journal of Politics* 51(3): 713–29.

Zaller, John. 1992. *The Nature and Origins of Mass Opinion.* New York: Cambridge University Press.

Chapter Four | Inequality and Public Policy

Jacob S. Hacker
Suzanne Mettler
Dianne Pinderhughes

THE PAST HALF century has witnessed wrenching changes in American politics and society that have provoked sharply conflicting conclusions about the fate of the American democratic experiment. On the one hand, long-standing restrictions on formal equality of citizenship have all but vanished. Women and minorities, once denied the right to freely vote, work, and associate, now enjoy guarantees of equal protection in a broad array of domains in which discrimination was once the norm. On the other hand, *economic* inequality has increased substantially in recent decades, reaching levels not seen since the Gilded Age (Jencks 2002). How these two great shifts, operating in tandem, have affected our nation's democratic life is perhaps the most vexing question facing students of American politics today. Yet, as this volume shows, it is a question that remains surprisingly underexamined and unnecessarily shrouded in uncertainty and doubt.

This chapter takes up one crucial aspect of the relationship between economic and political equality—the role of public policy—and shows that scholars know both more and less than they think they do about the subject. They know more, because in the last decade or so, a remarkable and growing body of research has examined how major programs of social provision affect family and personal income, attaching concrete numbers to relationships that had previously been the stuff of assumption and indirect inference. And yet, what scholars know about the impact of public policy only scratches the surface of what they could know (Lenz and the Princeton University Working Group 2003). Though a growing number of studies chart the effects of policies on *economic* inequality, knowledge of policies' effects on *racial and gender* inequality has simply not kept pace. And scholars know even less about the *political* effects of public policies—how, that is, policies shape political power and participation once they are put in place.

The discussion that follows outlines what we know about public policy and inequality, and suggests what we need to know and where we might look to find it. In developing our case, we build on recent scholarship on "policy feedback, " the study of how "policies, once enacted, restructure subsequent political processes" (Skocpol 1992). The concept of policy feedback pushes scholars to step beyond the traditional focus on the first-order socioeconomic effects of policies to consider how policies, once created, shape politics and policymaking down the line. This requires understanding not only the immediate socioeconomic effects of policies, but also the ways in which these effects shape power, participation, and policy in the future.

The first part of the chapter takes up the initial half of this two-way relationship—the effects of public policies on American inequality. We begin by presenting the state of the art in research on the wealth and income effects of U.S. public policies. We then briefly examine research on educational and health inequalities. Finally, we consider scholarship on the ways in which these income effects are mediated by differences of race, ethnicity, and gender.

The second part of the chapter moves to the political consequences of these policy effects, the heart of policy-feedback claims. We first showcase recent illustrative works that suggest the considerable utility of policy-feedback arguments for work on civic participation. Building on these studies, we then explore the sometimes contradictory effects on equality of several major examples of government policy in the post–World War II period. We conclude the analysis of postwar policy with a more general discussion of how recent changes in public policy have affected political equality.

The chapter closes by drawing these strands of research together into a set of larger claims about the interrelationships between public policy, inequality, and American civic life. Our first conclusion is that U.S. public policy, though certainly not the only cause of rising inequality, is indeed powerfully implicated in the trend. U.S. social programs and tax policies reduce inequality less than do similar programs and policies abroad, and they have done less to blunt the post-1970s increase in inequality. Moreover, while U.S. programs have remained largely intact, they have grown less capable of dealing with key risks to family income (Hacker 2004).

Our second major conclusion is that public policies do in fact have major effects on political as well as economic equality. Program design can profoundly influence political resources, conceptions of citizenship, definitions of interest, and assessments of efficacy—both among the targets of policies and among citizens more generally. These effects are as large as or larger than the correlates of political activity most research fixes on, and they indicate that the first-order socioeconomic effects of programs may well be deeply mediated by their second-order political effects. Perhaps most important, the evidence suggests that these second-order effects have increasingly exacerbated, rather than offset, disparities in political influence between the advantaged and less advantaged. It also suggests that the recent explosion of economic inequality has undercut some of the important gains in formal political equality experienced by groups that have historically faced discrimination.

Our final conclusion—and the one that we most want to emphasize to social scientists—is that surprisingly little systematic research asks how policies shape and refract inequality's social and political effects. Like the blind men and the elephant, commentators have explored parts of the puzzle but mostly failed to take in the larger picture. This may be an area in which small building blocks will not add up to a coherent whole. Scholars will also need to ask big questions about the future of civic life in a paradoxical age of increasing legal equality yet decreasing economic equality.

U.S. PUBLIC POLICY AND INEQUALITY IN COMPARATIVE PERSPECTIVE

Perhaps the most striking feature of discussions of the distributional effects of U.S. public policy is the extent to which, until recently, they have proceeded without much hard evidence of any kind. Harold Wilensky's seminal *The Welfare State and Equality* (1975), for example, actually had little to say about the welfare state and equality. Well into the 1980s, informed works like Benjamin Page's *Who Gets What from Government?* (1983) had to piece together various scattered evidence to come to even a preliminary judgment. Some commentators, indeed, questioned whether the welfare state—and not just the American welfare state—redistributed income at all. Others argued that a middle-class bias characterized social policy, but again without much evidence (Goodin and LeGrand 1987). As Frances Castles noted a decade ago, "the centrality of the welfare state in the comparative public policy literature has until now drawn its rationale from plausible inferences concerning the impact of government intervention on distributional outcomes. . . . However, in the absence of any independent measure of outcomes, both aggregate expenditures and types of instruments necessarily became proxies for distributional consequences, making any serious distinction between means and ends impossible" (Castles and Mitchell 1993, 96).

U.S. Inequality and Its Causes

We now know far more about the income effects of social policies, thanks in large part to the development of the Luxembourg Income Study (LIS)— a cross-national analysis of income and demographics that began in 1983 and now encompasses twenty-five nations, with data in some cases spanning three decades.[1] The LIS assembles and harmonizes data from cross-sectional surveys of households—which, we shall see, have strengths as well as limits for assessing public policy effects. Besides a variety of demographic variables, the LIS dataset includes fairly comprehensive measures of household and personal income and expenditures (but not in-kind benefits, such as health care). This allows the LIS data to be used to construct intuitive measures of the effect of government taxes and transfers on inequality.

The inequality of income both before and after government taxes and transfers for available nations and years, as measured by the well-known Gini index, is depicted in table 4.1.[2] The United States clearly has higher levels of inequality, both before taxes and transfers and afterward. It is also evident that inequality rose sharply in the United States and several other nations in the 1980s. The trend, however, appears to be largely the result of shifts in pre-tax and -transfer income; the amount by which taxes and transfers reduce inequality has not markedly changed, though it has certainly not increased.

The first important point to make, then, is that public policy is not directly responsible for the general rise in economic inequality in recent decades. That is to say, if we focus simply on redistribution of private income, and not on the ways in which government might shape the distribution of private income, it is shifts in private income, not changes in taxes and transfers, that are critical in explaining the rise in inequality.

To be sure, isolating private income from government intervention is not entirely possible. Public policies can and do shape the distribution of private income, and there seems little question that they are implicated in the rise in the inequality of private income, although this remains hotly contested. The decline in the real value of the minimum wage, for example, undoubtedly helps explain why the level of pay in low-wage jobs has improved little over the past thirty years. Nonetheless, private-income inequality differs surprisingly little between the United States and comparable nations, and in a range of nations with very disparate policies, it rose in the 1980s and 1990s.

What is clear, however, is that taxes and transfers in the United States have done considerably less than those in other nations to offset the rises

(Text continues on p. 163.)

Table 4.1   Income Inequality

Country and Year	Private Income Inequality (Gini Index; Higher Numbers Indicate Greater Inequality)	Income Inequality After Taxes and Transfers (Gini Index)	Percentage Reduction in Inequality Due to Taxes and Transfers
Australia			
1981	0.396	0.281	29%
1985	0.417	0.292	30
1989	0.428	0.304	29
1994	0.452	0.311	31
Mean	0.423	0.297	30
Belgium			
1992	0.449	0.224	50
1996	0.483	0.260	46
1997	0.481	0.260	46
Mean	0.471	0.248	48
Canada			
1981	0.370	0.284	23
1987	0.387	0.283	27
1991	0.405	0.281	31
1994	0.419	0.285	32
1997	0.417	0.291	30
1998	0.429	0.305	29
2000	0.413	0.302	27
Mean	0.406	0.290	28
Denmark			
1987	0.398	0.254	36
1992	0.426	0.236	45
1995	0.441	0.263	40
1997	0.432	0.257	41
Mean	0.424	0.253	40
Finland			
1987	0.393	0.209	47
1991	0.407	0.210	48
1995	0.438	0.226	48
2000	0.430	0.247	43
Mean	0.417	0.223	47

Table 4.1   Continued

Country and Year	Private Income Inequality (Gini Index; Higher Numbers Indicate Greater Inequality)	Income Inequality After Taxes and Transfers (Gini Index)	Percentage Reduction in Inequality Due to Taxes and Transfers
France			
1981	0.370	0.288	22%
1984	0.469	0.298	37
1989	0.474	0.287	40
1994	0.485	0.288	41
Mean	0.450	0.290	35
Germany			
1981	0.388	0.244	37
1983	0.385	0.260	33
1984	0.445	0.249	44
1989	0.405	0.247	39
1994	0.442	0.261	41
2000	0.459	0.264	43
Mean	0.421	0.254	39
Italy			
1986	0.424	0.306	28
1991	0.407	0.289	29
1995	0.468	0.342	27
Mean	0.433	0.312	28
Netherlands			
1983	0.470	0.260	45
1987	0.475	0.256	46
1991	0.448	0.266	41
1994	0.459	0.253	45
1999	0.440	0.248	44
Mean	0.458	0.257	44
Norway			
1986	0.352	0.233	34
1991	0.374	0.231	38
1995	0.400	0.238	41
2000	0.406	0.251	38
Mean	0.383	0.238	38

(Table continues on p. 162.)

Table 4.1   Continued

Country and Year	Private Income Inequality (Gini Index; Higher Numbers Indicate Greater Inequality)	Income Inequality After Taxes and Transfers (Gini Index)	Percentage Reduction in Inequality Due to Taxes and Transfers
Sweden			
1981	0.411	0.197	52%
1987	0.428	0.218	49
1992	0.461	0.229	50
1995	0.459	0.221	52
2000	0.447	0.252	44
Mean	0.441	0.223	49
Switzerland			
1982	0.382	0.309	19
1992	0.376	0.307	18
Mean	0.379	0.308	19
United Kingdom			
1986	0.476	0.303	36
1991	0.476	0.336	29
1994	0.502	0.339	33
1995	0.503	0.344	32
1999	0.500	0.345	31
Mean	0.491	0.333	32
United States			
1986	0.432	0.335	23
1991	0.440	0.336	24
1994	0.465	0.355	24
1997	0.475	0.372	22
2000	0.469	0.368	22
Mean	0.456	0.353	23

Source: Luxembourg Income Study, courtesy of Vincent Mahler, Timothy Smeeding, and David Jesuit.

Notes: "Private" income encompasses all reported non-governmental sources of income, including alimony and child support. These figures are for all households (after adjustment for household size), including households headed by persons older than sixty-five. The small number of households without any reported disposable income are excluded, on the assumption that their income is not accurately reported.

in inequality during this period. Averaging across the thirteen other countries in table 4.1, for example, the reduction in inequality created by taxes and transfers increased 4.5 percent between the first and last observation. In the United States, by contrast, taxes and transfers reduced inequality by 4.4 percent less by the end of the series than at the outset.

Economic inequality is, of course, less worrisome to the extent that the lowest strata are relatively well off. An obvious question, therefore, is whether America's greater per-capita income translates into higher incomes at all rungs on the economic ladder. The answer is no. Although median income is indeed higher in the United States, far more Americans are poor relative to that median than their counterparts abroad. And despite America's high average income, absolute poverty (based on cross-nationally equivalent standard-of-living measures) is much higher in the United States than in other advanced industrial democracies (Smeeding and Rainwater 2001). Moreover, these measures understate the gap because they do not account for America's unusually high rates of incarceration, which removes a not-inconsequential share of poor males from the surveyed population (Irvine and Xu 2002).

It is sometimes suggested that the rise in economic inequality in the United States is an artifact of immigration or changes in family structures, or is offset by increases in economic mobility (Cox and Alm 1999; Easterbrook 2003). None of these statements is true. Regarding immigration, it is indisputable that immigration has added to the ranks of America's low-income families, and more disputable but highly possible that immigration has depressed wages at the low end of the pay scale (compare Borjas 1990; Card 1990). But since much of the overall increase in inequality is due to the growing gap in wages and income between the median household and the very rich, immigration simply cannot explain all or even most of the overall increase in economic inequality. Similarly, Gary Burtless (2003) has estimated that family changes (namely, the rise in single-parent families and increased correlation of spouses' earnings) explains only a third of the rise in income inequality from the late 1970s to the late 1990s—about the same proportion that he estimates is due to increased inequality in wages.

As for economic mobility, good data on changes in mobility are hard to come by, but a recent review in the *Journal of Economic Perspectives* makes clear that, however one judges current levels of mobility, there is no evidence that mobility has risen in tandem with increased economic inequality (Gottschalk 1997). As noted shortly, what evidence we have on over-time income dynamics suggests mostly greater economic volatility, rather than greater upward mobility.

There is no question that social welfare programs are an important cause of the large cross-national disparities in inequality. The United States, as table 4.1 indicates, has average private-income inequality levels only 7 percent higher than the average for the other country-years, but inequality after taxes and transfers is almost 30 percent higher—a reflection of a tax and transfer system that is 36 percent less effective at reducing inequality. Across rich nations, inequality is highly correlated with public social welfare spending, and U.S. public social spending is much lower than average.[3]

It is also worth noting that U.S. social provision is also more targeted on the aged than is social provision in other nations. The United States lacks universal family allowances, provides limited public day care and housing, and is the only nation with a national health program limited to the elderly. Julia Lynch (2001) has constructed the best comparative measures. She finds that public transfers and tax breaks are overwhelming directed toward the aged in the United States, with only Greece and Japan exhibiting more of an age skew. Lynch's simplest measure, the elderly to nonelderly spending ratio for 1993, shows that the United States spends more than 37 times as much per elderly citizen as per nonelderly citizen. According to her data, this figure has not changed much since 1980.

Two Complications: Wealth and Intertemporal Variation

The LIS data have weaknesses (for a full assessment, see Atkinson, Brandolini, and Smeeding 2002). One obvious shortcoming is that they contain measures of income, not wealth, and wealth inequality is by all measures much larger than income inequality—and arguably as, if not more, important.[4] Moreover, the case for thinking that wealth inequality is influenced by public policy is strong, and the case for thinking that wealth inequality affects politics and policymaking is even stronger. Wealth is also a better indicator than income of long-run economic security—a powerful indirect measure of the extent to which families can weather temporary income shocks caused by unemployment and other negative events.

The most comprehensive work on twentieth-century wealth inequality comes from Edward Wolff (2002), who finds a significant concentration of wealth in the 1980s and 1990s. By the end of the 1990s, the top 1 percent of wealth holders controlled 38 percent of total household wealth—higher than at any point since 1929. This made the United States the most unequal of any industrialized country.

While Wolff's research does not investigate the sources of the growing wealth differential, the role of public policy in influencing wealth inequality is unquestionably powerful. According to Carole Shammas (1993, 428), "the share claimed by the top 1 percent is highly correlated with progressive tax rates." She notes that high-income levies were all introduced on the eve of World War I, when wealth inequality first fell. The share held by the top 1 percent, according to Shammas, rose with the proliferation of exemptions and the decrease in the top tax rate after World War II, exploding in the 1980s, as large marginal rate reductions and tax benefits for the affluent took effect. In the mid-twentieth century, the lower rungs of the wealth ladder were lifted up by laws encouraging unions, expanded educational opportunities, subsidized home ownership, and the creation of social programs that protected household wealth. As later sections of this memo will show, some of these policies promoting wealth formation among lower- and middle-income Americans have eroded, contributing to a marked rise in debt at lower ends of the income scale.

Another, and more subtle, weakness of the LIS data are their reliance on cross-sectional surveys, which provide only point-in-time "snapshots" of the distribution of income in any given year—both before and after government taxes and transfers. In other words, these data can tell us how much of the population is poor or rich in any given year, but not whether the same people are poor or rich from year to year. Similarly, they can tell us how much redistribution transfers and taxes create at a specific time, but not how much redistribution occurs over the life cycle or across risk classes or between those experiencing an adverse event and those not experiencing it.

Responding to these shortcomings, scholars have started to turn to an alternative source of evidence: panel studies of income dynamics (Bradbury, Jenkins, and Micklewright 2001; Goodin et al. 2000). These are studies that repeatedly interview the same families and individuals over many years—in the case of the longest such study, the U.S. Panel Study of Income Dynamics (PSID) over more than thirty years. To date, only a small handful of studies attempt to use panel income data to analyze the effects of welfare states.[5] Yet these studies have already contributed at least three important insights. The first is that there is in fact a great deal of variability in family income from year to year. For this reason, point-in-time estimates of the redistribution effected by public programs almost certainly overstates the extent to which welfare state policies take from the rich and give to the poor. Over time, the population at the lower and higher ends of the income scale change considerably. One year's benefactor may be next year's beneficiary (Goodin et al. 2000).

Second, spells of poverty are longer in the United States than elsewhere, particularly among children. Across the rest of the income spectrum, however, social mobility does not appear markedly different than in Europe (Bradbury, Jenkins, and Micklewright 2001; Gottschalk 1997).

Third, household income is considerably less stable in the United States than in Germany and the Netherlands, partly because Americans are subject to greater labor- and family-related income shocks and partly because the U.S. social insurance system is less extensive (DiPrete and McManus 2000; Goodin et al. 2000).

Unfortunately, although this research is longitudinal, it does not at present allow for robust assessments about the extent to which income dynamics in the 1990s are different from those in the 1970s or 1980s. This is in part because of limited historical reach of foreign panel studies. Yet even those who have limited their attention to the U.S. data, which go back to 1968, have not attempted to examine the trend in family income dynamics over recent decades. This is a serious oversight, for increasing evidence suggests that one crucial change in social policy over the past three decades is the increasing mismatch between existing social welfare programs and the "new social risks" to income that are arising out of the labor market and family (Esping-Andersen 1990; Hacker 2004).

Risk-Benefit Mismatch

Despite many observations about the "new social risks," the changing ability of social policies to deal with major life contingencies has not been studied intensively. There can be little question, however, that the constellation of risks that citizens face has changed significantly in the past three decades due to linked changes in work and family—including rising levels of earnings inequality and volatility, increased structural (rather than cyclical) unemployment, rising rates of divorce and separation, and the dramatic movement of women into paid employment.[6] Together, these changes have placed new strain on social protections constructed during an era in which the risks that families faced flowed almost entirely out of the employment status of the male breadwinner. In the new worlds of work and family, even stable full-time employment of household heads is not a guarantee of economic security, and citizens are barraged with a host of risks that arise from within their families.

Perhaps the most powerful evidence of increased risks to family income is the growing *instability* of male earnings over the past two decades—an increase driven more by instability of wages than by instability of employment (Moffitt and Gottschalk 2002). In addition, Jacob Hacker (2004) has shown that not only male wages, but also family incomes have grown more volatile since the 1970s—and, indeed, they have grown more volatile faster than the well-known increase in income inequality of recent decades. This is a potent indication of the increased risks to income that American families confront.

In principle, U.S. social policy could have adapted to changing social realities. In the last two decades, some nations have dramatically increased their provision of public protections that assist the entry of women into the labor force and help families balance work and childrearing, while tackling the new realities of the labor market with active public employment and training polices (Huber et al. 2001; Levy 1999; Orloff 1993; Stetson and Mazur 1995). Putting aside some important exceptions, however, the United States did not follow this path. Increases in the Earned Income Tax Credit (EITC) for low-wage workers, shifts of money from cash assistance to child care and job retraining, expanded public health insurance coverage, and new family leave legislation were all steps toward a response. But lower-wage workers continued to receive only modest public supports in comparative terms. The welfare reform legislation of 1996, though failing to uphold the dire predictions of critics, nonetheless removed important elements of the safety net for the most disadvantaged workers. Family leave rules did not apply to small employers and, more important, did not provide any income support to leave-takers. Government assistance for child care remained scant, and unavailable even for families eligible for it (Levy and Michel 2002). Despite longer spells of unemployment and new forms of job insecurity, unemployment insurance contracted in reach, particularly for lower-income and intermittently employed workers (General Accounting Office 2000). Perhaps most striking was a massive decline in employment-based health and pension protections among lower-wage workers (Hacker 2004).

The declines in private pension and health protection are quite large and surely worthy of policy analysis, given the roughly $300 billion in forgone tax revenue that now subsidizes these private employment-based benefits (EBRI 2004). Although the American welfare state has long been viewed as a "laggard" in comparative perspective, the picture looks quite different when publicly regulated and subsidized private social benefits are taken into account (Hacker 2002). Indeed, figure 4.1 shows that U.S. social spending is not all that much smaller as a share of the economy than the levels found in even the most generous of European welfare states when private benefits and relative tax burdens are factored in.

But while social spending in the United States is comparable to that in other nations, its distribution is not (Hacker 2002). In the United States, a much larger share of the duties that are carried out by government elsewhere are instead left in the hands of private actors, particularly employers. This pattern has major distributional effects, because private social benefits are distributed much less equally than public benefits. For one, private benefits are generally distributed in rough accordance with pay. For another, they are subsidized through exclusions and deductions in the

Figure 4.1   After-Tax Public and Private Social Welfare Expenditures in Eleven Nations, 1995

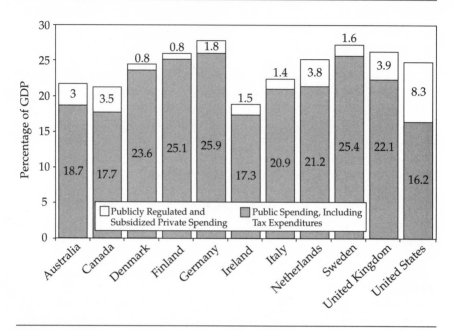

Source: Jacob S. Hacker (2002) calculated from Adema (1999).
Notes: Public social welfare expenditures exclude education. They include cash benefits for a wide range of social contingencies—disability, old age, death of a spouse, occupational injuries, disease, sickness, childbirth, unemployment, poverty—as well as spending on housing, health care, services for the elderly and disabled, active labor-market policies, and other similar social benefits. Private social welfare expenditures are payments for the same purposes made by employers and other nongovernmental organizations, provided that such benefits are mandated, subsidized, or regulated by government. To prevent double-counting, tax breaks for private benefits are not included in the public spending estimate.

tax code worth more to high-income tax filers—who generally receive more generous private benefits, are more likely to itemize their deductions, and are in higher income tax brackets.

In recent decades, moreover, the private side of America's hybrid benefit system has eroded as corporations have eliminated and restructured benefits to cut costs and encourage self-reliance. This erosion has taken two forms: drops in benefit coverage and generosity, and changes in the character of benefits that have shifted risk from collective intermediaries, such as employers and insurers, onto workers and their families (Hacker 2002, 2004).

In sum, the new climate of economic and family risks means that the welfare state has had to run to stay still—to do more merely to secure past gains. In the United States, it has not done more, and when we examine the broader framework of American social protection, a strong case can be made that it has done less.

Tax Policy

Beyond social policy, nothing directly affects disposable income more than tax policy. Indeed, among married couples, taxes have a greater effect than public transfers in reducing lifetime income inequality (Fitzgerald and Maloney 1990). Yet it is difficult to reach firm conclusions about the effect of tax policy on inequality, because effective tax rates (which include exemptions, deductions, and credits) are often quite different than statutory rates. One of the best recent studies of federal effective tax rates, for example, shows that despite the large decrease in marginal rates at the top of the income scale in the 1980s (from a 70 percent statutory rate to a 30 or 40 percent rate), effective tax rates (including federal income, corporate, estate, excise, and payroll taxes) have remained relatively stable (Congressional Budget Office 2001).

None of these studies, however, takes into account the 2001 and 2003 federal tax cuts, which are certain to shift the distribution of taxes in a regressive direction. Estimates placed the ten-year cost of the 2001 tax cut as high as $2.1 trillion, with a skewed distribution: 36 percent of that total will accrue to the richest 1 percent of Americans and 63 percent to the top 20 percent, while just over 20 percent will go to the bottom 60 percent (Citizens for Tax Justice 2002).[7] The 2003 tax bill is estimated to cost more than $1 trillion in the first ten years, and its benefits are similarly concentrated on higher-income taxpayers (Greenstein, Kogan, and Friedman 2003). Credible estimates indicate that, once the long-term financing cost of the tax cuts is taken into account, "the bottom four-fifths of households . . . would lose more than they gain from the tax cuts" (Gale, Orszag, and Shapiro 2004).

It is more difficult to track changes in state and local tax policy, but two conclusions seem warranted from the available evidence. First, the share of total tax revenues that is made up by state and local taxes has risen significantly since the 1970s. Second, state and local taxes are, on balance, much less progressive than federal taxes. State sales and excise taxes, for example, are a primary source of revenue for almost all states, but they hit lower-income residents much harder than higher-income residents, who spend a smaller share of their income on consumption goods. The combination of these two realities—higher state and local taxation, and the generally less progressive character of state and local taxes—have blunted any movement toward greater progressivity at the federal level.

Education Policy

The idea that education, rather than explicit redistribution, is the key to fostering opportunity and equality is a touchstone of American thinking. The United States pioneered universal public education, and U.S. spending on education ranks as relatively generous in comparative perspective. Moreover, there has been a significant growth in federal spending on education in the past few decades.

Despite the popular consensus that education encourages economic equality, the contribution of U.S. education policy to equality has long been contested (Jencks 1972), and relatively limited research has been conducted on the relationship between the growing economic inequality and educational equality. Nonetheless, there is suggestive evidence that rising economic inequality has exacerbated the gap in educational achievement as well. One study of educational attainment between 1970 and 1990 concludes that "growing income inequality raised mean educational attainment but also exacerbated disparities in educational attainment between rich and poor children" (Mayer 2001, 22). Economic inequality within school districts also appears to harm educational outcomes for all students in high-inequality districts. All else equal, a student's performance declines as the proportion of his or her classmates who are from poor household increases (Duncombe and Yinger 1998).

What is clear is that education's contribution to equality remains limited by a number of factors. Because American public education is built around a notion of local control and, consequently, funded largely by local property taxes, educational inequality is directly related to larger forces of social inequality and segregation. Despite Brown v. Board of Education, de facto segregation along racial lines within public schools has increased, with black children more likely to be in majority-black schools today than they were before Brown (Frankenberg, Lee, and Orfield 2002).

To be sure, the effects of resource inequality and racial segregation are variable and complex, and there is significant dispute over whether spending differentials truly translate into differences in educational opportunities. Yet there is some agreement that greater resource equality would at least marginally bolster educational equality. As Jennifer Hochschild and Nathan Scovronick explain, "higher per pupil expenditures, lower pupil ratios in lower grades, higher reported adequacy of teacher reported resources, higher levels of participation in public pre-kindergarten, and lower teacher turnover all show positive, statistically significant effects on achievement" (2003, 55). In fact, if districts with high poverty rates are to achieve the same educational outcomes as other districts, they would need to spend more than others, in order to overcome the enormous obstacles imposed on them by the environment (Duncombe and Yinger 1998).

At the level of higher education, U.S. public policy has also evidenced a commitment to educational opportunity for all citizens, at least since the 1970s. At the federal level, numerous programs attempt to enable lower and middle-income citizens to go to college (Gladieux, Astor, and Swail 1998)—most notably, so-called Pell Grants, which, since their creation in 1972, have come to represent the largest source of federal aid for needy undergraduates who had not yet earned their bachelor's or professional degree (King 2000, 7). At the subnational level, states have also poured extensive resources into higher education, particularly by expanding public universities and colleges. In 1940, fewer than half (46 percent) of all college students attended public institutions; by 1970, 75 percent did (Weir 2002, 183–84).

Since the 1970s, however, public funding has failed to increase with the rise in tuition. Accounting for all sources of public aid, support per student has just kept pace with inflation, but real costs per student have grown by about 40 percent.[8] At the federal level, the number of Pell Grant recipients has grown steadily, reaching 8.3 million students in the 1998 to 1999 academic year, but its value for individuals has diminished. In 1975, a Pell Grant covered about 80 percent of tuition, fees, and room and board at the average public four-year institution and 40 percent at the average private four-year school. By 1999, its share had fallen to about 40 percent and 15 percent, respectively (King 2000, 9–10).

Even as federal funding has stagnated, many states have continued to increase their contributions to higher education. Mounting fiscal pressures over the last two decades, however, have increasingly constrained spending. To make matters worse, states tend to increase the tuition at public colleges particularly during periods of recession, compounding the financial challenges faced by needy students (National Center for Public Policy and Higher Education 2002, 8–9, 12, 22–30).

What is crucial to recognize is that college education has become less affordable precisely at a time when its economic value has become more pronounced. In the mid-century and through the 1970s, a college degree did not offer the promise of economic well-being much greater than that attainable through jobs requiring less education. During the 1980s, however, the "college premium," grew tremendously. College graduates, between 1979 and 1994, witnessed a 5 percent increase in their weekly earnings, whereas high school graduates' earnings fell by 20 percent (Weir 2002, 10).

While enrollment in four-year colleges has grown sharply in recent years among students from high-income families, it has increased much less among their middle-class counterparts, and has actually declined slightly among students from the least advantaged backgrounds (Ellwood and Kane 1999, 286). In addition, among those who enroll, college completion rates have declined in recent decades; the lowest completion rates are among "underrepresented" minority groups.[9] In sum, even as higher education has become more clearly the road to economic success in the United States, those from less advantaged and middle-class backgrounds find their chances of attending college to be increasingly less favorable than those of their wealthy peers.

Health Inequality

The relationship between socioeconomic status and health has received less attention than the effect of income on education. Yet new research suggests that the link may well be profound. One recent study observed "a robust inverse association between SES and health status dates back to our earliest records and exists in all countries where it has been examined" (Williams and Collins 1995, 350).[10] Indeed, all manifestations of low health are present to a greater degree in poorer locales, particularly infant mortality, the most relied-upon indicator of the well-being of a population. In addition, minorities tend to receive lower quality care than nonminorities, even when controlling for income and insurance status (Smedley, Stith, and Nelson 2003). Mental health also varies greatly according to socioeconomic status and race (Holzer et al. 1986). Finally, the evidence suggests that mortality differences across socioeconomic lines have increased over recent decades (Williams and Collins 1995).

To summarize, then, economic inequality in the United States is greater than in other nations in part because U.S. public policy is less focused on trying to ensure equality. As for the rise in inequality over the past two decades, it can by no means be fully explained by public policy, because almost all of the rise occurred in private incomes, rather than incomes after government intervention. There is, however, considerable evidence that government policy has contributed to the rise. U.S. taxes and transfers have grown less redistributive in the same period, as have other key areas of policy—particularly private social benefits and government subsidies for them. And American education policies appear less capable of providing equality of opportunity to American's youth than they once did. More important, American policymakers have not, as have leaders in many other rich democracies, updated public policies to counteract the increase in market income inequality. It is failures of action as well as specific policy interventions that require attention in investigations of the relationship between public policy and inequality (Hacker 2004).

Economic equality is not, however, the same as political equality. The next section considers how the expansion of legal rights of citizenship over the past century has intersected with rising economic inequality. We conclude that declining economic opportunity has undercut some of the heralded expansions of political rights for historically disadvantaged groups, particularly among less affluent Americans.

ECONOMIC INEQUALITY MEETS THE "RIGHTS REVOLUTION"

In comparative perspective, the United States was a democratic pioneer, granting white men political rights regardless of whether or not they owned property by the 1830s. Yet the nation proceeded far more slowly and haltingly in extending rights to African Americans and women. Indeed, as late as the mid-twentieth century—a period celebrated for the relatively high degree of equality of income—entrenched forms of race and gender inequality persisted, either unhindered by public policy or, in the case of Jim Crow segregation, inscribed in law.

In the 1960s and 1970s, however, a "rights revolution" roiled these prevailing laws and practices. Through landmark legislative achievements, the civil rights and feminist movements succeeded in dismantling the most overt discriminatory rules. The Civil Rights Act of 1964 remains the biggest breakthrough, outlawing discrimination in public accommodations (Title II), prohibiting federal funding of educational institutions if they discriminated (Title VI), and forbidding discrimination by employers—whether in the public or private sector—as well as by unions (Title VII). Meanwhile, the Voting Rights Act of 1965 outlawed numerous practices that had been used to prevent African Americans from voting and also established a legal structure designed to forestall new discriminatory practices. Other policy achievements of the era include the Elementary and Secondary Education Act of 1965, which granted federal funds to poverty-stricken public schools; the Fair Housing Act of 1968, which outlawed discrimination in real estate transactions; the Educational Amendments of 1972 (Title IX), which prohibited sex discrimination in educational institutions receiving federal funds; and the Emergency School Aid Act of 1972, which granted financial aid to schools attempting desegregation.

The "rights revolution" has gone far in making the promise of equal opportunity a reality for many Americans. A vast array of formal policies and practices that granted second-class citizenship to men of color and women have simply disappeared from the political landscape, treated today not merely as illegal, but as socially retrograde.

These advances can be seen most clearly in the American professional class. Many better-off blacks and women have gained education and employment in fields that were, for the most part, closed to them until recent decades. The presence of African American men in the highest income categories has improved in recent decades, though they remain strikingly underrepresented (Welch 2002, 185–90). The number of women in managerial and professional jobs nearly doubled between 1974 and 1994 (Ford 2002, 216). At the ninety-fifth percentile, women's wages increased by 52 percent between 1979 and 2000, compared with 26.5 percent for men (Mishel, Bernstein, and Bushey 2003). Between 1967 and 1996, the proportion of African American women with wages in the top quartile increased from 0.7 to 7.5 percent, a tenfold increase (Welch 2002, 188, 190).

And yet, for many women and vast numbers of African Americans, equal opportunity remains elusive even at the start of the twenty-first century. To some extent, the limits on the "rights revolution" for these citizens reflects the reversal or curtailments of some of the relevant rights-oriented policies in recent decades—a topic that has been treated quite thoroughly by numerous scholars (for example, Klinkner and Smith 1999; Orfield, Eaton, and the Harvard Project on School Desegregation 1996).

What has received less attention, however, is the effect of rising economic inequality on the reach and impact of the "rights revolution." At the very same moment that the "rights revolution" ended many legally institutionalized patterns of racism and sexism, new forms of inequality emerged based less on legal discrimination and more on stratification of income and wealth. And while these disparities did not develop neatly along lines of either race or gender, women and minorities were still most likely to find themselves disadvantaged by these trends. As a consequence, many lower-income women and minorities found themselves lacking the resources to exercise their new rights effectively.

Race and Inequality

The post–World War II period represented a time of considerable social opportunity for American males of European ancestry. Yet African American males—including well over a million who fought in World War II—fared quite differently. In the first decades after the war, educational institutions in the South continued to segregate, relegating blacks to inferior facilities. Nationwide, African Americans faced rampant discrimination in job markets. Although federal reforms opened some government jobs in the 1950s, blacks still found employment only in a narrow range of jobs that offered low pay and low status (Klinkner and Smith 1999; Mettler, forthcoming). Even highly educated black men received less of a boost from advanced degrees than their white counterparts (Featherman and Hauser 1978, 481; Miller 1960). Though growing quickly, median black family income hovered at just above half the level of the median white family from the late 1940s through the early 1960s, and gaps in black and white educational attainment, home ownership, wealth, and occupational status were even more glaring (Hochschild 1995; Mishel, Bernstein, and Bushey 2003, 42).

It is important to recognize that a number of major twentieth-century government programs that aimed to reduce economic inequality reinforced rather than ameliorated racial inequality. For example, core elements of the New Deal, as well as of housing and urban renewal policy in the 1950s and 1960s, created new resources for middle- and lower-class white Americans that were largely inaccessible to African Americans (Jackson 1985; Anderson 1964, 7–8). Prior to the rights revolution, then, the failure of many inequality-reducing policies to reach blacks reinforced the link between racial and economic inequalities—in ways that proved difficult to undo once economic inequality among all Americans began to rise sharply in later decades.

The "rights revolution," initially, seemed to promise fundamental improvement in the well-being of African Americans. The Civil Rights Act of 1964 ushered in a brief period during which the racial wage gap rapidly narrowed (Donahue and Heckman 1990; Heckman and Payner 1989). After the late 1970s, however, the trend of dramatic progress in diminishing inequality between blacks and whites stopped or was reversed. The racial wage gap exploded—by the 1980s, it had returned to levels found in the 1950s. And unemployment spiked among African Americans, averaging 14.7 percent throughout the 1980s, more than twice the average rate for whites (6.2 percent)—a ratio that has persisted.

The high economic growth period of the late 1990s greatly benefited African Americans (the black-white income ratio rose to an historical high of 63.5 percent), but the economic well-being of blacks still lags well behind that of whites (Mishel, Bernstein, and Bushey 2003, 218–21, 41–2). As of 2001, 31.2 percent of black workers were employed in jobs paying less than poverty-level wages, compared with 21.2 percent of white workers.

Amid deindustrialization and other economic shifts, black men were especially likely to be squeezed out of jobs offering middle-class salaries. One quarter of black men (25.7 percent) worked for poverty level wages in 2001 compared to only 14.5 percent of white men, and poverty rates among African Americans generally remain much higher than among whites. In short, after the immediate gains that followed the banning of discrimination, relative income gains among African Americans slowed dramatically (Hochschild 1995; Thernstrom and Thernstrom 1997).

Yet that is not the whole story. Unlike the period before the Civil Rights movement, the extent to which African Americans' well-being lags behind that of whites now depends heavily on the interaction of race and other factors, particularly educational attainment. Highly educated blacks, like highly educated whites, have seen increasing returns to their education. And many are considerably better off today than they were in the early 1970s. These disparate trends highlight ways in which growing inequality cuts across all racial groups. Yet they also point to ways in which public policies have aided some members of minority groups more than others—a point we pursue in later sections of this chapter. For example, affirmative action has been especially helpful to highly educated and professional African Americans (Wilson 1999, 20). Conversely, programs that previously offered strong support to working-class and low-income Americans have grown considerably weaker, with particularly harmful effects on African Americans.

Residential segregation is a powerful example of the important intersection of race and class. Although the residential isolation of blacks has declined somewhat over the last two decades, it continues to be higher than among any other ethnic group in the United States (Iceland, Weinberg, and Steinmetz 2002). According to Douglas Massey and Nancy A. Denton (1993), black urbanites did not dwell in segregated neighborhoods before 1900. Rather, such enclaves emerged by 1940 through a combination of individual and collective discriminatory actions that had few parallels in the treatment of other ethnic groups. Once established, this extreme residential segregation persisted, despite fair housing laws. Some recent studies downplay such outcomes, ascribing them to individual choice (Thernstrom and Thernstrom 1997). Yet careful empirical studies offer evidence that discrimination in housing is still a common experience for blacks and Hispanics (Yinger 2001).

At the same time, growing income inequality has fostered greater economic segregation. One study reports that "economic classes are becoming more spatially separate from each other, with the rich increasingly living with other rich people and the poor with other poor" (Dreier, Mollenkopf, and Sandstrom 2001, 1). While much of the emphasis has been on the "gated communities" that have appeared across the nation over the last few decades, the main reason for growing economic segregation is that income disparities between neighborhoods have grown more exaggerated in direct relationship to growing inequality in the population (Mayer 2001).

Economic and racial segregation exacerbate each other in predominantly black neighborhoods, perpetuating numerous and intertwined forms of disadvantage, including high poverty rates and limited educational and economic opportunities. The cumulative disadvantages include high rent burdens, poor quality housing and associated health risks, and lack of access to housing wealth or equity. Segregated neighborhoods also undermine employment opportunities, creating a spatial mismatch between residence and quality available jobs (Yinger 2001). Neighborhood effects also appear to harm individuals' life opportunities by, for example, undermining children's chances of academic achievement and exposing residents to crime and other social pathologies (Borjas 1995; Yinger 2001). And housing values in poor communities fail to appreciate over time at levels comparable to those in middle-class communities, deflating the local property tax base, with all the vast implications already discussed for the relative quality of educational institutions.

Gender and Inequality

Gender equality might appear less affected by growing income differences than racial inequality has been. Yet while women have indeed made significant economic gains over the last three decades, they remain unequal in economic status to men, and the gap is most severe for women lower on the economic ladder. Moreover, policies aimed at fostering gender equality have been seriously undermined by growing economic inequality.

Amid the tide of growing income inequality, women's economic progress stands out. Overall, women's median wages have increased in real terms—from $9.24 per hour in 1973 to $11.40 in 2001. In contrast, men's real median wages fell between the mid-1970s and mid-1990s, rising to their pre-1975 level of about $15 only in 2001. As a result, the ratio between women's and men's wages has narrowed substantially, though the narrowing is due as much to stagnation of men's wages as to improved women's wages.

These shifts have varied, to be sure, with occupational sector, income level, familial situation, and other factors. Just as white-collar men have gained economically in recent decades while their blue-collar counterparts have seen their real wages fall, wages grew most rapidly among women in the highest-paying jobs (Mishel, Bernstein, and Bushey 2003). Nonetheless, gender inequality persists in the workforce at all levels, with women earning substantially lower wages than men in each occupational sector (Mishel, Bernstein, and Bushey 2003) and women much more likely to earn poverty-level wages. The persistence of an especially high gender wage gap in the United States is usually linked to occupational segregation, discrimination, and women's role in raising children. Yet these factors actually explain less of the gap in the United States than they do in other nations. One recent analysis found that the gap is largely attributable to the high level of U.S. wage inequality, which especially penalizes those in the bottom half of the wage distribution (Blau and Kahn 2000).

Most vulnerable, for a variety of reasons, are single mothers. Among married couples, wives' earnings as a percentage of family incomes have grown from about 25 percent in the early 1970s to about 34 percent in 2000 (Mishel, Bernstein, and Bushey 2003, 103–4). At the same time, women with children are far more likely to be raising them alone than they were three decades ago. And despite the fact that female-headed households are better off financially now than in the past, they are still likely to live at just below twice the poverty line (Mishel, Bernstein, and Bushey 2003, 49–50).

Women with low incomes are assisted by a variety of government programs, but huge gaps remain. Given their greater likelihood of working for low wages, women are especially vulnerable to the diminished real value of the minimum wage. In fact, women comprise well over half of workers earning wages within a dollar of the present minimum wage. Moreover, 94 percent of women in low-wage jobs are not unionized (Mishel, Bernstein, and Bushey 2003, 196–201). In the absence of stronger labor regulations, a crucial safety net has been provided by the Earned Income Tax Credit, which lifted perhaps two million children out of poverty in 1996 (Center on Budget and Policy Priorities 1998). Meanwhile, however, public assistance has provided sharply declining support (Mishel, Bernstein, and Bushey 2003, 342–44). To the extent, then, that single mothers are better off now than in past decades, it is primarily because they are working more outside of the home and because their pay is supplemented by the EITC. Finally, despite Medicaid, the share of women lacking health insurance has increased over the last twenty years—from less than 14 percent of women in the late 1980s to more than 18 percent in the late 1990s (Misra 2001).

The situation of elderly women also deserves emphasis. While social programs aimed toward the elderly have proven important in lifting women out of poverty, women continue to reach older adulthood with considerably less in private savings and pensions than men. They also live longer after retirement, making them especially vulnerable to poverty. For this reason, Social Security provides a vital safety net for elderly women.

Overall, then, the most spectacular gains in women's economic status have, for the most part, affected highly educated professional women. In the top income quintile of households, both men's and women's wages have increased dramatically over the past two decades, with women's wages rising by a stunning 80 percent, fully a third faster than men's. Yet in the lowest income quintile, men's wages actually fell while women's wages rose by only 20 percent (Mishel, Bernstein, and Bushey 2003). It can be said that far greater gender equality exists today than thirty years ago. As with African Americans, however, the fruits of the rights revolution have disproportionately reached more privileged women.

Indeed, many of the rights secured by feminists—though applying to all women in principle—can be exercised only by those with financial means. For example, the Family and Medical Leave Act of 1993 offers unpaid leave to workers to care for a newborn, child, or other relative. Yet lower income women are typically unable to afford to exercise this right (Phillips 2002). Similarly, while new public policies aim to allow women to escape from domestic violence and press charges, low-income women are less likely to feel sufficiently independent in economic terms to leave a violent relationship (Kelly 1991). In essence, growing income inequality has undermined some of the key successes of the movement for gender equality. More important, it has distributed these successes quite unequally across the income scale.

The postwar years are often viewed as a golden age of growing economic equality. But we should not forget that this era also featured two levels of citizenship, divided along the fault lines of race and gender. The "rights revolution" of the 1960s and 1970s powerfully attacked this ascriptive citizenship regime. But in its wake, three decades of growing economic inequality have created disparities of wealth and income that have reinforced some of the very disadvantages the "rights revolution" aimed to eliminate. What political consequences ensue from this brave new world of equal formal rights yet increasingly unequal economic standing?

POLICY FEEDBACKS AND POLITICAL EQUALITY

The Civil Rights movement offered the hope of not only leveling access to social opportunity, but also of reducing political inequality. The initial record, of course, was one of stunning success: The extension of basic citizenship rights directly enabled and encouraged political participation among historically excluded groups. Nonetheless, the political playing field still remains tilted, and the immediate gains of the Civil Rights movement have not yielded sustained equalization of political voice. As chapter 2 points out, whites continue to participate much more frequently than African Americans and Latinos, and men continue to participate more frequently than women. This is principally because racial and gender inequalities continue to mark education, employment, income, and other factors that are critical in distributing the skills, networks, and resources that make participation possible and productive.

Most of the differences in voice that mark American politics today, therefore, are not due to explicit exclusion of groups from the public sphere, but from educational inequities, differential employment rates, and other factors that affect the distribution of civic skills and political opportunities. It remains the case, however, that these inequities and differences significantly undermine equality of voice. And it is almost certainly the case that rising inequality—because it has been especially disadvantageous to groups helped by the Civil Rights movement—has limited the gains in political equality that the movement aimed to foster.

Here we consider these intertwined factors by examining how the evolution of American public policy over the past half century has shaped both social and political equality. To examine the relationship between public policy and political equality requires an understanding not just of policies' social consequences, but also of their long-term political effects— a subject increasingly explored by political scientists under the label *policy feedbacks*. We begin, therefore, by reviewing the growing body of scholarship on how public policies affect citizens' political resources, capacities, and interests. We then examine the impact on American citizenship of a number of twentieth-century policies particularly associated in the public and scholarly mind with social and political equality. Finally, we bring together the findings of these sections to explore how U.S. public policy promoted (and responded to) social and political equality in the immediate postwar years. This discussion then sets the stage for our final major section, which argues that this "virtuous cycle" seems to have eroded significantly in recent decades.

Studying Policy Feedback Effects

The idea that policies reshape the political environment has a long legacy. In 1935, E. E. Schattschneider suggested that "new policies create a new politics" (Schattschneider 1935, 288). More recently, historical institutionalists have coined the term "policy feedback" to illuminate such dynamics. Most analyses to date focus on how new policies alter the calculus and priorities of public officials and interest groups, such that the next round of policymaking assumes different dynamics (Orloff 1988; Skocpol 1992).

The approach has antecedents in Charles Lindblom's observation that public officials build on existing policies incrementally, and on Hugh Heclo's argument that policymakers engage in learning from existing policies (Heclo 1974; Lindblom 1959). As Margaret Weir explains it, "decisions at one point in time can restrict future possibilities by sending policy off onto particular tracks, along which ideas and interests develop and strategies adapt" (1992, 19).

Scholars of American welfare state development have embraced the policy feedback approach, using it to explain several seeming anomalies of the U.S. case. They have told us, for example, why policymakers in the early twentieth century failed to enact a "paternalist" welfare state like that of most European nations; why most programs within the Social Security Act of 1935 were made subject to joint national-state administrative arrangements but Old Age Insurance was endowed with fully national level authority; why American employment policy, over time, moved increasingly away from efforts to promote full employment and features only remedial efforts for those at the lower end of the labor market; why national health insurance has been so much more difficult to achieve in the United States than elsewhere; and why the United States has increasingly sanctioned and regulated private forms of social provision rather than bolstering public benefits (Hacker 1998; 2002; Mettler 1998; Orloff 1993; Skocpol 1992; Weir 1992). These prominent examples primarily emphasize policy feedback effects on administrative and political elites.

In contrast, relatively little scholarship has explored the boundary between public policy and mass political behavior. In a seminal theoretical analysis, Paul Pierson suggested that the effects of policies on mass publics could take two main forms: resource effects, as policies shape the costs and benefits associated with particular political strategies; and interpretive effects, as policies shape information and meaning, with implications for political learning (1993). Understanding such effects requires careful attention to the details of policy design (Ingram and Schneider 1993). Already scholars know that policies seem to vary in terms of their consequences for civic engagement (Verba, Schlozman, and Brady 1995). The nascent literature on policy feedback for mass publics begins to illuminate the mechanisms through which policy designs produce such variation in political outcomes.

There are many such possible mechanisms. For example, it is well known that advanced education and higher levels of socioeconomic status foster, in turn, cultivation of those skills and predispositions that make citizens more engaged politically (Verba, Schlozman, and Brady 1995). In addition, recipients of benefits are sought after in mobilization efforts by political parties and interest groups, thus amplifying their voice in the political process (Rosenstone and Hansen 1993). And policies may have interpretive effects by conveying messages to citizens about their status in the polity, the relationship of government to people like them, and their rights and obligations as citizens. Joe Soss (1999) found, for instance, that when recipients of Social Security disability insurance (SSDI) sought benefits, they encountered a rule-bound agency that, though cumbersome to deal with, generally proved responsive. Conversely, beneficiaries of Aid to Families with Dependent Children (AFDC) found the program to be administered by agencies that were unresponsive and even hostile to client demands. Soss argues that recipients of both SSDI and AFDC experienced the program from which they benefited as a microcosm of the political system, one that conveyed critical lessons to them about their relationship to government.

In a recent article, Suzanne Mettler and Joe Soss (2004) suggest four principal ways in which policies may affect the citizenry. First, policies shape civic affiliations, status, and the degree of unity among the citizenry. Policies delineate groups in the polity, defining their boundaries and infusing them with political meaning. (Neither "welfare mothers" nor "taxpayers," for example—both potent sources of political symbolism—would exist without public policy.) Second, policies affect civic capacity, altering the incentives, skills, resources, and beliefs of citizens. They may create material incentives for mobilization, build and distribute civic capacities, and supply resources for political mobilization. Third, policies have feedback effects through the citizenry that shape issue framing and political agenda setting. As policymakers approach social problems through particular solutions and not others, they effectively frame issues, shaping the way citizens perceive the problem and the legitimate role of government in relation to it. Finally, public policies structure political participation itself, influencing the extent to which individuals or groups are mobilized and the form their participation takes. They define the universe of participants and demand makers, create new arenas for political action, and shape political group and party affiliations.

To what extent are these four relationships between policy and political influence seen in the landscape of twentieth-century policies? The remainder of this section offers some concrete answers to this question by exploring a handful of major government policies that have shaped inequality and its political effects in the post–World War II era: the G.I. Bill, Social Security and Medicare, the War on Poverty, and the Voting Rights Act. These policies were chosen for analysis not because they are representative of all government activities, but because their role in affecting inequality is acknowledged and because a growing amount of research explores their second-order political effects. We conclude these mini-case studies by offering some reflections on the relationship between policy and economic and political equality in the postwar era. This sets the stage for us to consider how the relationship between policy and political equality has changed in the wake of the rights revolution and the post-1970s trend toward sharply rising economic inequality.

The G.I. Bill

The Serviceman's Readjustment Act of 1944—commonly known as the G.I. Bill—significantly fostered social and political equality in the post–World War II era. While grounded in the long-standing American tradition of providing social benefits to military servicemen, the G.I. Bill parted from earlier veterans' programs by offering a wide array of immediate benefits to all who served: education, vocational and on-the-job training, unemployment compensation, and loan guarantees to assist in the purchase of homes, farms, or businesses. Similar benefits were offered to veterans of later wars, but the original bill was far more generous and extensive, and stands out today as one of the most important postwar programs promoting equality.

Under its renowned inclusivity and generosity, any veteran was eligible for benefits as long as he had served for at least 90 days and had a discharge status other than dishonorable. All veterans were entitled to a "mustering-out" payment of $100 to $300 per person. They also qualified for up to a year of unemployment benefits that were far more generous and easier to obtain than unemployment benefits in most states. Loan guarantee provisions were also offered—and widely used: 4.3 million veterans purchased homes at low-interest rates, and 200,000 purchased farms or started businesses, giving construction an enormous boost. By 1955, nearly one-third of the new housing starts nationwide owed their backing to the Veterans' Administration (VA).

Just over half of all World War II veterans, some 7.8 million individual men and women accepted the education and training benefits the VA offered. Beneficiaries could attend the educational institution of their choice as long as they gained admission through the standard procedures. Approximately 28 percent attended colleges and universities; 45 percent went to schools below the college level, especially trade and vocational training programs; and the remainder undertook on-the-job or on-the-farm training. The G.I. Bill covered tuition and provided monthly stipend payments for up to four years, depending on the veteran's length of service (Mettler 2005).

The effects of the higher education provisions were dramatic indeed. Colleges were inundated with students, with veterans comprising half of the undergraduate population nationwide by 1949. Before the war, higher education had been limited primarily to the sons of the elite. The G.I. Bill provided access to college for large numbers of Jews, Catholics, African Americans, immigrants and the children of immigrants, and members of working- and middle-class families (Mettler 2005). Given the rapid rise in high school graduation rates just prior to the war, the average veteran had already completed high school and therefore could choose whether to opt into the higher education benefits (Goldin 1998, 371) . The financial assistance of the G.I. Bill, in turn, served to weaken the prevailing class determinants of who went to college and how much education they received. In turn, the program greatly boosted educational attainment among beneficiaries—indeed, by as much as three years, with other key determinants held constant (Behrman, Pollack, and Taubman 1989).

The vast majority of veterans on the G.I. Bill flocked to the sub-college programs, prompting the number of vocational training schools in the nation to triple within six years. Through these programs, veterans acquired training in a wide array of vocations. Thousands also attended flight and business schools or completed their primary or secondary education. Veterans with less prior education were especially likely to use the vocational benefits. And while such programs did not increase beneficiaries' formal education, they enabled them to advance in their careers and reach supervisory or managerial positions that typically guaranteed middle-class wages and health, pension, and other benefits (Mettler 2005).

The G.I. Bill—through both its World War II and Korean War versions—extended educational opportunity to the vast majority of males of the World War II generation (that is, men born in the 1920s), 80 percent of whom served in the military. Though blacks were somewhat underrepresented in the military, due largely to explicit discrimination, as well as to inferior schooling and health in the Jim Crow era, black veterans actually used the education and training benefits at higher rates than white veterans—in the South and, indeed, throughout the nation.[11] While institutionalized segregation persisted in the South, tens of thousands of black veterans crowded into the historically black colleges and separate vocational programs. Others seized the opportunity to move to the North or West, and utilized their benefits to attend integrated institutions of higher education. Granted, black G.I. Bill users in the South did not exhibit the same advances in formal educational attainment as white users, but that is because they had less education to begin with and therefore were more likely to sign up for vocational training programs. In the North, moreover, the program did advance black educational attainment (Sampson and Laub 1996). All told, black male veterans were even more likely than white male veterans to regard the program as a turning point in their lives (Mettler, forthcoming).

By contrast, the G.I. Bill had little direct impact on women's lives. Women comprised only 2 percent of the military, and gender norms promoted educational advancement mostly among men. Forty percent of female veterans used the education and training provisions, though typically for shorter periods of time than male veterans and with less likelihood of receiving degrees (Mettler 2005).

Today, political scientists view the World War II generation as the great exemplar of twentieth-century civic engagement. Did the G.I. Bill have any role in creating this celebrated civic generation? The evidence indicates that it did, and powerfully so. As it extended generous benefits, the G.I. Bill also prompted higher levels of subsequent involvement in civic and political activity. Although the higher education levels that the G.I. Bill prompted were an important cause of this effect—and one worth emphasizing, given that avenues for educational advancement had generally been closed to less advantaged Americans in the past—there is also evidence that the G.I. Bill encouraged civic engagement through the lessons that it carried about citizenship and common cause. Comparing two non-black male veterans with the same socioeconomic background and level of educational attainment, for example, the veteran who used the G.I. Bill's education and training benefits joined 50 percent more civic organizations and participated in 30 percent more political activities during the postwar era (Mettler 2002).

How can we explain this remarkable effect? It appears that that the policy design of the program—particularly its universalism, generosity, and message of equal citizenship— made beneficiaries much more inclined toward civic involvement. These "interpretive effects" were most pronounced for those from low to moderate socioeconomic backgrounds, who felt, often for the first time, that they were fully incorporated into the polity as first-class citizens (Pierson 1993). Interpretive effects also proved strong among vocational education beneficiaries, and—strikingly—among African American veterans, who became especially active in the civil rights movement of the 1950s and 1960s and, subsequently in electoral politics and political organizations (Mettler, forthcoming). Although the interpretive effects of the G.I. Bill largely faded by the mid-1960s, beneficiaries' civic engagement remained high, thanks to enhanced educational levels, skills, and networks that allowed them to engage successfully in public life (Mettler and Welch 2004).

The G.I. Bill served as a template for later legislative efforts to help veterans of the Korean War (1952), the Cold War (1966), and the Vietnam War (1967). Each bill's educational and training benefits were extended on somewhat less generous terms than those of its predecessor. In 1984, Congress established a comparatively modest system of educational benefits

for veterans of the all-volunteer military that has proved much less suc-
cessful than the original G.I. Bill was in bridging the significant educa-
tional gap that now exists between veterans and nonveterans (Cohen,
Warner, and Segal 1995). Nonetheless, the G.I. Bill still looms large in
American public consciousness, demonstrating that policies that affect
economic inequality and opportunity can also have profound effects on
American civic life. This conclusion is greatly reinforced when we turn to
Social Security and Medicare.

Social Security and Medicare

Social Security and Medicare—technically, old-age, survivors', disability,
and health insurance, or OASDHI—stand out as the privileged core of
American social provision. Enacted during the New Deal, the original old-
age insurance program (henceforth called "Social Security") represented
the first national program of retirement protection available to private
workers across the industrial economy. Medicare, passed in 1965 as an
amendment to the Social Security program, provides hospital coverage
(Part A) and physicians' insurance (Part B) to eligible U.S. residents older
than 65 and, since 1972, the disabled. Although Social Security initially excluded many workers—most notably, agricultural and domestic employees—it is now essentially universal. Medicare, since its inception, has covered virtually all of the aged.

Both programs are also generally quite favorable to lower- and middle-
income workers. Social Security bases its benefits on a formula that provides higher benefits to lower-income workers relative to the taxes they
pay into the program. Medicare's medical benefits do not seem so starkly
redistributive. For beneficiaries with similar health histories, for example,
higher-income beneficiaries consume more—and more costly—Medicare-
funded services (Gornick et al. 1996). But Medicare's financing is more
progressive than Social Security's. Part A is financed by a small tax on
wages that applies to all wage income, rather than the first $90,000 or so,
as is the case with Social Security's payroll tax. Part B is principally financed by general tax revenues, which in turn are principally financed by
the progressive income tax. And both Social Security and Medicare are
complemented by special supplementary programs for the indigent
aged—Supplemental Security Income in the case of Social Security, and
Medicaid for elderly Americans who are "dually eligible" for Medicare
and Medicaid.

A clear illustration of this progressivity is provided by the extensive research on the role of Social Security in lifting elderly Americans out of
poverty. Census data show that without Social Security, nearly half—47.6

percent—of the U.S. population age sixty-five and older would have been poor in 1997. By lifting more than eleven million senior citizens out of poverty, Social Security lowered the elderly poverty rate by three-quarters that year—making it the most effective of all government programs in reducing poverty. To be sure, these statistics cannot answer the question of what senior citizens' incomes would have been if Social Security did not exist and elderly Americans had not been able to count on its income in retirement during their working lives. Yet it is impossible to argue that Social Security is not vital to increasing income, and equality of income, among the aged. Social Security makes up approximately 80 percent of the income of both the poorest fifth of elderly people and the next-to-the-poorest fifth, provides 62 percent of the income of those in the middle fifth of the elderly population, and even provides 41.5 percent of the income of the elderly in the next-to-highest income fifth (Porter, Larin, and Primus 1999).

Moreover, when the risk of needing the benefits that the programs provide are taken into account, both Social Security and Medicare appear even more favorable to workers on the lower half of income ladder. Private pensions are often unavailable for lower-income workers, who also rarely have tax-favored private savings accounts, in part because the tax breaks that such accounts offer are worth relatively little to workers in low income tax brackets. Lower-income workers are also much more likely to use Social Security's survivors' insurance, which aids dependents of deceased workers. These survivors' benefits, in fact, more than offset the fact that the more affluent tend to live longer, and thus collect Social Security longer after retirement (Aaron et al. 2001; Coronado, Fullerton, and Glass 2000; Gustman and Steinmeier 2000).

The story is similar with regard to Medicare. Average health status generally gets worse as one moves down the income ladder, making Medicare's guarantee of basic benefits without regard to prior health experience extremely valuable to less affluent Americans. Private health insurance for the aged is nearly impossible to obtain, especially for senior citizens who are less healthy than average, and retiree health coverage is mostly limited to highly paid and unionized workers.

That said, the taxes that fund Social Security and Medicare Part A are proportional, flat levies—which in the case of Social Security, stop at a certain standard of income. And, for most workers, they are far and away the largest portion of the federal tax bill paid. While many workers hit hard by the tax will disproportionately benefit from the Social Security and Medicare programs, it cannot be denied that the OASDHI payroll taxes are a serious blow to their disposable income during their working lives.

And because both programs pay current benefits using the contributions of current taxpayers, the program also disadvantages, relatively speaking, smaller generations of workers vis-à-vis larger ones. If present benefit levels are to be maintained when the large baby boom generation retires, taxpaying workers will need either to be markedly more productive than their predecessors or to pay higher levies. This points to a crucial feature of Medicare and Social Security: they redistribute across generations rather than across classes. Nonetheless, within generations, and even taking into account the heavy burden of the payroll tax on workers' current incomes, the thrust of the two programs is clearly progressive.

Research on the effects of Social Security across lines of race and gender is more scattered and sketchy. Initially, Social Security excluded most African Americans and many women (Lieberman 1998). Today, however, it is generally quite favorable to both groups. To the extent that women and blacks are more likely to have low incomes during their working lives and in retirement, Social Security's progressive, guaranteed benefits offer disproportionately valuable assistance. While it is often argued that blacks do poorly under the program because they generally do not live as long as whites, the overall distribution of benefits remains in their favor when the progressivity of the benefit structure and survivors' benefits are taken into account (Aaron et al. 2001).

As for women, Social Security (and Medicare) are increasingly crucial and generous to them, because the progressive benefit structure, because of generous spousal benefits (which despite their gender-neutrality are disproportionately received by women), and because women tend to live longer than men after retirement. Thus women receive 53 percent of Social Security benefits, while paying 38 percent of the program's payroll taxes. In 1997, nearly two-thirds of elderly women received a majority of their income from Social Security, and for almost one-third of elderly women, Social Security provided at least 90 percent.[12]

The effects of Medicare across lines of race and gender are even less well understood. There is considerable evidence, however, that African Americans and other minorities are disproportionately among the uninsured within the nonelderly population (with rates of uninsurance two to three times as high as for whites); thus, the guaranteed, universal benefits offered by the Medicare program are arguably more valuable to these groups than whites. That said, recent studies suggest that racial disparities in access to care that exist for the nonelderly are by no means eliminated by Medicare. Blacks covered by Medicare appear to receive less appropriate treatment than whites, controlling for income—although these disparities are much less severe than for the nonelderly (Gornick et al. 1996). Barriers to prompt access to appropriate care that affect nonelderly women no doubt also carry over, to some extent, to female Medicare patients.

Until recently, both Social Security and Medicare have remained relatively stable. (In 2003, however, Medicare was reformed to add a prescription drug benefit and increase the role of private health plans, and, after the 2004 election, President George W. Bush called for partial privatization of Social Security, but the fate of this proposal remains uncertain.) The main changes in the 1980s and 1990s were in the direction of cost containment, which in some cases reduced benefits. Social Security's replacement rates—the share of preretirement income provided to retirees by the program—has declined, and Medicare covers a smaller share of senior citizens' medical costs today than it did at its inception (though, of course, total costs are now much larger and some of this gap will be closed by the new drug benefit). In Medicare, the growth of private health plans contracting with the program has increased benefits for some, but there is evidence that private plans discriminate against sicker patients, and that those in private plans are less supportive of program upgrading than those who remain in the traditional program (Kronick and DeBeyer 1999).[13]

This last point raises the issue of Social Security and Medicare's political effects. It would seem difficult for two programs this large, visible, and politically salient not to have significant political effects, and indeed a new body of research demonstrates profound civic consequences. Perhaps most telling is the recent work of Andrea Campbell, which shows how Social Security has helped create the actively engaged population of senior citizens that so marks American politics today. Not only are levels of participation among the aged remarkably high, but in addition, the aged are the one group for which a marked participatory bias favoring the affluent and educated does not exist. As Campbell (2003,138) argues, Social Security and Medicare have "materially enhanced [senior citizens'] participatory capacity" and, in doing so, "fundamentally altered the American democratic landscape."

Not only were senior citizens themselves activated by government efforts to help the aged; the popularity—and the weaknesses—of these programs helped give rise to extremely important watchdog groups representing senior citizens, notably, the American Association for Retired Persons (which now operates only under its acronym, AARP). It is a relatively little known fact that the AARP gained its current prominence mainly by selling supplemental policies that filled the gaps in the Medicare program. This reinforces the more general argument outlined in the previous section—that what government does (and does not do) can create important organizing opportunities for civic groups, shaping the organizational landscape of American politics decades after the initial impetus for a program fades.

In short, Medicare and Social Security have continued to foster civic engagement much as the G.I. Bill did in the immediate postwar era—first, by providing material resources that generate higher rates of participation; second, by providing the basis for group mobilization; and third, by providing interpretive signals that both shape and reinforce public perceptions of government and the worth of political action. These effects have been, in many respects, overwhelmingly positive, and they certainly help account for the political resilience of the Medicare and Social Security programs. Yet the age bias in U.S. social policy noted earlier suggests that the active mobilization of the aged is not an unmitigated good for efforts to address rising inequality for all Americans. With poverty and inequality concentrated increasingly among the working aged and young, the lack of parallel civic engagement among the nonelderly probably reinforces the tendency of political leaders to focus on the preservation and improvement of programs for the aged, rather than the formulation of broader measures emphasizing young and old alike.

Nonetheless, the broad support for public programs for the aged, and the relative political equality among the aged that they appear to have fostered, provide a clear example of success in building participatory potential and capacities among once-vulnerable citizens. One reason for this success, surely, is that these programs are highly inclusive, rather than focused simply on the poor or disadvantaged, as well as that they are received by groups in American society that are widely viewed with sympathy and favor. These reasons for success are worth keeping in mind as policymakers consider reforms of Social Security and Medicare—such as private individual accounts within Social Security—that could undercut the sense of shared political fate that these programs have so far fostered. They are also worth keeping in mind as we turn from Social Security and Medicare to the very different policy and political consequences of President Lyndon Johnson's War on Poverty—another prominent example of a government initiative that has shaped American inequality and its political ramifications.

The War on Poverty

The War on Poverty is notable for three reasons. First, launched amid the civil rights movement's greatest breakthroughs, it challenged racial inequalities much more directly than previous social policies. Second, it also departed from previous policies in attempting to affect directly the political capacities of lower-income citizens through programs of organization and empowerment. And, third, many of the embodiments and legacies of the War on Poverty became highly controversial, and some were abandoned, repudiated, or stripped of substantial financing. It is thus important to ask today, with clear eyes, what the War on Poverty actually attempted and accomplished in affecting inequality and poverty in the United States.

The specific programmatic results of the War on Poverty were extensive and diverse, and involved a variety of interlocking and mutually reinforcing policies and programs (Henderson 1995; Perry, Ambeau, and McBride 1995). Housing policies included the creation of the Department of Housing and Urban Development, the Model Cities program, and the Fair Housing Act of 1968. Health policies included Medicaid, the public assistance counterpart of Medicare. Employment and job training policies included the Job Corps and Neighborhood Youth Corps, though neither ever received much funding. The Johnson administration also encouraged compliance with Title VII of the 1964 Civil Rights Act related to nondiscrimination in employment and, when labor unions balked, issued Executive Order 11246, which permitted affirmative action in federal contract compliance and led to the development of affirmative action in education, employment, and a number of other areas.

A number of educational programs focusing on the disadvantaged also originated with the War on Poverty, including Head Start and Upward Bound. The 1964 Economic Opportunity Act (EOA) included a wide range of antipoverty policies; Food Stamps was created during this period. In addition to expanding antipoverty efforts, the EOA established more than a thousand Community Action Agencies—nonprofit groups, city agencies, and community-controlled groups designed to encourage "maximum feasible participation" of the poor in the administration of the act. This exemplified the War on Poverty's focus on civil rights and political participation, and indeed the 1964 Civil Rights Act and the 1965 Voting Rights Act, though not formally part of the War on Poverty, bolstered the emerging focus of the antipoverty program agenda on urban black poverty and played an important part in mediating its political effects.

Discerning the effects of all these complex and interwoven programs is difficult, despite the wealth of studies that have been done. The initial record was one of significant improvements in income and reductions in poverty. Research by Linda Williams finds large reductions in poverty and increases in college completion among both blacks and whites based on analysis of U.S. census data. Perhaps the clearest effect of the War on Poverty was in the area of black employment: many of the new public-sector jobs created within government during the period went to African Americans (Williams 2003, esp. 150). Nonetheless, improvements in income and living conditions were not sustained because of the confluence of the economic downturn and industrial transformation of the 1970s, failure to maintain relatively high levels of initial spending, and weaknesses in the programs themselves.

Although the War on Poverty has been criticized for exerting little sustained effect on poverty, most experts agree that the spending was never great enough to have a major impact on cash income. Most agree, too, that macroeconomic trends were far more important than the program's effects, positive or negative, in shaping poverty and inequality in the 1970s and after. Plus, the focus on poverty rates alone is misleading. Many of the most politically resilient programs that resulted from the War on Poverty—Medicaid, Food Stamps, Head Start—do not have much direct effect on poverty, providing as they do in-kind benefits rather than cash.

The political effects of the War on Poverty are even more difficult to judge. In each area in which the War on Poverty extended its programmatic reach, there were increased efforts to empower citizens and enforce civil rights reforms. The Community Action Program aimed at community involvement and complemented the changes brought about by the Civil Rights Act and Voting Rights acts of 1964 and 1965. The Model Cities Program aimed at improving housing and was complemented by the Fair Housing Act of 1968, as well as by the elevation of the policy area of housing from an agency to a cabinet-level department. Title VI of the 1964 Civil Rights Act, which gave the federal government considerable discretion in ensuring nondiscrimination in federal education spending, was complemented by new education programs at a variety of levels, such as Head Start and Upward Bound.

At the same time, however, the War on Poverty clearly sparked a political backlash that compromised its own aims as well as the continued political popularity of activist government. Many of the community empowerment efforts backfired badly, alienating local Democratic leaders. With the campaign of Governor George Wallace and Nixon's Southern Strategy, the South moved steadily into the Republican fold. And whatever its achievements, the perception of the War on Poverty not only as unsuccessful, but as a set of giveaways to urban black communities poisoned the well for future antipoverty efforts and negatively shaped public views of existing programs, such as Aid to Families with Dependent Children (Gilens 1999; Skocpol 1995). In all these respects, the War on Poverty showcased the inextricable link between poverty and skin color. Sadly, it also showcased the political risks of programs too focused in the public mind on the plight of the poor in general and the black poor in particular.

The Voting Rights Act of 1965

The Voting Rights Act of 1965 offers a powerful example of policy feedback effects; but it is of a different character than the other cases we have discussed. Voting rights legislation addresses the political status of groups suffering discrimination directly rather than indirectly. In this sense, it is inherently designed to have long-term effects on political power and participation. Still, the act has had a number of second-order policy feedback effects that extend well beyond its immediate impact on the participation of previously marginalized groups. These include mobilizing organizations concerned with voting rights; setting the agenda of voting rights policy (which shifted from an emphasis on basic rights to a concern with the actual election of minority candidates); and creating precedents that were extended to other racial and ethnic groups and even to new protected categories, such as so-called language minorities (groups speaking or reading languages other than English) and populations whose differing physical abilities limit their access to the polls.

The Voting Rights Act of 1965 originated in a moment of high politics driven by the moral and political challenge created by the African American Civil Rights movement. The act gave the federal government the power to require states and localities to curtail laws and practices that prevented the South's sizable African American population from exercising its political rights (Davidson and Grofman 1994). The 1965 act has been amended repeatedly and, in the process, extended in both intent and reach—to counteract other challenges to equal electoral rights and to reach other regions and groups.

In the wake of the 1965 act, federal observation of voter registration led to rapid increases in the size of the black southern electorate in the 1960s and 1970s. Nonetheless, southern states (especially Mississippi) implemented new electoral strategies to minimize "black electoral success" even after African Americans were registered and active.[14] In response, legal defense organizations and civil rights attorneys developed new strategies for ensuring that registration and voting actually led to shifts in electoral outcomes. Perhaps the most prominent and most controversial of these innovations was the concept of majority-minority districts designed to increase the number of black elected officials.

The most immediate consequence of the Voting Rights Act was a massive improvement in the electoral participation of previously excluded minorities. Voting and registration by African Americans, once only a small fraction in the South, now rivals the white population's (Guinier 1994; Parker 1991).[15] Reported registration in November of 2000, for instance, was 67.5 percent for blacks, 71.6 percent for white non-Hispanics, and 70.4 percent for whites. Voting, however, was lower: 53.5 percent among blacks, 60.4 percent among non-Hispanic whites, and 56.4 percent among whites in the 2000 presidential election (Jamieson, Shin, and Day 2002, 12). Among other groups, the numbers are somewhat less encouraging: voter registration in 2000 was 57.3 percent for Hispanics and 52.4 percent for Asian Pacific Islanders, while voting in the 2000 presidential race was reported as 27.5 percent among Hispanics and 25.4 percent among Asian Pacific Islanders.

Elected officials from these varying racial and ethnic groups have also increased dramatically. African Americans, with 1,469 elected representatives at all levels of government in 1970 (when such data was first reported by the Joint Center for Political and Economic Studies), had reached 8,936 representatives by 1999. The census, which reported Latinos had 3,147 elected officials in 1985, counted 4,432 by 2001 (Bositis 2000; Lien, Conway, and Wong 2004; National Association of Latino Elected Officials Educational Fund 2002). Indeed, while focused on voting rights and elections, the act has also had significant spillover effects on the nonelectoral participation of African Americans, Latinos, and Asian Americans. This includes participation in appointive government offices and in important nongovernmental organizations, such as state and federal legal and public-interest groups that monitor the act's effects. Perhaps most notably, the election of racial and ethnic minorities to public office has opened the doors to expanded representation within the executive and judicial branches—at all levels of government (Wasby 1995; Rich 2004; Ricci 1993; Pinderhughes 1995).

Although voting rights legislation was originally targeted at racial discrimination in southern states, its reach has dramatically expanded since 1965. The act now aims to encourage the political participation not just of African Americans, but also of American citizens who either are members of language minorities or have physical disabilities. This huge expansion, in turn, has involved a substantial growth in federal observation of electoral activities. Originally the act covered just seven states, all in the South—Alabama, Arizona, Georgia, Louisiana, Mississippi, South Carolina, Virginia—and portions of North Carolina. The language minority provisions, however, added all of Alaska, Arizona, and Texas, as well as portions of California, Florida, New York, South Dakota, and Michigan to the list (U.S. Department of Justice 2004).

Perhaps the most important way in which the Voting Rights Act of 1965 has fed back into American politics is through its effect on electoral outcomes themselves. The act fundamentally reshaped regional and national partisan competition. Reacting to the Democratic Party's support for civil and voting rights at the national level, many southern white Democrats shifted their partisan identification toward the GOP, making the South a two-party region for the first time and establishing the region as a powerful base for the national Republican Party.

But the feedback effects of the act extend beyond its consequences for election outcomes. The Voting Rights Act has also prompted frequent, and frequently fierce, new struggles to shape those outcomes through the redefinition of district boundaries and electoral rules. Indeed, the debates over the design of electoral systems and legislative districts prompted by the act represent a remarkable example of high-level democratic theory meeting real-world political struggles. These debates led, in particular, to the creation of majority-minority districts, in which a majority of voters are members of minority groups. Responding to the concern that expanded voting rights did not lead to the election of minority candidates, the Voting Rights Act Extension of 1982 allowed the creation of majority-minority districts under certain conditions. Partly as a result, the U.S. census count became an increasingly important event on the voting rights agenda, triggering as it did a new round of state, local, and federal redistricting. As the size of the black and Latino populations increased, voting rights litigators and groups seized the opportunity to draw majority-minority districts after the census in 1990 and then again in 2000 (see Grofman 1998; Willingham 2002).

The debate over majority-minority districts showcases the important ways in which the Voting Rights Act prompted new deliberation about appropriate electoral forms for enhancing electoral participation and control. Scholars and activists debated and discussed the logic of a variety of possible reforms, including cumulative voting and proportional representation (Pinderhughes 1987).[16] They did not always agree, of course, about which paths of reform were most feasible—or even desirable. (Some researchers have subsequently noted, for example, that majority-minority districts have packed black voters, who vote predominantly for the Democratic Party, into fewer districts, thereby helping elect Republicans elsewhere (Lublin 1997; Swain, Borrelli, and Reed 1998; Swain 1993)). In recent years, the debate over electoral reform appears to have stalled after decades of litigation, as the Supreme Court has sharply limited the conditions under which majority-minority districts can be drawn for black voters. However, redistricting based on partisan considerations, according to several recent decisions—including the recent ruling in Vieth v. Jubelirer, the Pennsylvania redistricting case—remains acceptable.

Today, controversies continue to swirl around the act—for example, on issues related to gerrymandering (including both its partisan and racial forms) and the accurate counting of racial and ethnic minorities in the U.S. census. Although the Supreme Court affirmed the constitutionality of the original Voting Rights Act in 1965, the current bench has offered declining support for strategies to strengthen and expand protections for the voting rights of racial and ethnic minorities (Pinderhughes 1997). The controversy over the 2000 presidential election in Florida and the Supreme Court's ruling in Bush v. Gore thrust voting rights back into the headlines.

It also prompted a new wave of voting rights legislation. The Help America Vote Act of 2002, for example, created an Election Assistance Commission, provided funds to reform and to improve state election procedures, and to set new minimum standards for the conduct of elections. With the special powers of the Voting Rights Act due to expire in 2007, disagreements over its future—and over its feedback effects on the participation of racial and ethnic groups—are all but certain.

In sum, the Voting Rights Act of 1965 had profound policy feedback effects. It shaped civic affiliations and capacities, reframed issues, altered the political agenda, and restructured political participation—both among minority citizens and among whites.

Policy Feedback and Postwar American Democracy

In the interaction between equality and engagement in postwar America, public policy was crucial and, for the most part, conducive to expanded participation. In the mid-twentieth century, Americans exhibited higher levels of civic activity than they have more recently. They held more interest in public affairs and greater confidence in government. They also participated more frequently in a wide range of political activities, including voting, working for political parties or on campaigns, contacting elected officials, or serving on a local committee (Putnam 2000; Rosenstone and Hansen 1993; Teixeira 1992; Wattenberg 2002).

It is significant that the period that has been called the "golden age of civic engagement" was also—in socioeconomic terms—the most egalitarian of the twentieth century (Putnam 2000). One analysis shows that 1950 marked the moment of greatest equality among American workers in the twentieth century. Inequality remained at a historic low point for the next two decades until it began to ascend dramatically from the mid-1970s to the present. Educational level proved much less of a predictor of earnings in the mid-century than it is currently. The sharp increase in high-school educated individuals entering the labor market after the war depressed the wages of white-collar jobs somewhat. Meanwhile, less-skilled workers saw increases in their standard of living (Goldin 1998; Goldin and Katz 1999; Goldin and Margot 1992).

This relatively high degree of income equality resulted not only from technological advances and shifts in the economy, but also, as we have seen, from increasingly well-established regulatory and redistributive policies. Various programs enacted during the New Deal era were strengthened and broadened, and thus began to have important consequences for large portions of the populace. The real value of the minimum wage standard, established under Fair Labor Standards Act of 1938, was raised considerably throughout the 1950s and 1960s, enhancing the wages of low-wage workers. Organized labor, emboldened by the National Labor Relations Act of 1935, grew to its highest levels, comprising over 20 percent of the workforce from the early 1940s through the 1970s. Social Security coverage grew rapidly during the 1950s and 1960s after Congress extended it to more sectors of the workforce and to the disabled, and the benefits value grew steadily. The G.I. Bill's educational provisions, extended in generous form to World War II and Korean War veterans, helped elevate educational levels among males. In addition, greater equality was facilitated by the postwar demand for construction workers, aided largely by the housing provisions of the G.I. Bill, FHA loans, and other government programs (Bound and Turner 2002a; Goldin and Margot 1992; Jackson 1985; Mettler 1998; Mettler and Milstein 2003).

Should such policies also be credited with helping to stimulate the high levels of political involvement among citizens in the mid-twentieth century? Given our discussion of resource and interpretive policy feedback effects, and our discussion of specific programs, it is reasonable to assume this to be the case. The resources offered through public policies and programs, especially to less advantaged members of the polity who are most lacking in the factors that lead to participation, are likely to have been highly instrumental in enhancing civic skills and networks, prompting citizens to be more interested in politics, and stimulating political parties and interest groups to mobilize such individuals politically. In addition, to the extent that these programs featured universalistic and visible policy designs, they are likely to have enhanced individuals' civic status, promoted unity within the polity, and prompted beneficiaries to have a greater sense of political efficacy and inclination to participate politically.

In short, the universal design and redistributive effects of public policies of the mid-twentieth century may have been critical in fostering the vibrant civic and political life that flourished in the United States at that time. We next argue that there is reason to believe that this positive role has been less in evidence in recent decades.

Inequality, Public Policy, and American Democracy

In *The New American Voter*, Warren E. Miller and J. Merrill Shanks (1996) observe that while voting rates have declined generally over recent decades, the change can be largely accounted for by compositional changes in the electorate over time. Interestingly, those who came of age during the Great Depression and World War II—the very Americans who benefited from the kinds of programs discussed above—have participated at high levels throughout their lives, continuing to do so even recently.

Those who grew up during the 1950s and 1960s, in contrast, have voted at considerably lower levels. Most strikingly, less advantaged members of the younger cohorts vote at considerably lower levels than the older cohort groups with the same level of education. Of members of the post–New Deal generation who have less than a high school diploma, turnout rates are drastically below those of the comparably educated members of the older generation, even at the same points in their life cycle (Miller and Shanks 1996; Putnam 2000, chaps. 2, 14). Other scholarship confirms that the tilt toward participatory inequality today extends beyond voting to numerous other areas of civic and political activity (Schlozman, Verba, and Brady 1995; Wuthnow 2002).

Five trends in policy development that we have explored in previous sections of this chapter help to explain the transformation in civic engagement. First, direct spending programs targeted primarily toward elderly Americans have remained relatively vibrant. Social Security benefit rates for retired workers and survivors held largely constant, owing to the cost-of-living adjustments mandated in 1972, and coverage rates persisted. Both Medicare and Medicaid have generally grown in coverage and value over the same period of time, though not enough to offset fully declines in private protections or increases in medical costs. Similarly, veterans' disability compensation benefits, under which the majority of beneficiaries have been members of the New Deal generation, have also increased in value over the period.

Scholars have marveled at the persistently high rates of participation among the "civic generation" (Miller and Shanks 1996; Putnam 2000). Some of the participation of these older Americans can be explained by the resources they gained from generous programs in the mid-century, which reaped long-term effects by fostering subsequent development of civic skills, networks, and resources (Mettler and Welch 2004). In addition, as earlier sections argued, the civic mobilization of older Americans has been sustained by Social Security, Medicare, and veterans' compensation (Campbell 2003). The relatively generous and dependable nature of those benefits boosts their civic capacity and yields positive interpretive effects as well. The impact of government programs on these Americans is especially strong among less advantaged seniors, the same socioeconomic strata within which younger citizens have simultaneously become so disengaged politically.

A second trend in policy development since the 1970s is that several forms of social provision and economic regulation targeting less advantaged nonelderly Americans have been subject to retrenchment. Unionization rates began to plummet in the early 1980s, falling from 23 percent of the labor force in 1980 to 13.5 percent in 2003 as government support withered. In constant 2002 dollars, the value of the minimum wage fell from $8.28 per hour in 1968 to $5.15 in 2003. The real value of unemployment insurance benefits descended from high levels of $240 or more for weekly average benefits in the early 1970s to around $220 throughout most of the 1990s. Average individual benefits for Food Stamps, also in real terms, declined from $144 per month in 1981 to $91 in 2000. Finally, individual benefits under Aid to Families with Dependent Children lost one-third of their value between 1970 and the mid-1990s (Mettler and Milstein 2003). At that time, in 1996, the states regained increased authority over key features of the program as part of welfare reform, and beneficiaries were also made subject to strict work requirements and time limits.

Third, compared with other rich democracies, U.S. public policy has changed relatively little to reflect the changing character of the risks faced by American families as the job market and family relations have changed (Hacker 2004). Not only has the American tax and social welfare framework not followed the lead of other national frameworks in moderating the rise in private income inequality, there has also been a sharp decline in the generosity of antipoverty programs (with the notable exception of the EITC) and a massive fall in the scope and risk-spreading capacity of private workplace benefits among low-wage workers.

Fourth, the period has witnessed the persistence of the "hidden welfare state" of tax expenditures and the increasing reliance of higher-income Americans on private forms of social provision that are regulated by public policy (Hacker 2002; Howard 1997). Most of these benefits—again, with the exception of the Earned Income Tax Credit—tend to further advantage already advantaged citizens economically (Howard 1993). In terms of political effects, the results are less clear. Certainly the programs bestow important resource effects among users, perhaps helping to explain why participation among post–New Deal generations today is strongly tilted toward more advantaged citizens (Schlozman, Verba, and Brady 1995). On the other hand, the less visible nature of such programs may undermine a wide array of interpretive effects. In fact, the obscurity of the EITC means that the program is underused by the low-income working population it targets, because so many are unaware of it. Presumably the hidden nature of such programs also thwarts broad-based efforts at citizen mobilization (Hacker 2002). In addition, citizens are unlikely to develop positive attitudes toward the political process and a stronger sense of political efficacy on the basis of such programs because the government's role is so camouflaged and the fact that they are social benefits is less clear to many beneficiaries.

Finally, the nature of civic participation has changed over the past three decades in ways that likely accentuate the trends just described. While these changes defy simple assessment, one prominent strand within them has been a shift from civic-mobilization strategies premised on widely distributed and tightly knit local groups with active memberships toward national civic organizations reliant on direct mail, media appeals, foundation grants, and dues-paying members (Skocpol 2003). Associational reliance on direct mail, media appeals, and mailing lists is especially attractive for highly educated citizens, and there is some evidence that mailing-list organizations are increasingly targeting well-to-do potential contributors. Throughout much of U.S history, associations claiming to speak for the public or broad categories of citizens typically had to try to involve large numbers of people in their efforts. Today, however, civic elites can become influential by looking "upwards"—to wealthy donors and foundations—and by centering their activities in national headquarters close to the media and federal government. If this is indeed the direction of civic evolution, it would represent a major shift in the associational universe—one that is likely to shape profoundly the prospects for political mobilization around issues that intersect with America's widening inequality gap.

Considering the cumulative effect of these developments, it appears that the positive role of government has diminished in the lives of less advantaged, nonelderly Americans. The voices of older Americans continue to be well heard in the political process, at least in part because of the ways in which policies have bestowed positive resource and interpretive effects on them throughout their lifetimes and continue to do so today. Among younger generations, however, major declines in participation are manifest among less advantaged citizens, who have suffered disproportionately not only from economic transformations but also from the simultaneous departure of government assistance in their lives. The decline in participation among these individuals may have much to do with their perception that government is not responsive to or representative of people like them. Meanwhile, the enduring high levels of participation of advantaged citizens may emanate in part from the fact that they continue to derive important resources from government. Ironically, however, the policies that most benefit them feature government in a hidden role, such that they are unlikely to credit government with the benefits they receive.

A large and promising research agenda looms for political scientists interested in better informing policymakers and the public about the consequences of public policy for the well-being of American democracy. We have tried to give a sense of the scope of this agenda, while demonstrating that substantial research exists. The conclusions that emerge from this review defy simple summary, as befits the complexity of the subject. Yet two must be emphasized in closing. First, public policy is powerfully implicated in American economic, racial, and gender inequality. Although policy has made a great dent in each of these intertwined inequalities over the past half century, the last two to three decades have seen an erosion of its capacity to promote equal opportunity.[17] Second, the effects of public policies on the political standing and capacity of citizens is at least as profound as the impact of public policies on social conditions and relationships. Public policy shapes citizenship just as citizenship shapes public policy, and will continue to shape it in the future.

In addition to the comments of our colleagues on the Task Force that helped guide our work, we wish to thank John DiIulio, Faye Williams, and Jared Bernstein, who provided extensive and extremely helpful comments on an earlier draft of this memo; Vincent Mahler, Timothy Smeeding, and David Jesuit, who offered extremely helpful data on redistribution from the Luxembourg Income Study; Joe Soss, who contributed greatly to the ideas presented in the section on policy feedback; Nigar Nargis, who helped develop the index of income volatility; Andrew Milstein, who helped compile the data presented about changes in the value and coverage of various policies over time; David Mayhew, who offered extensive and thoughtful comments on a previous draft; Peter Orzag, who helped with the discussion of the causes of rising inequality in the United States; and Nelson Gerew, Rachel Goodman, Pearline Kyi, Joanne Lim, Natalie Wigg, and, especially, Alan Schoenfeld, who provided valuable research assistance.

NOTES

1. For additional information, see http://www.lisproject.org.
2. Incorporating the elderly into statistics on redistribution poses the problem that in countries with very high replacement rates, the elderly make little or no provision for old age, inflating the redistributive effect of taxes and transfers. Excluding the elderly, however, seems equally likely to distort measures of redistribution, since intergenerational transfers are a crucial component of all welfare states' activities.
3. For summaries of the relevant scholarship, see Bradley, Huber, and Stephens (forthcoming); Kenworthy (1999).
4. Wealth is calculated by adding together the current value of all assets a household owns—such as bank accounts, stocks and bonds, life insurance savings, mutual funds, houses and unincorporated businesses, cars and major appliances, and the value of pension rights—and then subtracting from that total mortgage balances and other outstanding debt.
5. Because most of these are cross-national in focus, they are limited by the

availability of panel data comparable to the PSID, the gold standard in the field. Since only two other long-term panel studies of comparable scope and consistency exist (the German and Dutch Socioeconomic Panel surveys), and because neither is available before 1984, researchers interested in longer-term patterns have essentially found themselves forced to focus their cross-national analyses on the period between the mid-1980s and mid-1990s—all years that postdate the major shocks to the welfare state and economy of the 1970s and early 1980s.

6. The next few paragraphs draw on Esping-Andersen (1999) and Skocpol (2000).

7. These figures take the bill as written, ignoring future changes in the Alternative Minimum Tax, which would raise the estimate of upper-income benefits.

8. See http://www.rand.org/publications/CAE/CAE100/ (accessed April 21, 2005).

9. See http://www.gseis.ucla.edu/heri/darcu_pr.html (accessed April 21, 2005). Perhaps these outcomes, too, relate to the mounting financial challenges faced by students and the greater necessity for many to be employed during their college years.

10. Evidence linking economic inequality to poor health status is not universally accepted. The main counterargument is that persistent poverty or racial discrimination, rather than inequality, is responsible for the United States' comparatively poor health outcomes (Mellor and Milyo 2001; Jencks 2002; Burtless and Jencks 2003; House 2001). Although the poorest Americans do bear a disproportionately high burden of illness and premature mortality compared to the rest of society, the unequal distribution of income and wealth—as distinct from the low absolute levels of each—appears to exert an independent, harmful effect on the health of Americans (Kawachi 2004; Morone and Jacobs 2004).

11. This finding contradicts previous analyses that were based largely on anecdotal evidence, as in Cohen (2003). It comes from primary sources, including U.S. Congress, Committee on Veterans' Affairs, "Readjustment Benefits: General Survey and Appraisal: A Report on Veterans' Benefits in the United States by the President's Commission on Veterans' Pensions," Staff Report No. IX, Part A (Washington: U.S. Government Printing Office, 1956, 72); U.S., Veterans Administration, "Benefits and Services Received by World War II Veterans under the Major Veterans Administration Programs," pp. 13, 20, Records of the Office of Management and Budget (RG 51), ser. 39.20a, box 9, National Archives. See also Michael K. Brown, *Race, Money, and the American Welfare State* (1999, 189–190 and table 11). In contrast to the educational and training provisions, the low interest mortgage program did not prove equally accessible to African Americans, given that it was administered largely through local banks adhering to red-lining procedures or other forms of discrimination (Bound and Turner 2002b).

12. See data at http://research.aarp.org/econ/ib31_sswomen.pdf.

13. The evidence on differential support between private plans and traditional Medicare is from work in progress by Mark Schlesinger, Yale University.

14. Davidson and Grofman's (1994) work surveys these changes throughout the south; Parker (1991) discusses the program of legislation the Mississippi legislature created to limit the power of its large black population:. The phrase "black electoral success" is drawn from Guinier's (1994) analysis of Voting Rights conflicts.

15. National Urban League (2004, 32–4) presents an "Equality Index" composed of several subindices: economics, health, education, social justice, and civic engagement. Civic engagement, composed of several measures, including voting in the last election, was the only subindex in which African American political status exceeded whites (at 1.08).

16. Illinois used cumulative voting to elect state representatives for more than a century.

17. Subsequent inquiries, for example, must go beyond social policy—our main concern in preceding sections. For instance, incarceration rates in the United States have quadrupled since 1975, over the course of an era featuring a vigorous anticrime policy agenda and strict sentencing laws. As a result, 4.7 million individuals are currently prohibited from voting because they are felons, or, in some states, ex-felons. Christopher Uggen and Jeff Manza (2001) found that such disenfranchisement likely altered the outcomes of several gubernatorial and U.S. Senate elections and at least one presidential election. Campaign finance laws and tax rules governing nonprofit organizations and foundations are two others areas of policy that are not explored in this memorandum but which are likely to shape the constellation of political forces surrounding public policymaking in the United States.

REFERENCES

Aaron, Henry J., Alan S. Blinder, Alicia H. Nunnell, and Peter R. Orszag. 2001. Perspectives on the Draft Interim Report of the President's Commission to Strengthen Social Security. Washington, D.C.: Center on Budget and Policy Priorities and The Century Foundation.

Adema, Willem. 1999. "Net Social Expenditure." *Labour Market and Social Policy-Occasional Papers No. 39* (August): 30. Paris: OECD.

Anderson, Martin. 1964. *The Federal Bulldozer: A Critical Analysis of Urban Renewal, 1949–62.* Cambridge, Mass.: MIT Press.

Atkinson, Tony, Andrew Brandolini, and Timothy Smeeding. 2002. "Producing Time Series Data for Income Distribution: Sources, Methods and Techniques." Luxembourg Income Study Working Paper 295. Syracuse, N.Y.: Maxwell School of Citizenship and Public Affairs, Syracuse University.

Behrman, Jere, Robert Pollack, and Paul Taubman. 1989. "Family Resources, Family Size, and Access to Financing for College Education." *Journal of Political Economy* 97(2): 398–419.

Blau, Francine D., and Lawrence M. Kahn. 2000. "Gender Differences in Pay." NBER Working Paper 7732. Cambridge, Mass.: National Bureau of Economic Research.

Borjas, George J. 1990. *Friends or Strangers: The Impact of Immigrants on the U.S. Economy.* New York: Basic Books.

———. 1995. "Ethnicity, Neighborhoods, and Human Capital Externalities." *American Economic Review* 85(3): 365–90.

Bositis, David A. 2000. *Black Elected Officials: A Statistical Summary 1999.* Washington, D.C.: Joint Center for Political and Economic Studies.

Bound, John, and Sarah Turner. 2002a. "Going to War and Going to College: Did the G.I. Bill Increase Educational Attainment?" *Journal of Labor Economics* 20(4): 784–815.

———. 2002b. "Closing the Gap or Widening the Divide: The Effects of the G.I. Bill and World War II on the Educational Outcomes of Black Americans." NBER Working Paper W9044. Cambridge, Mass.: National Bureau of Economic Research. Available at: www.nber.org/papers/w9044 (accessed April 19, 2005).

Bradbury, Bruce, Stephen P. Jenkins, and John Micklewright, eds. 2001. *The Dynamics of Child Poverty in Industrialized Countries.* Cambridge: Cambridge University Press.

Bradley, David, Evelyne Huber, and John D. Stephens. Forthcoming. "Distribution and Redistribution in Post-Industrial Democracies." *World Politics.*

Brown, Michael K. 1999. *Race, Money, and the American Welfare State.* Ithaca, N.Y.: Cornell University Press.

Burtless, Gary. 2003. "Has Widening Inequality Promoted or Retarded US Growth?" *Canadian Public Policy - Analyse de Politiques* 29(January, supp.): S185–S201.

Burtless, Gary, and Christopher Jencks. 2003. "American Inequality and Its Consequence." Luxembourg Income Study Working Paper 339. Syracuse, N.Y.: Maxwell School of Citizenship and Public Affairs, Syracuse University.

Campbell, Andrea Louise. 2003. *How Policies Make Citizens: Senior Political Activism and the American Welfare State.* Princeton, N.J.: Princeton University Press.

Card, David. 1990. "The Impact of the Mariel Boatlift on the Miami Labor Market." *Industrial and Labor Relations Review* 43(2): 245–57.

Castles, Francis G., and Deborah Mitchell. 1993. "Worlds of Welfare and Families of Nations." In *Families of Nations: Patterns of Public Policy in Western Democracies,* edited by Francis G. Castles. Sydney: Dartmouth.

Center on Budget and Policy Priorities. 1998. "Strengths of the Safety Net: How the EITC, Social Security and Other Government Programs Affect Poverty." Washington, D.C.: Center on Budget and Policy Priorities.

Citizens for Tax Justice. 2002. "Year-by-Year Analysis of the Bush Tax Cuts Growing Tilt to the Very Rich." Washington, D.C.: Citizens for Tax Justice.

Cohen, Jere, Rebecca L. Warner, and David R. Segal. 1995. "Military Service and Educational Attainment in the All-Volunteer Force." *Social Science Quarterly* 76(1): 88–104.

Cohen, Lizabeth. 2003. *A Consumer's Republic.* New York: Alfred A. Knopf.

Congressional Budget Office. 2001. "Effective Federal Tax Rates, 1979–1997." Washington: U.S. Government Printing Office.

Coronado, Julia Lynn, Don Fullerton, and Thomas Glass. 2000. "The Progressivity of Social Security." NBER Working Paper 7520. Cambridge, Mass.: National Bureau of Economic Research.

Cox, W. Michael, and Richard Alm. 1999. *Myths of Rich and Poor: Why We're Better Off Than We Think.* New York: Basic Books.

Davidson, Chandler and Bernard Grofman, eds. 1994. *Quiet Revolution in the South: The Impact of the Voting Rights Act, 1965–1990.* Princeton, N.J.: Princeton University Press.

DiPrete, Thomas A., and Patricia A. McManus. 2000. "Family Change, Employment Transitions, and the Welfare State: Household Income Dynamics in the United States and Germany." *American Sociological Review* 65(3): 343–70.

Donahue, John J., and James Heckman. 1990. "Continuous Versus Episodic Change: The Impact of Civil Rights Policy on the Economic Status of Blacks." *Journal of Economic Literature* 29(4): 1603–43.

Dreier, Peter, John Mollenkopf, and Todd Swanstrom. 2001. *Place Matters: Metropolitics for the Twenty-First Century.* Lawrence: Kansas University Press.

Duncombe, William, and John Yinger. 1998. "Financing Higher Standards in Public Education: The Importance of Accounting for Educational Costs." Center for Policy Research Briefs Working Paper 10. Syracuse, N.Y.: Syracuse University, Maxwell School of Citizenship and Public Affairs. Available at: http://www-cpr.maxwell.syr.edu/pbriefs/pb10.pdf (accessed April 21, 2005).

Easterbrook, Gregg. 2003. *The Progress Paradox: How Life Gets Better While People Feel Worse.* New York: Random House.

Ellwood, David T., and Thomas Kane. 1999. "Who is Getting a College Education? Family Background and the Growing Gaps in Enrollment." In *Securing the Future,* edited by Sheldon Danziger and Jane Waldfogel. New York: Russell Sage Foundation.

Employee Benefit Research Institute (EBRI). 2004. "Tax Expenditures and Employee Benefits: An Update from the FY2005 Budget." Washington, D.C.: Employee Benefit Research Institute.

Esping-Andersen, Gøsta. 1990. *The Three Worlds of Welfare Capitalism.* Princeton, N.J.: Princeton University Press.

———. 1999. *Social Foundations of Postindustrial Economies.* New York: Oxford University Press.

Featherman, David L., and Robert M. Hauser. 1978. *Opportunity and Change*. New York: Academic Press.

Fitzgerald, John, and Tim Maloney. 1990. "The Impact of Federal Income Taxes and Cash Transfers on the Distribution of Lifetime Household Income, 1969–1981." *Public Finance Quarterly* 18(2): 182–97.

Ford, Lynne E. 2002. *Women and Politics: The Pursuit of Equity*. Boston: Houghton-Mifflin.

Frankenberg, Erica, Chungmei Lee, and Gary Orfield. 2002. "A Multiracial Society with Segregated Schools: Are We Losing the Dream?" Cambridge, Mass.: Harvard Civil Rights Project.

Gale, William G., Peter R. Orszag, and Isaac Shapiro. 2004. "Distributional Effects of the 2001 and 2003 Tax Cuts and Their Financing." Washington, D.C.: Tax Policy Center. Available at: http://www.taxpolicycenter.org/publications/template.cfm?PubID=8888 (accessed April 19, 2005).

General Accounting Office. 2000. *Unemployment Insurance: Role as Safety Net for Low Wage Workers is Limited*. Washington: U.S. Government Printing Office.

Gilens, Martin. 1999. *Why Americans Hate Welfare: Race, Media, and the Politics of Antipoverty Policy*. Chicago: University of Chicago Press.

Gladieux, Lawrence E., Bart Astor, and Watson Scott Swail. 1998. *Memory, Reason, Imagination: A Quarter Century of Pell Grants*. New York: College Entrance Examination Board.

Goldin, Claudia. 1998. "America's Graduation from High School: The Evolution and Spread of Secondary Schooling in the Twentieth Century." *Journal of Economic History* 58(2): 345–74.

Goldin, Claudia, and Lawrence Katz. 1999. "The Returns to Skill in the United States Across the Twentieth Century." NBER Working Paper 7126 (May). Cambridge, Mass.: National Bureau of Economic Research. Published as: "Egalitarianism and the Returns to Education During the Great Transformation of American Education." *Journal of Political Economy* 107(6): S65–S94.

Goldin, Claudia, and Robert Margot. 1992. "The Great Compression: The Wage Structure in the United States at Mid-Century." *Quarterly Journal of Economics* CVII(February): 1–34.

Goodin, Robert E., Bruce Headey, Ruud Muffels, and Henk-Jan Dirven. 2000. *The Real Worlds of Welfare Capitalism*. Cambridge: Press Syndicate of the Cambridge University Press.

Goodin, Robert E., Julian LeGrand, eds. 1987. *Not Only the Poor*. London: Allen & Unwin.

Gornick, Marian E., Paul W. Eggers, Thomas W. Reilly, Renee M. Mentnech, Leslye K. Fitterman, Lawrence E. Kucken, and Bruce C. Vladeck. 1996. "Effects of Race and Income on Mortality and Use of Services among Medicare Beneficiaries." *New England Journal of Medicine* 335(11): 791–99.

Gottschalk, Peter. 1997. "Inequality, Income Growth, and Mobility: The Basic Facts." *The Journal of Economic Perspectives* 11(2): 21–40.

Greenstein, Robert, Richard Kogan, and Joel Friedman. 2003. "New Tax Cut Law Uses Gimmicks to Mask Costs: Ultimate Price Tag Likely to be $800 Billion to $1 Trillion." Washington, D.C.: Center on Budget and Policy Priorities.

Grofman, Bernard, ed. 1998. *Race and Redistricting in the 1990s.* New York: Agathon Press.

Guinier, Lani. 1994. *The Tyranny of the Majority: Fundamental Fairness in Representative Democracy.* New York: The Free Press.

Gustman, Alan, and Thomas Steinmeier. 2000. "How Effective is Redistribution under the Social Security Benefit Formula." Paper presented at Second Annual Joint Conference of the Retirement Research Consortium. Washington, D.C. (May 17–18).

Hacker, Jacob S. 1998. "The Historical Logic of National Health Insurance: Structure and Sequence in the Development of British, Canadian, and U.S. Medical Policy." *Studies in American Political Development* 12(1): 57, 130.

———. 2002. *The Divided Welfare State: The Battle over Public and Private Social Benefits in the United States.* New York: Cambridge University Press.

———. 2004. "Privatizing Risk Without Privatizing the Welfare State: The Hidden Politics of Social Policy Retrenchment in the United States." *American Political Science Review* 98(2): 243–60.

Heckman, James J., and Brook S. Payner. 1989. "Determining the Impact of Federal Antidiscrimination Policy on the Economic Status of Blacks: A Study of South Carolina." *American Economic Review* 79(1): 138–77.

Heclo, Hugh. 1974. *Modern Social Politics in Britain and Sweden: From Relief to Income Maintenance.* New Haven, Conn.: Yale University Press.

Henderson, Lenneal J., Jr. 1995. "Budgets, Taxes and Politics: Options for African American Politics." In *Blacks and the American Political System,* edited by Huey L. Perry and Wayne Parent. Gainesville, Fla.: University Press of Florida.

Hochschild, Jennifer L. 1995. *Facing Up to the American Dream: Race, Class, and the Soul of the Nation.* Princeton, N.J.: Princeton University Press.

Hochschild, Jennifer L., and Nathan Scovronick. 2003. *The American Dream and the Public Schools.* Oxford: Oxford University Press.

Holzer, C., B. Shea, J. Swanson, P. Leaf, J. Myers, L. George, M. Weissman, and P. Bednarski. 1986. "The Increased Risk for Specific Psychiatric Disorders Among Persons of Low Socioeconomic Status." *American Journal of Social Psychiatry* 6: 259–71.

House, James. 2001. "Relating Social Inequalities in Health and Income." *Journal of Health Politics, Policy and Law* 26(3): 523–32.

Howard, Christopher. 1993. "The Hidden Side of the American Welfare State." *Political Science Quarterly* 108(3): 403–36.

———. 1997. *The Hidden Welfare State: Tax Expenditures and Social Policy in the United States, Princeton Studies in American Politics.* Princeton, N.J.: Princeton University Press.

Huber, Evelyne, John D. Stephens, David Bradley, Stephanie Moller, and Francois Nielsen. 2001. *The Welfare State and Gender Equality.* Syracuse, N.Y.: Maxwell School of Citizenship and Public Affairs.

Iceland, John, Daniel H. Weinberg, and Erika Steinmetz. 2002. "Racial and Ethnic Residential Segregation in the United States: 1980–2000." Paper read at Annual Meeting of the Population Association of America. Atlanta (May 9–11).

Ingram, Helen, and Anne Schneider. 1993. "Constructing Citizenship: The Subtle Messages of Policy Design." In *Public Policy for Democracy,* edited by Helen Ingram and. Steven Rathgeb Smith. Washington, D.C.: Brookings Institution.

Irvine, Ian, and Kuan Xu. 2002. "Crime, Punishment and the Measurement of Poverty in the United States, 1979–1997." LIS Working Paper 333. Syracuse, N.Y.: Maxwell School of Citizenship and Public Affairs, Syracuse University.

Jackson, Kenneth T. 1985. *Crabgrass Frontier: The Suburbanization of the United States.* New York: Oxford University Press.

Jamieson, Amie, Hyon B. Shin, and Jennifer Day. 2002. "Voting and Registration in the Election of 2000." *Current Population Reports,* series P20, no. 542. Washington: U.S. Government Printing Office for U.S. Census Bureau.

Jencks, Christopher. 1972. *Inequality: A Reassessment of the Effect of Family and Schooling in America.* New York: Basic Books.

———. 2002. "Does Inequality Matter?" *Daedalus* 131(1): 49–65.

Kawachi, Ichiro. 2004. "Why The USA is not Number 1 in Health." In *Healthy, Wealthy, and Fair: Health Care and the Good Society,* edited by James A. Morone and Lawrence R. Jacobs. New York: Oxford University Press.

Kelly, Rita Mae. 1991. *The Gendered Economy.* Newbury Park, Calif.: Sage Publications.

Kenworthy, Lane. 1999. "Do Social-Welfare Politics Reduce Poverty?: A Cross-National Assessment." *Social Forces* 77(3): 1119–39.

King, Jacqueline E. 2000. *2000 Status Report on the Pell Grant Program.* Washington, D.C.: American Council on Education.

Klinkner, Philip A., and Rogers M. Smith. 1999. *The Unsteady March: The Rise and Decline of Racial Equality in America.* Chicago: University of Chicago Press.

Kronick, Richard, and Joy DeBeyer. 1999. *Medicare HMOs: Making them Work for the Chronically Ill.* Chicago: Health Administration Press.

Lenz, Gabriel, and the Princeton University Working Group. 2003. "The Policy Related Causes and Consequences of Income Inequality." New York: The Russell Sage Foundation. Available at: http://www.russellsage.org/programs/proj reviews/si/revlenz01.pdf.

Levy, Denise Urias, and Sonya Michel. 2002. "More Can Be Less: Child Care and

Welfare Reform in the United States." In *Child Care Policy at the Crossroads: Gender and Welfare State Restructuring*, edited by Sonya Michel and Rianne Mahon. New York: Routledge.

Levy, Jonah. 1999. "Vice into Virtue? Progressive Politics and Welfare Reform in Continental Europe." *Politics and Society* 27(2): 239–73.

Lieberman, Robert. 1998. *Shifting the Color Line*. Cambridge, Mass.: Harvard University Press.

Lien, Pei-Te, M. Margaret Conway, and Janelle Wong. 2004. *The Politics of Asian Americans*. New York: Routledge.

Lindblom, Charles E. 1959. "The Science of 'Muddling Through.'" *Public Administration Review* 19(2): 79–88.

Lublin, David. 1997. *The Paradox of Representation*. Princeton, N.J.: Princeton University Press.

Lynch, Julia. 2001. "The Age Orientation of Social Policy Regimes in OECD Countries." *Journal of Social Policy* 30(3): 411–36.

Massey, Douglas S., and Nancy A. Denton. 1993. *American Apartheid*. Cambridge, Mass.: Harvard University Press.

Mayer, Susan. 2001. "How Did the Increase in Economic Inequality Affect Educational Attainment?" *American Journal of Sociology* 107(1): 1–32.

Mellor, Jennifer M., and Jeffrey Milyo. 2001. "Reexamining the Evidence of an Ecological Association Between Income Inequality and Health." *Journal of Health Politics, Policy and Law* 26(3): 487–522.

Mettler, Suzanne B. 1998. *Dividing Citizens: Gender and Federalism in New Deal Public Policy*. Ithaca, N.Y.: Cornell University Press.

———. 2002. "Bringing the State Back into Civic Engagement: Policy Feedback Effects of the G.I. Bill for World War II Veterans." *American Political Science Review* 96(2): 351–65.

———. 2005. *Soldiers to Citizens: The G.I. Bill and the Making of the Greatest Generation.*. New York: Oxford University Press.

———. Forthcoming. "'The Only Good Thing was the G.I. Bill': Policy Feedback Effects on African American Veterans' Political Participation." *Studies in American Political Development*.

Mettler, Suzanne, and Andrew Milstein. 2003. "'A Sense of the State': Tracking the Role of the American Administrative State in Citizens' Lives Over Time." Paper read at Annual Meeting of the Midwestern Political Science Association. Chicago (April 3–6).

Mettler, Suzanne, and Joe Soss. 2004. "The Consequences of Public Policy for Democratic Citizenship: Bridging Policy Studies and Mass Politics." *Perspectives on Politics* 2(1): 55–73.

Mettler, Suzanne, and Eric Welch. 2004. "Civic Generation: Policy Feedback Effects of the G.I. Bill on Political Involvement over the Life Course." *British Journal of Political Science* 34(July): 497–518.

Miller, Herman P. 1960. *Income Distribution in the United States. A 1960 Census Monograph*. Washington: U.S. Government Printing Office.

Miller, Warren E., and J. Merrill Shanks. 1996. *The New American Voter*. Cambridge, Mass.: Harvard University Press.

Mishel, Larry, Jared Bernstein, and Heather Boushey. 2003. *The State of Working America, 2002–2003*. Ithaca, N.Y.: Cornell University Press.

Misra, Dawn. 2001. *Women's Health Data Book*. 3rd ed. Washington, D.C.: Jacobs Institute of Women's Health and the Henry J. Kaiser Family Foundation.

Moffitt, Robert, and Peter Gottschalk. 2002. "Trends in the Transitory Variance of Earnings in the United States." *Economic Journal* 112(March): C68–C73.

Morone, James A., and Lawrence R. Jacobs, eds. 2004. *Healthy, Wealthy, and Fair: Health Care and the Good Society*. New York: Oxford University Press.

National Association of Latino Elected Officials Educational Fund. 2002. *2000 National Directory of Latino Elected Officials*. Washington, D.C.: National Association of Latino Elected Officials Educational Fund.

National Center for Public Policy and Higher Education. 2002. *Losing Ground: A National Status Report on the Affordability of American Higher Education*. San Jose, Calif.: National Center for Public Policy and Higher Education.

National Urban League. 2004. *The Complexity of Black Progress: The State of Black America 2004*. New York: The National Urban League.

Orfield, Gary, Susan E. Eaton, and Harvard Project on School Desegregation. 1996. *Dismantling Desegregation: The Quiet Reversal of Brown v. Board of Education*. New York: New Press.

Orloff, Ann Shola. 1988. "The Political Origins of America's Belated Welfare State." In *The Politics of Social Policy in the United States*. Princeton, N.J.: Princeton University Press.

———. 1993. *The Politics of Pensions: A Comparative Analysis of Britain, Canada, and the United States, 1880–1940*. Madison: University of Wisconsin Press.

Page, Benjamin I. 1983. *Who Gets What from Government?* Berkeley: University of California Press.

Parker, Frank R. 1991. *Black Votes Count*. Chapel Hill: University of North Carolina Press.

Perry, Huey L., Tracey L. Ambeau, and Frederick McBride. 1995. "Blacks and the National Executive Branch." In *Blacks and the American Political System*, edited by Huey L. Perry and Wayne Parent. Gainesville: University Press of Florida.

Phillips, Katherin Ross. 2002. "Working for All Families? Family Leave Policies in the United States." In *The Economics of Work and Family*, edited by Jeanne Kimmel and Emily P. Hoffman. Kalamazoo, Mich.: W. E. Upjohn Institute for Employment Research.

Pierson, Paul. 1993. "When Effect Becomes Cause: Policy Feedback and Political Change." *World Politics* 45(4): 595–628.

Pinderhughes, Dianne. 1987. *Race and Ethnicity in Chicago Politics: A Reexamination of Pluralist Theory*. Urbana: University of Illinois Press.

———. 1995. "Black Interest Groups and the 1982 Voting Rights Extension." In *Blacks and the American Political System*, edited by Huey L. Perry and Wayne Parent. Gainesville: University Press of Florida.

———. 1997. "Voting Rights Policy and Redistricting: An Introductory Essay." In *Symposium: Race and Representation* in *Race and Representation*, edited by Georgia Persons. New Brunswick, N.J.: Transaction Publishers.

Porter, Kathryn H., Kathy Larin, and Wendell Primus. 1999. *Social Security and Poverty Among the Elderly*. Washington, D.C.: Center for Budget and Policy Priorities.

Putnam, Robert D. 2000. *Bowling Alone: The Collapse and Revival of American Community*. New York: Simon & Schuster.

Ricci, David M. 1993. *The Transformation of American Politics: The New Washington and the Rise of Think Tanks*. New Haven, Conn.: Yale University Press.

Rich, Andrew. 2004. *Think Tanks, Public Policy, and the Politics of Expertise*. New York: Cambridge University Press.

Rosenstone, Steven J., and John Mark Hansen. 1993. *Mobilization, Participation, and Democracy in America*. New York: Macmillan.

Sampson, Robert J., and John H. Laub. 1996. "Socioeconomic Achievement in the Life Course of Disadvantaged Men: Military Service as a Turning Point, Circa 1940–1965." *American Sociological Review* 61(3): 347–67.

Schattschneider, Elmer Eric. 1935. *Politics, Pressures and the Tariff : A Study of Free Private Enterprise in Pressure Politics, as Shown in the 1929–1930 Revision of the Tariff*. New York: Prentice-Hall.

Schlozman, Kay Lehman, Sidney Verba, and Henry E. Brady. 1995. "Participation's Not a Paradox: The View from American Activists." *British Journal of Political Science* 25(1): 1–36.

Shammas, Carole. 1993. "A New Look at Long-Term Trends in Wealth Inequality in the United States." *American Historical Review* 98(2): 412–31.

Skocpol, Theda. 1992. *Protecting Soldiers and Mothers: The Political Origins of Social Policy in the United States*. Cambridge, Mass.: Belknap Press of Harvard University Press.

———. 1995. *Social Policy in the United States: Future Possibilities in Historical Perspective*. Princeton, N.J.: Princeton University Press.

———. 2000. *The Missing Middle: Working Families and the Future of American Social Policy*. New York: W. W. Norton.

———. 2003. *Diminished Democracy: From Membership to Management in American Civic Life*. Norman: University of Oklahoma Press.

Smedley, Brian D., Adrienne Y. Stith, and Alan R. Nelson, eds. 2003. *Unequal Treatment: Confronting Racial and Ethnic Disparities in Health Care*. Washington, D.C.: National Academy of Sciences.

Smeeding, Timothy M., and Lee Rainwater. 2001. *Comparing Living Standards Across Nations: Real Incomes at the Top, the Bottom and the Middle.* Syracuse, N.Y.: Maxwell School of Citizenship and Public Affairs, Syracuse University.

Soss, Joe. 1999. "Lessons of Welfare: Policy Design, Political Learning, and Political Action." *American Political Science Review* 93(2): 363–80.

Stetson, Dorothy McBride, and Amy G. Mazur, eds. 1995. *Comparative State Feminism.* Thousand Oaks, Calif.: Sage Publications.

Swain, Carol. 1993. *Black Faces Black Interests: The Representation of African Americans in Congress.* Cambridge, Mass.: Harvard University Press.

Swain, John W., Stephen A. Borrelli, and Brian C. Reed. 1998. "Partisan Consequences of the Post-1990 Redistricting for the U. S. House of Representatives." *Political Research Quarterly* 51(December): 945–67.

Teixeira, Ruy A. 1992. *The Disappearing American Voter.* Washington, D.C.: Brookings Institution.

Thernstrom, Stephan, and Abigail Thernstrom. 1997. *America in Black and White: One Nation, Indivisible.* New York: Simon & Schuster.

Uggen, Christopher, and Jeff Manza. 2001. "Democratic Contraction: The Political Consequences of Felon Disenfranchisement Laws in the United States." *American Sociological Review* 67(December): 777–803.

U.S. Department of Justice. 2004. "Section 5 Covered Jurisdictions." Voting Rights Act of 1965. Available at: http://www.usdoj.gov/crt/voting/sec_5/about.htm (accessed on May 8, 2004).

Verba, Sidney, Kay Lehman Schlozman, and Henry Brady. 1995. *Voice and Equality: Civic Voluntarism in American Politics.* Cambridge, Mass.: Harvard University Press.

Wasby, Steven. 1995. *Race Relations Litigation in an Era of Complexity.* Charlottesville: University of Virginia Press.

Wattenberg, Martin P. 2002. *Where Have All the Voters Gone.* Cambridge, Mass.: Harvard University Press.

Weir, Margaret. 1992. *Politics and Jobs: The Boundaries of Employment Policy in the United States.* Princeton, N.J.: Princeton University Press.

——. 2002. "The American Middle Class and the Politics of Education." In *Postwar Social Contracts Under Stress: The Middle Classes of America, Europe and Japan at the Turn of the Century,* edited by Oliver Zunz, Leonard Schoppa, and Nobuhiro Hiwatari. New York: Russell Sage Foundation.

Welch, Finis. 2002. "Half Full or Half Empty? The Changing Economic Status of African Americans, 1967–1996." In *Beyond the Color Line: New Perspectives on Race and Ethnicity in America,* edited by Abigail Thernstrom and Stephan Thernstrom. Stanford, Calif.: Hoover Institution Press.

Wilensky, Harold L. 1975. *The Welfare State and Equality: Structural and Ideological Roots of Public Expenditures.* Berkeley: University of California Press.

Williams, David R., and Chiquita Collins. 1995. "U.S. Socioeconomic and Racial

Differences in Health: Patterns and Explanations." *Annual Review of Sociology* 21: 349–86.

Williams, Linda Faye. 2003. *The Constraint of Race: Legacies of White Skin Privilege in America*. University Park: Pennsylvania State University Press.

Willingham, Alex, ed. 2002. *Beyond the Color Line? Race, Representation and Community in the New Century*. New York: Brennan Center for Justice, New York University School of Law.

Wilson, William Julius. 1999. *The Bridge over the Racial Divide: Rising Inequality and Coalition Politics*. Berkeley: University of California Press.

Wolff, Edward. 2002. *Top Heavy: A Study of Increasing Inequality of Wealth in America*. New York: Twentieth Century Fund.

Wuthnow, Robert. 2002. "The United States: Bridging the Privileged and Marginalized?" In *Democracies in Flux*, edited by Robert D. Putnam. New York: Oxford University Press.

Yinger, John. 2001. "Housing Discrimination and Residential Segregation as Causes of Poverty." In *Understanding Poverty in America*, edited by Sheldon Danziger and Robert Haveman. Cambridge, Mass.: Harvard University Press.

Chapter Five | Studying Inequality and American Democracy: Findings and Challenges

Lawrence R. Jacobs
Theda Skocpol

SOCIAL SCIENTIFIC research at its best performs "the vital function of helping our democracy to know itself better" (Herring 1953, 71).[1] Earlier generations of scholars grappled with the impact of industrialization, urbanization, immigration, and ethnic variety on American democracy; probed the processes by which modern party and governmental practices challenged nineteenth-century patronage politics; investigated how well U.S. national government coped with the challenges of world war and depression; and reflected on the changing meaning and prospects of American democracy in the eras of the Cold War and the Civil Rights movement. Today, scholars who study American politics work in an era of new challenges and paradoxes. In the wake of the rights movements of the 1960s and 1970s, U.S. democracy has become in many ways more equal and inclusive. Yet the polity must also function in an era of sharply rising disparities of income and wealth, even as new waves of immigration and new kinds of social tensions are roiling American society.

How do the momentous economic and social transformations of our time affect patterns of political participation and government responsiveness? What difference do government policies make for economic and political inequalities? Is American politics becoming more disproportionately attentive to the needs and values of the privileged few, rather than the majority? As U.S. government does less than it once did to expand opportunity and ensure widespread security in an era of rapid, market-driven changes, are ordinary Americans becoming disillusioned with government and convinced that political participation has little to offer—thus creating the risk of a self-reinforcing cycle of democratic decline?

Much current research speaks to these pressing questions, yet the an-

214

swers are far from clear-cut. Each core chapter in this volume has pieced together findings synthesized from many specialized literatures and studies—findings that sometimes add up to larger conclusions and sometimes leave major gaps. Fundamental questions and challenges remain to be tackled by future research in political science and beyond. Social scientists today must resist the temptations of overspecialization and in-group reference to remain true to the broader mission of "helping our democracy to know itself better."

Rich research literatures document inequalities in American democracy in the overlapping arenas of political voice, governance, and public policy. After reviewing key findings in each area, we reflect on lacunae in current literatures and the pressing issues that remain to be addressed.[2]

UNEQUAL VOICE

The social and economic roots of citizens participating and expressing opinions in American politics have been the object of extensive research and careful theorization. We know a lot about the extent and determinants of unequal participation and differential attitudes at any one time. But we know much less than we need to know about changes over time and about the ways in which changing institutional contexts and organizational strategies affect citizen behavior and attitudes.

Political Participation

As chapter 2 documents, disparities in citizen voice are a consistent theme across an array of quite different political activities—ranging from contacting officials, to voting and giving money, to protesting. All these activities are stratified—including protesting, despite the fact that it is often considered a "weapon of the weak."

Voting is of special interest, in part because political scientists have long focused on it, and in part because it is the most widespread political activity and hence has the greatest equalizing potential. Nevertheless, in the United States turning out to vote remains quite stratified, a regular habit only for (most of) the more affluent and better educated. A clear gap in voting between the well-off and the less affluent is revealed in national surveys (for example, Verba, Schlozman, and Brady 1995) and in analyses based on census data and validated votes (Freeman 2004; Leighley and Nagler 1992). Certainly, a socioeconomic tilt in voter turnout is not new—and many questions remain about whether it has grown over recent decades. What is certain, however, is that American voting has not become more extensive or more equal across socioeconomic strata in that time—despite developments such as the Civil Rights movement, rising education levels, and lowered administrative barriers to registration that might have been expected to expand and equalize the electorate. Compared to whites, African Americans have made gains in voter participation since the 1950s, but progress has recently stalled. Scholars are exploring various reasons for this, including the differential racial as well as socioeconomic effects of felon disenfranchisement, which has a growing impact in a period of increased incarceration due to drug laws and other criminal sentencing measures toughened since the 1970s (see Uggen and Manza 2002).

Debates continue about how American voluntary associations and civic life have changed over the past half century, and why (for a summary of debates and research, see Skocpol 2004b). Yet there is considerable agreement that many broad-gauged, popularly rooted trade unions and voluntary membership associations have declined, while business and professional associations have continued to proliferate and professionally managed advocacy groups and nonprofit associations have flourished in unprecedented numbers. Except perhaps in the sphere of evangelical churches and associated voluntary federations active in the antiabortion and pro-gun movements, the experience of joining and meeting voluntarily in America may now be more tilted than ever toward the affluent and the best-educated. Organized interest groups and civic institutions may speak most loudly about the values and the needs of the middle class and the privileged (Berry 1999; Skocpol 2003, 2004a). According to a 1990 survey, only 29 percent of individuals in families with incomes under $15,000 are affiliated with a political organization, compared with 73 percent among those in families earning over $75,000 (Verba, Schlozman, and Brady 1995).

It is hard to find aspects of American political life that are not dominated by the better off. Even political parties—which generations of political activists and observers have held out as a vehicles for democratic mobilization—function nowadays in ways that often intensify participatory inequalities. Party operatives are less likely than they were decades ago to scour neighborhoods in search of every available voter. Instead, they use sophisticated data banks to locate voters who already lean their way and are inclined to vote (Schier 2000). The effect can be to reinforce decrements and inequalities in voter turnout.

Targeting the already active is a bipartisan endeavor. Americans who identify themselves as Republican and cast their ballots for GOP candidates tend to come from families with significantly higher income than Democrats. What is striking, however, is that when it comes to seeking campaign contributors and volunteers the Democratic Party converges on a similar group of affluent adherents. To find contributors and activists, both political parties concentrate on the same narrow segments of American society that are already well represented in the political process.

The Internet has been touted for its potential to overcome participatory inequalities—and this technology admittedly remains at an early stage of impact. So far, however, the potential of the Internet to broaden democracy has been at best imperfectly realized. It may make it easier to bundle large numbers of modest monetary contributions, but the affluent and the best educated are the biggest Internet users. This technology simplifies their efforts to gain political information, make political connections, and contribute money.

Public Opinion

Because of their capacity to register mass opinions in a more comprehensive way than voting does, public opinion surveys have been held out as a potential means for political equalization (Gallup and Rae 1940). Yet recent research suggests that the results of surveys are also biased toward over-representing the views of the better off (Berinsky 2002; Brehm 1993; Bartels 1996; Althaus 1998). Individuals with lower income and education levels are particularly prone to be uncertain or confused and to say "don't know" when interviewers ask their opinions, even though they also harbor real political wants, needs, and desires. This exclusionary bias tends to portray Americans as somewhat more conservative and antiegalitarian than they actually are on such issues as whether the government should "reduce income differences between the rich and the poor."

Frontiers of Behavioral Research

As this overview of key findings suggests, research on stratification in political behavior and public opinion has been especially fruitful. Nevertheless, key areas remain inadequately explored. The next generation of research on political behavior and public opinion needs to focus on economic correlates and causes, and also explore the impact of recent (legal and illegal) immigrant flows on political behavior and attitudes. It must also do a better job of linking individual opinions and behavior to broader contexts in order to explore potential threats to representative democracy.

Income levels and changes in income distributions deserve to be treated as variables of primary interest in many future studies. What are the direct and indirect effects of rising economic inequality on individual participation and collective actions? Studying changes in political behavior and public opinion is essential to evaluate the impact of rising economic inequality. This will require assembling over-time data on a comprehensive set of critical indicators—from public opinion and political behavior to trends in economic distributions and organizational activity.

Given the sharp rise in income disparities, we need to refocus research on the relationships between changing income distribution over time and individual and group behavior across a set of activities including voter turnout and vote choice. Cross-sectional studies of broadly defined "social and economic status" have been valuable, but may have distracted attention from examining the impact of changing income distribution as such. Important disputes remain about whether, when, and how changes in income inequality may have influenced voter turnout and behavior (as highlighted in the discussion between Freeman 2004 and Leighley and Nagler 1992). Immigration has markedly increased since 1965, and the effects of new legal and illegal immigrant flows interact with changes in economic disparities in complex ways. How much of declines in voter turnout and increased economic skew in voting can be explained by the effects of immigration—such as illegal status or the failure of legal arrivees to connect to U.S. political routines—and how must be attributed to other causes?

Understanding the dynamics of political behavior as economic inequality rises requires more cross-level research and, in particular, analysis of individual-level behavior that is informed by and linked to aggregate-level, institutional, and policy developments (as in Rosenstone and Hansen 1993; Campbell 2003). Psychology and its experimental methods have been used to study how individuals process information and reach decisions about politics. The field of political psychology has made a number of important contributions to understanding why individuals withdraw from political participation. Maximizing this potential, though, requires more attention to the larger context in which individuals operate. How has the perception and lived experience of rising economic inequality—as manifested, for example, in declining or terminated health benefits or in longer working hours—affected individual efficacy, political engagement, and confidence in political institutions? And what explains the political responses of white men with a high school education or less to the significant decline in their real economic position?

We also need research that relates individual-level behavior to changes in the broader organizational context. How are individual attitudes and behavioral options affected by changes in political party mobilization, interest group campaigning, and the formation of social movements? What difference does it make for the mobilization of ordinary citizens into politics if party or interest group organizations rely on impersonal versus networking techniques to arouse potential participants (Gerber and Green 2000)? As membership in unions has fallen below 10 percent of the private-sector labor force, what has been the impact on turnout, partisanship, and attitudes not just of union members and their families, but of citizens more generally? Similar questions can be asked about the rise of evangelical Protestant churches and associations. Analyses of variations across U.S. states as well as nations can shed new light on these issues (see Radcliff and Davis 2000).

Finally, behavioral research needs to take a questioning stance toward assumptions that citizens are autonomous first-movers. Behavioralist research often assumes that shifts in mass attitudes and behavior drive politics. And, of course, normatively speaking, representative democracy rests on the presumption that citizens can independently evaluate government policy and select among competitive candidates for public office. But—especially given recent advances in information technologies and public opinion research—rising economic inequality (along with elite polarization and other political developments) increases the incentives of politicians to use the capacities of government and allied organizations to manipulate the evaluations of voters. Attempts at voter manipulation may have intensified. Such attempts may make more headway with the least educated and privileged, although the better educated can also be manipulated precisely because they are heavier consumers of media content.

The formation of public opinion is one of the most important and understudied areas of research on democratic life. Some recent research treats public opinion as the dependent variable, documenting the often discrete impacts of the media, think tanks, and government manipulation on what citizens think (Zaller 1992; Page 1996; Smith 2000; Jacobs and Shapiro 2000; Druckman, Jacobs, and Ostermeier 2004; Jacobs and Burns 2004). What we need, however, are studies that analyze the overall process of public opinion formation in ways that integrate these discrete influences; and such synthetic studies must spell out implications for the workings of representative democracy.

UNEQUAL GOVERNMENT RESPONSIVENESS

The study of government responsiveness to the citizenry is central to democratic theory in general and to assessments of the health of U.S. democracy in particular. Americans expect government to respond to the needs and values of the majority. And Americans are, in effect, pragmatic statists (Free and Cantril 1967; Page and Shapiro 1992; Jacobs 1993; Jacobs and Shapiro 1999). In the abstract, Americans harbor reservations about active government, yet at the same time majorities consistently support government policies to deal with insecurities and disruptions in daily life. The result is that large majorities support government actions to expand security and opportunity in education, health care, and retirement; and large majorities also favor government policies to promote environmental protection.

In recent years, political scientists have paid less attention to issues of differential government responsiveness than they should. But fascinating and worrisome findings are emerging, laying the basis for much future work.

Government Inaction and Selective Responsiveness

As chapter 3 suggested, long-standing features of U.S. governance may have taken on new significance in an era of rising economic inequality. Because of its complexly divided institutions, U.S. government has never been easy to move. Forces interested in blocking action—especially comprehensive government initiatives—almost always have an easier time than proponents of strong government action. When U.S. government does act, moreover, it often distributes subsidies, tax breaks, and regulatory adjustments in fine-grained ways, targeted on the most vocal and well-organized.

Again, there is nothing completely new here. U.S. pork barrel politics—"bringing home the bacon"—has long targeted distributions of government money and services, delivering benefits across congressional districts and demonstrating to salient constituents back home that members of Congress are effectively fighting for their constituents. Yet, of late, institutional changes in Congress are facilitating more finely targeted government allocations to narrow factions that support the majority party and its elected officials. Members of the majority party disproportionately benefit from the distribution of funds for defense contracts, transportation projects and other kinds of federal subsidies and grants (Carsey and Rundquist 1999; Lee 2000; Balla et al. 2002). Favoritism toward districts of majority party members has been intensified by the efforts of members themselves to differentially funnel federal discretionary spending within their districts (Martin 2003). The targeted distribution of government money that has always favored well-organized particularistic groups has arguably become yet more selective.

Looking more generally at issues of representation and government responsiveness, a growing body of analysis demonstrates tilted government decisionmaking. Some research suggests that government responsiveness to overall public opinion has declined during the period of rising economic inequality (Jacobs and Shapiro 2000). Other research finds that members of Congress are disproportionately responsive to their most affluent constituents, especially on issues where more and less privileged Americans disagree (Bartels 2002; Gilens 2003). The poor are not the only ones that have a hard time getting response from legislators and government. Even the preferences of middle-strata citizens, this research shows, have much less sway over what government does than the most affluent (Gilens 2003). Additional research documents that business—more than experts, organized labor, or public opinion—consistently dominates U.S. foreign policy, including diplomatic and defense affairs as well as international economic measures (Jacobs and Page 2005).

Bias in U.S. governance toward inaction and selective responsiveness may well be compounded by the impact of big monetary contributions, which play an ever-greater role in electoral and policy campaigns. Recent campaign finance reforms aimed at curbing "soft money" have helped reduce the individual influence of those who once wrote million dollar checks to the two major political parties. But giving money to political campaigns—even in smaller denominations—is an activity still reserved for a rarefied subset of Americans. Only about 15 to 17 percent of American households make over $100,000 annually, yet this segment disproportionately accounts for substantial contributions. As wealth and income have become more concentrated and the flow of money into elections has grown, campaign contributions give the affluent a means to express their voice that is, in practice, unavailable to most citizens.

Political scientists have been interested in what difference, exactly, monetary contributions make in politics. Research consistently shows that legislators are not usually directly bribed today by political contributors or moneyed interests. But big contributors have the power to help some candidates, rather than others, run effectively for office. And they reap attention from politicians in office, gaining opportunities to meet, to express their concern, and to press information on policymakers.

Challenges for Future Research on Responsiveness

Although the research summarized and synthesized in chapter 3 supports the provisional conclusions we have summarized, much more remains to be learned about the workings and responsiveness of government in an era of rising economic inequality. Issues about inequality and governance have not received as much attention from political scientists as questions about inequalities in political participation and voice. Institutional literatures have become specialized and focused on the internal workings of Congress, the executive, or the judiciary. The working group that pulled together chapter 3 faced a greater challenge of interpreting and synthesizing scattered literatures than the authors of chapters 2 or 4.

Furthermore, little research in this area has focused on changes over time (Jacobs and Shapiro 2000; Jacobs and Page 2005; Gilens 2004). Have disparities in government responsiveness to popular preferences—conceptualized along racial-ethnic, gender, and socioeconomic lines—changed or grown over time? And if so, why? Changes in government responsiveness are unlikely to have been parallel along all dimensions, so more dynamically conceived research will face not just daunting problems of finding appropriate data, but also conceptual challenges. This will be true even for studies that merely seek to descriptively document degrees of government responsiveness over time. The best future research will probably use combinations of methods, including case studies along with statistical models, to tease out shifting (and differential) patterns of responsiveness across disparate policy areas.

Potential causes of differentials and changes in government responsiveness also need much more investigation. Nowhere is the need for additional, more sophisticated research more obvious than for understanding how monetary contributions and flows of money affect U.S. politics and governance. For example, we know that campaign contributions influence which candidates win elections and how well challengers fare (Jacobson 1990, 1992, 1999). But knowing that money influences which candidates succeed opens a new series of questions. Which kinds of challengers raise competitive sums of money? What kind of policies and positions do these candidates favor? Put simply, what kind of candidates make it through the money filter—and have there been changes over recent decades? Have well-organized, ideologically motivated groups—ranging from the conservative Club for Growth to liberal advocacy groups—become more sophisticated and effective about using actual or threatened primary election challenges to influence candidate orientations?

Furthermore, although some research has examined the impact of campaign contributions in generating privileged access to officeholders (Hall and Wayman 1990), we need to learn more about how money affects legislative decisions other than floor votes—decisions about which issues to raise, which issues to push hard, and decisions about how to process bills in committees. We also need to know how big money contributors might influence the interpretation and implementation of legislation, after it is enacted. Statistical studies may not always be the best way to learn about such matters. Political scientists may also need to revitalize traditions of in-depth interviewing and ethnographic observation focusing on case studies. At the same time, they face the challenge of exploring these issues not just at any one point in time, but over time. Clever uses of long-standing records may be the way to do this.

Overall, there must be much more sophisticated theorizing about how giving money may affect the agendas of politics, not just discrete decisions. Much of politics is about influencing what government will attend to, or not, rather than just shaping the details of what is done. Our hypotheses and research models may have to consider indirect effects of money, not just net direct effects. For example, what are the substantive implications of looking for contribution effects after controlling for the ideology of politicians? Perhaps big money works most effectively in furthering the careers and magnifying the messages of politicians with certain ideologies, rather than others. Ideologically consistent teams of officeholders may, in turn, autonomously favor certain lines of policymaking, and rule out others, obviating the need for pressures (monetary or otherwise) targeted on particular legislative votes. As the foregoing suggests, we need new theorizing about how money might matter in politics—and then we need research designs capable of exploring indirect and interactive effects.

Better theorizing and research to explore processes that may link unequal voice to bias in government responsiveness are also needed. We now have studies showing that legislative votes and government policies are more highly correlated with the preferences of the privileged than with the preferences of the poor or the middle class. But why is this true? What, exactly, are the mechanisms that may cause government to respond differentially to constituents with different characteristics and resources? Do officials simply not hear from some groups of citizens—such as those who do not vote or organize as often as others? Do officials respond more assiduously to the concerns of those who can give money—and, if so, how does this work when large numbers of voters have contrary preferences and the intensity of their preferences vary? Or are there other reasons for differential responsiveness? In what ways has responsiveness increased, or decreased, over recent decades.

Issues of government responsiveness have an important normative dimension. Joseph Schumpeter (1947) famously argued that democracy is simply a "method"—the use of elections to select among competing teams of elites with the expertise and wisdom to design reasonable policies for a complex world. Robert Dahl (1989), Hannah Pitkin (1967), and others disagree, arguing that democratic governance is defined by the substantive content of its decisions and, specifically, their general conformity with the wishes of citizens. In normative as well as empirical literatures, political scientists need to renew research on American governance that critically wrestles with competing views of democratic representation. What is the standing of a form of government that uses the "method" of democracy by fielding competing teams of candidates but allows money to act as a systematic filter on which candidates run for office? How representative is

American government if its substantive decisions are often at odds with the views of the majority?

PUBLIC POLICY, INEQUALITY, AND DEMOCRATIC LIFE

What government does—or does not do—is obviously at the center of research on both government responsiveness and public policymaking. Scholarship on government decisions tends to focus on the effects of government policies, including the effects of policies that are not pursued by particular nations. Rich literatures by political scientists, sociologists, and economists have had much to say about the effects of U.S. policy choices on socioeconomic inequalities.

Political scientists have recently launched an exciting new line of research on the "feedback" effects of policies on the political process itself, especially on mass political participation. Much has been learned, but as usual, much remains to be done.

The Economic and Political Impact of U.S. Policies

Across many nations in recent decades, changes in private markets, along with demographic factors, have propelled rising economic inequality. But governments vary in how they respond to mitigate such effects. Economic inequality has risen faster in the United States than other advanced industrialized nations in part because American government has failed to enact new social policies or adequately adjust existing policies in the face of market and demographic changes. Chapter 4 draws on the latest empirical research—especially the Luxembourg Income Studies—documenting various degrees to which advanced-industrial nations have used government transfer policies to mitigate poverty or equalize post-transfer income distributions. Overall, the United States does much less to mitigate poverty or equalize incomes than other advanced nations.

The picture becomes more complex when specific policy areas and slices of the population are examined, as chapter 4 details. For example, U.S. social programs for the retired elderly—especially Social Security— do much more to relieve poverty and raise incomes for the retired elderly than other U.S. social programs do to protect children or working-aged adults.

The most innovative aspect of the research synthesis offered in chapter 4 is its focus on the political effects of government social programs. Here is where the analysis of inequality and American democracy tends to come full circle. What government does—or does not do—not only affects the economic well being of the citizenry; public policies also influence citizen participation and attitudes toward the role of government. Public policies have resource and interpretive effects, both of which can affect political behavior (Pierson 1993; Mettler 2002; Mettler and Soss 2004). For example, social programs can enhance security or opportunity for large numbers of citizens, making it easier for them to engage in the political process; conversely, if government fails to aid citizens in insecure circumstances, that can dampen political participation. Similarly, social programs that reach broad categories of people and deliver benefits as a matter of "rights" can enhance citizens' sense that they are deserving recipients of public succor and encourage them to participate fully in the polity. By contrast, programs that deliver meager supports to slices of people who must go through complicated, demeaning procedures to qualify can leave citizens feeling like disempowered, undeserving recipients.

This line of theorizing has been fruitfully applied to reveal the political as well as economic equalizing impacts of broad social programs enacted from the 1930s to the 1960s in the United States. At the end of World War II, for example, the United States instituted the "G.I. Bill of Rights" of 1944, which (among other things) opened up educational opportunities to 16 million veterans. Not only did this major social program help to equalize educational opportunities—and thus facilitate subsequent occupational success for many from less privileged backgrounds who received occupational or college training—the G.I. Bill also empowered recipients to become more active citizens (Mettler 2002). It did this in part by enhancing individuals' skills and capacities, and in part by reinforcing their sense of themselves as deserving, engaged citizens. The G.I. Bill may also have helped to buoy the fortunes of voluntary membership associations in the postwar period, because it increased the likelihood that recipients would join civic organizations of various kinds.

Similarly, the expansion of Social Security and the enactment of Medicare and other programs for the U.S. elderly in the 1960s and 1970s have been shown to have political as well as economic effects. Social Security and Medicare have raised the stakes of politics and fostered a sense of efficacy and commitment to political participation among seniors, largely offsetting the differences between rich and poor found in the general population (Campbell 2003). U.S. seniors have become unusually active and attentive citizens, with low-income and lower-middle-income seniors much more likely to vote than their younger adult counterparts. Less privileged strata of seniors have an unusually strong stake in active, inclusive government policy—and they know it.

In short, when government responds to the many rather than the privileged few, it matters. Broad social supports delivered as a matter of citizenship right not only enable citizens to better take care of themselves and their families. They also empower citizens—increasing their sense of stake in positive actions by government and conveying the message that they are worthy and efficacious political actors. In this way, inclusive government can build the political and institutional conditions for its own continuance into the future.

The converse may also be true. Today the educational and training benefits for America's all-volunteer military are relatively modest and, as a result, have made less impact in boosting the schooling of veterans to the level of nonveterans. Higher education is becoming less affordable for poor and lower-middle-class families in the face of rising tuition, the declining value of individual Pell Grants, and budget cuts imposed on state universities. These muted government responses may dampen democratic participation. Failure to continue government programs that widen opportunity and security removes a spur to political engagement for Americans who are not elderly.

Emerging Areas of Research on the Effects of Policies

Although chapter 4 charts the comparatively small impact of U.S. transfer policies on stemming widening gaps in market incomes among nonelderly Americans, more attention needs to be paid to ways in which government policies influence market incomes and practices in the workplace (see Freeman 1994). In Europe, for instance, government policy is aggressive not only in setting wage rates but also in supporting unionization and employer-employee bargaining regimes. A fuller understanding of how government influences socioeconomic inequalities requires analysis of the determinants of market as well as post-transfer income. It also requires us to explore the impact of divergent national policy regimes on the effects of growing global economic linkages. Internationalization of finance and investment has been identified as one source of rising market-income inequalities, but internationalization does not proceed entirely apart from government policy choices. Tax regimes, trade policies, and policies to compensate or retrain displaced workers all can have an impact.

Moving on to think about the effects of government policy choices in the political realm, research on the mass political effects of social policies is a growing new area in which exciting challenges loom (Mettler and Soss 2004). Welfare policies, for example, seem to function very differently than more universal programs, not just in distributing resources, but also in affecting political beliefs and attitudes (Soss 1999; but see Grogan and Patashnik, forthcoming). This fertile line of research can potentially also be expanded to "hidden welfare state" policies (Howard 1997; Hacker 2002). Social policymaking through tax breaks, for example, is increasingly common in U.S. politics—witness the expansion of the Earned Income Tax Credit in recent times. How do such relatively invisible programs influence citizen perceptions of government and their likelihood of becoming politically engaged? The same questions can be posed about more long-standing "hidden welfare policies" such as government-backed yet privately managed educational loans or tax breaks given to employers who provide health or retirement benefits. U.S. government policies play a central role in stimulating and channeling such indirectly managed social benefits, but do citizens perceive government's role? What does it mean for policy feedbacks in general that the overall mix of new social policies has shifted in recent times toward measures that reduce regulation and taxes, and away from direct social expenditures?

Research on policy feedbacks can focus on organizational as well as aggregate individual-level effects. When government launches new lines of policymaking, or shifts the modalities of policy—for example, substituting regulations for direct expenditures—that is likely to influence the goals and capacities of social movements and voluntary organizations, not just individual citizen behavior. Government policies obviously affect the prospects for trade unions to organize and flourish, not to mention the stances that trade union leaders are likely to take in partisan politics. More generally, considerable work has already been done on ways in which U.S. government policies in the 1960s and afterward stimulated the proliferation of voluntary associations, encouraged the professionalization of associations, and both fostered the proliferation of nonprofit institutions and drew them into closer partnerships with government (for example, Baumgartner, Leech, and Mahoney 2003; Berry and Arons 2003; Skocpol 2004a; Walker 1991). But much more can be learned about the reciprocal, temporally unfolding relationships between government action and the goals and capacities of organizations in civil society. And such research is likely to have important implications for our understandings of political equality, because the disparate organizational capacities and orientations of different slices of the citizenry have important consequences for the messages politicians and government officials hear, and the degrees of support they are likely to receive for difference lines of public action.

FOCUSING ON THE BIG PICTURE

From the 1950s into the early 1970s, research on democracy in the United States and beyond was often guided by a set of overarching theories that highlighted interrelationships between society and politics and, at least implicitly, offered critical perspectives on the health of democracy (Task Force on Inequality and American Democracy 2004). From pluralism and its critics to Weberian analysis, systems theory, and Marxism, contending perspectives focused on connections between society and government and reflected on the implications of empirical findings for democratic life. Even studies dealing with discrete components of the society–government nexus—such as political parties, social movements, interest groups, or the legislative process—were informed by larger macro models of democracy.

By the 1980s, especially in the discipline of political science, macro theories were falling from fashion, having been subjected to persuasive critiques about the deterministic relationships they posited or about the overly abstract and general levels of analysis at which some of these perspectives operated. Key concepts were seen as underspecified, and various macro theories were seen to neglect government institutions and historical variety, or else distract attention from human agency. Macro theorizing was somewhat discredited, with scholarship shifting toward micro as well as behavioralist perspectives—although historical institutionalists and students of American political development did continue to analyze institutional configurations and policy processes unfolding over long stretches of time.

When we think about the challenges involved in better understanding changes in American political participation, governance, and public policymaking in an era of rapidly shifting social and economic inequalities, it becomes clear that students of U.S. politics may have overreacted to critiques of macro-theorizing. In understandably recoiling from overly abstract, static, and determinist grand theories, scholars focusing on American politics may sometimes have lost sight of our need to understand large-scale transformations and shifts in state-society relationships. We cannot afford to forsake asking questions about the big picture and simply retreat into pursuing very specialized, atemporal studies about this or that specific institution or process. We have to be able to hypothesize about, and investigate, the direct and indirect reverberations in politics of momentous societal changes such as rising economic inequalities since the 1970s; and we have to be able to think through the direct and indirect effects on society and democratic political engagement of major lines of policymaking pursued, or not, by national and state governments.

If carefully honed to inform middle-level and rigorously empirical theorizing and research, earlier macro perspectives may offer useful conceptual insights for conducting research on the interactions among shifts in political voice, governance, and policy effects in an age of rising inequality. And the door remains open to fresh theorizing that goes beyond any early macro perspective.

Two agendas offer challenges and promising opportunities for reconnecting the study of American society and government to critical analysis of democratic life.

First, we need to know more about the ways in which society and government condition one another. Societal conditions do not simply represent the "environment"—an input into the black box of governance that is converted into policy. The reality is that society and government influence and limit each other; each is an "environment" to the other. Research on political voice demonstrates the impact of economic conditions on the political attitudes and behaviors of masses of Americans—just as the analysis of policy feedbacks reveals the influence of government policy on economic conditions and political attitudes and behavior. Government institutions, furthermore, have long been understood to influence the demands, orientations, and alliances of politically active social groups, movements and organizations (see Vogel 1978; Kitschelt 1986), just as groups and movements obviously influence the shape of government institutions and the policies government actors undertake.

There is, however, an imbalance in existing literatures that address state-society relationships. Behaviorists in political science and political sociology are very much in the lead. Students of political participation and public opinion have long paid attention to class, gender, and racial influences on aggregate individual behavior—and, nowadays, such research is expanding to consider the impact of new streams of immigration and shifting patterns of religious adherence. Also, of late, students of the effects of public policies have started to pay attention to the effects of policies on mass political participation and attitudes, as well as to the impacts of social programs on the socioeconomic life chances of different social groups. Behavioralism and institutionally informed policy studies are speaking to one another, and we can expect rich veins of new theorizing and empirical research to continue to unfold.

By contrast, in current political science literatures focused on particular formal institutions such as Congress there is far less attention to interrelationships between society and politics—and such attention as there is often ignores issues of inequality. This is beginning to change, as we have seen, but there is a long way to go before regularly accumulating specialist literatures yield empirically and normatively important insights about the larger democratic polity.

The second major area in which there are rich possibilities for new theorizing and research has to do with disentangling relationships among changes playing out over substantial stretches of time. Sometimes coterminous changes will be causally related to one another; in other instances, they will be separate trends that nevertheless interact in their implications for the larger polity. A good example of the latter situation may well be the relationship between rising economic inequalities since the 1970s, and shifts from membership mobilization toward professional staff management in U.S. civic associations and institutions. There is little evidence that rising economic inequalities directly caused civic reorganizations (those reorganizations were well under way in the 1960s). Nevertheless, recently proliferating advocacy groups and other professionally managed civic institutions place a great deal of emphasis on fundraising, ideally from major donors, and this shift in the direction and goals of civic groups may very well interact with the expansion of the ranks of very wealthy Americans. The wealthy may have gained much more leverage over organizations that set agendas in politics and deliver key services in U.S. community life.

A word about data. In each of our commentaries in the sections above, we have noted that cross-sectional research is more advanced than cross-temporal research—though there certainly are important exceptions to this generalization, such as *The Macro Polity* by Robert Erikson, Michael MacKuen, and James Stimson (2002) and *How Policies Make Citizens: Senior Political Activism and the American Welfare State* by Andrea Louise Campbell (2003). Any serious effort to evaluate the impacts—direct, indirect, and interactive—of shifting social inequalities on American politics and governance requires a major and sustained professional commitment to collecting and analyzing over-time data. Such data is especially needed on the living conditions, attitudes, and political behavior and experiences of minorities, women, and less affluent (as well as very elite) Americans. And we should also place a high value on the preparation of data sets that track legislative enactments, agendas of public attention, associations, and executive initiatives over (at least) several decades of time. In quantitative research, our methods of times series analysis outstrip our data on medium- to long-term trends in society and government.

As scholars pay more attention to macro relationships and large-scale transformations to better grasp the implications of shifting societal inequalities for democratic politics, such efforts will challenge the fragmentation of social science disciplines into fields, subfields, and competing approaches to research. In fact, arenas of research and approaches often tend to line up with one another. Thus, most students of political participation tend to be behavioralists who often rely on cross-sectional surveys; many students of institutions tend to be rational-choice analysts who model choice sets and elite strategic maneuvers; and many students of policy effects and feedbacks tend to be historical institutionalists (for more on these approaches, see Pierson and Skocpol 2002). But such alignments only tend to discourage investigation of linkages among participation, governance, and policy effects. And they deprive scholars working in any one area of the theoretical insights and empirical strategies of their colleagues who pose and answer questions in a different way. Overspecializing and adhering to only one research approach also tends to encourage scholars to confine their investigations to particular data sets or kinds of data, rather than using multiple sources as necessary to fully examine hypotheses or relationships of interest.

Expanding research on society-government links thus requires changes in scholarly behavior. Through funding and other steps we need to encourage problem-focused collaborations among scholars with different areas of expertise. Our criteria of evaluation in reviewing manuscripts and colleagues need to be recalibrated to give positive weight to scholarly contributions that cross disciplines and subfields and combine empirical approaches. At base, social scientists who care about pressing issues such as those raised in this book must understand that the genuine benefits of specialization can introduce significant costs in terms of narrowness and myopia. Cutting-edge research in the social sciences—as in other areas of scholarship—is most likely to be produced by individuals and research teams able to bridge specializations and research approaches.

What we need, in short, is a new generation of research devoted to *critical studies of democratic life* that reexamines what we study and how we do it.

CONCLUSION

Political science, sociology, and economics were all originally launched as organized and interdependent disciplines by reformers committed to improving democratic life. Generations of social scientists continued to marry rigorous research to broader debates about the quality of democracy and government in the United States and beyond. Peer-reviewed research is vital to social knowledge because it offers a unique check on self-serving ideologues and uninformed commentators. This contribution is especially valuable in an era of elite polarization and rising inequality that threatens continued progress in expanding democratic participation and government responsiveness.

Scholars today are called to carry forward the rich social science tradition of public-regarding research that treats democratic politics and policy not as givens but as an ongoing experiment subject to improvement and to reversals. This book points to worrisome, mutually reinforcing trends in American politics that deserve close attention. If disparities of participation and influence become further entrenched—and if average citizens give up on democratic government—unequal citizenship could take on a life of its own, prompting Americans to become increasingly discouraged about the effectiveness of democratic governance and spreading cynicism and withdrawal from elections and other arenas of public life. At present, the confluence of rising economic inequality and political disparities are reinforcing low and, in some cases, declining participation and involvement in the electoral and governing processes. Government inaction and selective benefits raise questions about the U.S. government's will and capacity to offset rising market inequalities.

The Declaration of Independence promised that all American citizens would enjoy equal political rights. Every generation has returned to this promise and struggled to elevate the performance of American democracy to its high ideals. But in our time, the promise of American democracy faces distinctive new threats—not the overt threat of formal barriers to equal participation conquered by earlier generations, but the threat that rising economic inequality will solidify long-standing disparities in political voice and influence, and perhaps exacerbate such disparities. U.S. government today is responsive mainly to the privileged and well-organized, and is often not a powerful instrument to correct social disparities or look out for the needs of the majority. If disparities of participation and influence become further entrenched, and if average citizens give up on democratic government as a tool to enhance security and opportunity for all, unequal citizenship could take on a life of its own, weakening American democracy for a long time to come. To help prevent such worrisome possibilities, our responsibility as citizen-scholars is to conduct rigorous research on the state of American democracy and report findings and their implications in plain and direct terms to our students and fellow citizens.

NOTES

1. This point was made in Herring's 1953 presidential address to the American Political Science Association. After having attended the 2003 centennial of the American Political Science Association, Herring died in August 2004 at the age of 100.
2. References in the research summations will be selective and incomplete, because readers can refer to chapters 2, 3, and 4 for more complete discussions and extensive lists of relevant references.

REFERENCES

Althaus, Scott. 1998. "Information Effects in Collective Preferences." *American Political Science Review* 92(3): 545–58.
Balla, Steven, Eric Lawrence, Forrest Maltzman, and Lee Sigelman. 2002. "Parti-

sanship, Blame Avoidance, and the Distribution of Legislative Pork." *American Journal of Political Science* 46(3): 515–25.

Bartels, Larry M. 1996. "Uninformed Votes: Information Effects in Presidential Elections." *American Journal of Political Science* 40(1): 194–230.

———. 2002. "Economic Inequality and Political Representation." Presented at the 2002 Annual Meeting of the American Political Science Association. Boston (August 29–September 1).

Baumgartner, Frank R., Beth L. Leech, and Christine Mahoney. 2003. "The Co-Evolution of Groups and Government." Paper delivered at the 2003 Annual Meeting of the American Political Science Association. Philadelphia (August 28–31).

Berinsky, Adam J. 2002. "Silent Voices: Social Welfare Policy Opinions and Political Equality in America." *American Journal of Political Science* 46(2): 276–87.

Berry, Jeffrey M. 1999. *The New Liberalism: The Rising Power of Citizen Groups.* Washington, D.C.: Brookings Institution.

Berry, Jeffrey M., and David F. Arons. 2003. *A Voice for Nonprofits.* Washington, D.C.: Brookings Institution.

Brehm, John. 1993. *The Phantom Respondents.* Ann Arbor: University of Michigan Press.

Campbell, Andrea Louise. 2003. *How Policies Make Citizens: Senior Political Activism and the American Welfare State.* Princeton, N.J.: Princeton University Press.

Carsey, Thomas, and Barry Rundquist. 1999. "Party and Committee in Distributive Politics: Evidence from Defense Spending." *Journal of Politics* 61(4): 1156–69.

Dahl, Robert Alan. 1989. *Democracy and Its Critics.* New Haven, Conn.: Yale University Press.

Druckman, James N., Lawrence R. Jacobs, and Eric Ostermeier. 2004. "Candidate Strategies to Prime Issues and Image." *Journal of Politics* 66(4): 1180–1202.

Erikson, Robert S., Michael B. MacKuen, and James A. Stimson. 2002. *The Macro Polity.* New York: Cambridge University Press.

Free, Lloyd, and Hadley Cantril. 1967. *The Political Beliefs of Americans: A Study of Public Opinion.* New Brunswick, N.J.: Rutgers University Press.

Freeman, Richard, ed. 1994. "Working Under Different Rules." A National Bureau of Economic Research Project Report. New York: Russell Sage Foundation.

———. 2004. "What, Me Vote?" In *Social Inequality,* edited by Kathryn M. Neckerman. New York: Russell Sage Foundation.

Gallup, George, and Saul Rae. 1940. *The Pulse of Democracy.* New York: Simon & Schuster.

Gerber, Alan, and Donald Green. 2000. "The Effects of Canvassing, Telephone Calls, and Direct Mail on Voter Turnout: A Field Experiment." *American Political Science Review* 94(3): 653–63.

Gilens, Martin. 2004. "Public Opinion and Democratic Responsiveness: Who Gets

What They Want from Government?" Paper presented at the 2004 Annual Meeting of the American Political Science Association. Chicago (September 2–5).

Grogan, Colleen, and Erik Patashnik. Forthcoming. "Between Welfare Medicine and Mainstream Entitlement." In *Healthy, Wealthy, and Fair*, edited by James A. Marone and Lawrence R. Jacobs. New York: Oxford University Press.

Hacker, Jacob S. 2002. *The Divided Welfare State: The Battle over Public and Private Social Benefits in the United States*. New York: Cambridge University Press.

Hall, Richard, and Frank Wayman. 1990. "Buying Time: Moneyed Interests and the Mobilization of Bias in Congressional Committees." *American Political Science Review* 84(3): 797–820.

Hartz, Louis. 1955. *The Liberal Tradition in America*. New York: Harcourt Brace Jovanovich.

Herring, Pendleton. 1953. "On the Study of Government." *American Political Science Review* 47(4): 961–74.

Howard, Christopher. 1997. *The Hidden Welfare State: Tax Expenditures and Social Policy in the United States*. Princeton, N.J.: Princeton University Press.

Jacobs, Lawrence R. 1993. *The Health of Nations: Public Opinion and the Making of Health Policy in the U.S. and Britain*. Ithaca, N.Y.: Cornell University Press.

Jacobs, Lawrence R., and Melanie Burns. 2004. "The Second Face of the Public Presidency: Presidential Polling and the Shift from Policy to Personality Polling." *Presidential Studies Quarterly* 34(3): 536–56.

Jacobs, Lawrence R., and Benjamin I. Page. 2005. "Who Influences U.S. Foreign Policy?" *American Political Science Review* 99(1): 107–23.

Jacobs, Lawrence R., and Robert Y. Shapiro. 1999. "Pragmatic Liberalism Meets Philosophical Conservatism: Americans' Reactions to Managed Care." *Journal of Health Policy, Politics and Law* 24(5): 5–16.

———. 2000. *Politicians Don't Pander: Political Manipulation and the Loss of Democratic Responsiveness*. Chicago: University of Chicago Press.

Jacobson, Gary C. 1990. "The Effects of Campaign Spending in House Elections: New Evidence for Old Arguments." *American Journal of Political Science* 34(2): 334–62.

———. 1992. *The Politics of Congressional Elections*, 3rd ed. New York: Harper Collins.

———. 1999. "The Effect of the AFL-CIO's 'Voter Education' Campaigns on the 1996 House Elections." *Journal of Politics* 61(1): 185–94.

Kitschelt, Herbert P. 1986. "Political Opportunity Structures and Political Protest: Anti-Nuclear Movements in Four Democracies." *British Journal of Political Science* 16(1): 57–85.

Lee, Frances. 2000. "Senate Representation and Coalition Building in Distributive Politics." *American Political Science Review* 94(1): 59–72.

Leighley, Jan E., and Jonathan Nagler. 1992. "Socioeconomic Class Bias in Turnout,

1964–1988: The Voters Remain the Same." *American Political Science Review* 86(3): 725–36.

Martin, Paul. 2003. "Voting's Reward: Voter Turnout, Attentive Publics, and Congressional Allocation of Federal Money." *American Journal of Political Science* 47(1): 110–27.

Mettler, Suzanne. 2002. "Bringing the State Back In to Civic Engagement: Policy Feedback Effects of the G.I. Bill for World War II Veterans." *American Political Science Review* 96(2): 351–65.

Mettler, Suzanne, and Joe Soss. 2004. "The Consequences of Public Policy for Democratic Citizenship: Bridging Policy Studies and Mass Politics." *Perspectives on Politics* 2(1): 55–73.

Page, Benjamin I. 1996. *Who Deliberates? Mass Media in Modern Democracy*. Chicago: University of Chicago Press.

Page, Benjamin I., and Robert Y. Shapiro. 1992. *The Rational Public*. Chicago: University of Chicago Press.

Pierson, Paul. 1993. "When Effect Becomes Cause: Policy Feedback and Political Change." *World Politics* 45(4): 595–628.

Pierson, Paul, and Theda Skocpol. 2002. "Historical Institutionalism in Contemporary Political Science." In *Political Science: The State of the Discipline*, edited by Ira Katznelson and Helen Milner. New York: W. W. Norton.

Pitkin, Hanna. 1967. *The Concept of Representation*. Berkeley, Calif.: University of California Press.

Radcliff, Benjamin, and Patricia Davis. 2000. "Labor Organization and Electoral Participation in Industrial Democracies." *American Journal of Political Science* 25(1): 137–43.

Rosenstone, Steven J., and John Mark Hansen. 1993. *Mobilization, Participation, and Democracy in America*. New York: Macmillan.

Schier, Steven E. 2000. *By Invitation Only: The Rise of Exclusive Politics in the United States*. Pittsburgh, Penn.: University of Pittsburgh Press.

Schumpeter, Joseph. 1947. *Capitalism, Socialism, and Democracy*, 2nd ed. New York: Harper & Brothers.

Skocpol, Theda. 2003. *Diminished Democracy: From Membership to Management in American Civic Life*. Norman: University of Oklahoma Press.

———. 2004a. "Voice and Inequality: The Transformation of American Civic Democracy." *Perspectives on Politics* 2(1): 3–20.

———. 2004b. "Civic Transformation and Inequality in the Contemporary United States." In *Social Inequality*, edited by Kathryn M. Neckerman. New York: Russell Sage Foundation.

Smith, Mark A. 2000. *American Business and Political Power: Public Opinion, Elections, and Democracy*. Chicago: University of Chicago Press.

Soss, Joe. 1999. "Lessons of Welfare: Policy Design, Political Learning, and Political Action." *American Political Science Review* 93(2): 363–80.

Task Force on Inequality and American Democracy. 2004. "American Democracy in an Age of Rising Inequality." *Perspectives on Politics* 2(December): 651–66.

Uggen, Christopher, and Jeff Manza. 2002. "Democratic Contraction: The Political Consequences of Felon Disenfranchisement Laws in the United States." *American Sociological Review* 67(6): 777–803.

Verba, Sidney, Kay Lehman Schlozman, and Henry Brady. 1995. *Voice and Equality: Civic Voluntarism in American Politics.* Cambridge, Mass.: Harvard University Press.

Vogel, David. 1978. "Why Businessmen Distrust Their State: The Political Consciousness of American Corporate Executives." *British Journal of Political Science* 8(1): 45–78.

Walker, Jack L, Jr. 1991. *Mobilizing Interest Groups in America: Patrons, Professions, and Social Movements.* Ann Arbor: University of Michigan Press.

Zaller, John. 1992. *The Nature and Origins of Mass Opinion.* New York: Cambridge University Press.

Index

Boldface numbers refer to figures and tables.

AARP, 189
Abramson, Paul R., 73*n*21, 76*n*45
advocacy organizations, 64. *See also*
  organized interests
affirmative action programs, 23, 191
AFL-CIO, 114
African American reparations movement, 66
African Americans: advances for upper income, 174; discrimination and
  segregation faced by, 174–77; economic inequality faced by, 5–7;
  equality, struggle for (*see* racial
  equality, struggle for); G.I. Bill educational benefits, use of, 184; inequalities faced by, public opinion
  regarding, 22; organized interests
  representing, 55; representation and
  redistricting, opinion regarding,
  132–33; Social Security and
  Medicare, benefits of, 188; unequal
  political voice, significance of, 42;
  voting rights and participation of,
  193–96, 216; the War on Poverty and,
  191–92. *See also* race/ethnicity
age: elderly women, disadvantages
  faced by, 178–79; explaining partici-

patory inequality associated with,
  41; participatory inequality associ-
  ated with, 39; political acts by, **39**;
  political participation and, 189–90;
  social welfare spending based on,
  164
Aid to Families with Dependent Chil-
  dren, 128, 182, 192, 199
Aldrich, John, 76*n*45
American Association for Retired Per-
  sons. *See* AARP
American governance. *See* government
American Medical Association, 111
American Political Science Association:
  Committee on Political Parties, 93,
  99; Task Force on Inequality and
  American Democracy, 1–2, 14*n*1
American Trucking Association, 115
Anderson, Barbara A., 73*n*21
Asian Americans, 40, 67

Barber, Ben, 14*n*1
Bartels, Larry, 14*n*1
behavioral research, frontiers of,
  217–19
Berry, Jeffrey, 54, 75*n*33
blacks. *See* African Americans

Boston Tea Party, 63
Brown v. Board of Education, 170
Burstein, Paul, 78n60
Burtless, Gary, 163
Bush, George W., 25, 189
Bush v. Gore, 195
business, influence of, 53–57, 221

campaign finance: election campaigns, growing expenditures on, 112–13; explaining participatory inequality among contributors, 40; impact of money on electoral outcomes, 113–15; influence of money on elected representatives, 11, 13, 115–17; legislative parties, emergence of and changed patterns of contributions, 96; money in politics, directions for future research regarding, 222–23; organized interests and, 108 (see also organized interests); participatory inequality among contributors, 33–35, 221; party mobilization efforts and, 59–60; political action committees (see political action committees); presidential donors, characteristics of significant, 50; public opinion regarding, 26; social characteristics of contributors, stability of over time, 49–50; soft money, increase in, 49
Campbell, Andrea Louise, 189, 230
Castles, Frances, 158
circularity, problem of, 27
citizens: attributes that matter for politics, 42–43; demobilization of, 58–61; government responsiveness to policy preferences of (see responsiveness of government); public policy and, 199–201 (see also policy feedbacks)
Civil Rights Act of 1964, 131, 173, 175, 191–92

Civil Rights movement: direct action campaigns of the, 63–64; formal discrimination, success in ending, 128, 173; internal dynamics of, 67; substantive representation, improvements in from advances in descriptive representation, 135; success and limits of, 179–80; the Voting Rights Act of 1965 and, 193
Claggett, William J. M., 77n58
class, socioeconomic: congressional responsiveness to, 126; participatory inequality and, 19–20, 40, 46–47, 215–17; partisanship and voting behavior based on, 95; party conflict and, 61–63; political voice and increasing stratification of, 45; upward mobility and increase in inequality, 163. See also economic inequality; income inequality; socioeconomic status
Clinton, Bill, 104–5, 110
collective action, 31–32, 89
Community Action Agencies, 191–92
conditional party government, 96–99, 104–6

Dahl, Robert, 91, 138n1, 223
defense policy, 121
democracy: critical studies of democratic life, need for, 227–31; direct, 133, 140n24; inequality, threat posed by, 1–2, 7–14; quality of and social science research, 231–32
Denton, Nancy A., 176
descriptive representation, 131–35
devolution of authority, 129
direct democracy, 133, 140n24
distributive politics, 106–8. See also redistributive policies and politics
Druckman, James N., 140n20

Earned Income Tax Credit, 92, 104, 167, 178, 199
economic inequality: consequences of, 7–14; distribution of income and wealth, 5; education as antidote to, 170–72; gender and, 177–79; growing in America, 2–7, 156–58; incomes, related to (*see* income inequality); public opinion regarding, 7–8, 23–25; public policy and, 156–58, 172–73, 224–25 (*see also* redistributive policies and politics); public policy impacts on, future research directions regarding, 226; race and, 131–32, 175–77 (*see also* racial equality, struggle for); reinforcement of the status quo, tendencies toward, 137; the "rights revolution" and, 173–74 (*see also* "rights revolution"); social movements and, 67–68
economic mobility, increase in inequality and, 163
Economic Opportunity Act of 1964, 191
education: campaign contributions and, 34; economic inequality and, 170–72; the G.I. Bill and, 183–85, 197; participatory inequality, as factor explaining, 40; Pell grants, 171; political voice and changing levels of, 44, 198; racial inequality and, 175–76; the War on Poverty and, 192
Educational Amendments of 1972, 173–74
elections: as check on legislators, 108; funding of campaigns (*see* campaign finance); incumbents in, 113–14, 139n12; racial redistricting, 132–33; shifting landscape of, 95–96; turnout for, 9, 44, 58–59, 76n43–45; the Voting Rights Act of 1965 (*see* Voting Rights

Act of 1965). *See also* political parties; voting
Electoral College, public opinion regarding, 25
Elementary and Secondary Education Act of 1965, 173
elite issue activism, rise of, 63
Emergency School Aid Act of 1972, 174
equal protection of interests, 29–30, 42
Equal Rights Amendment, 22
Erikson, Robert S., 120–21, 230
ethnicity. *See* race/ethnicity
exclusion bias, 26, 217

Fair Housing Act of 1968, 173, 192
Fair Labor Standards Act of 1938, 196
families: changes in and increasing inequality, 163; new social risks faced by, 166–67
Family and Medical Leave Act of 1993, 179
Federal Election Campaign Act, 56
Federal Election Commission, 56
federalism: distribution of the tax burden and, 169–70; policy responsiveness and, 127–29
Federalist No. 10, 29–30
feminist/women's movement, 65, 173
Fiorina, Morris, 14n1, 94
Freeman, Richard B., 9, 45, 74–75n28, 76n43

gender: economic inequality and, 177–79; explaining participatory inequality associated with, 40–41; inequalities based on, public opinion regarding, 22–23; inequality in political voice and, 20; participatory inequality associated with, 36–39; political activities by, 37–38. *See also* women
G.I. Bill, 183–86, 197, 225

government: diminishment of role
helping less advantaged citizens,
200; federal structure, policy implications of, 127–28; foreign policy
preferences, influences on, **125**; ideological distance in the House and
Senate, **98**; inequality and the
processes and institutions of, 88–90,
136–37; inequality in, challenges of
evaluating, 90–93; political parties
and, 93–94 (*see also* political parties);
public opinion regarding, 8, 27–28;
race and (*see* racial equality, struggle
for); responsiveness to the public (*see*
responsiveness of government); society and, need for research encompassing the linkages between,
227–31. *See also* public policy; redistributive policies and politics
Guinier, Lani, 203*n*14

Hacker, Jacob, 14*n*1, 166
Hansen, John Mark, 75*n*28, 76*n*45
health care policy: federalism and, 128;
interest groups, impact of, 110–11;
Medicaid, 191–92, 198; Medicare,
111, 136, 186–90, 198, 225; public
opinion regarding, 72*n*11; race relations and, 135–36; socioeconomic
status and health status, relationship
of, 172, 202*n*10; women lacking
health insurance, 1178
Heclo, Hugh, 14*n*1, 181
Help America Vote Act of 2002, 196
Hero, Rodney, 14*n*1
Herring, Pendleton, 91
Hispanics. *See* Latinos
Hochschild, Jennifer, 170
homosexuality, public opinion regarding, 23
housing: racial segregation in, 176–77;
the War on Poverty and, 191–92

ideology, polarization of activists, 49,
95–99
image responsiveness, 140*n*20
immigration, increase in inequality
and, 163
incarceration rates, 203*n*17
income inequality: comparative perspective on, 159–64; family income
growth, **4**; gender and, 177–79; intertemporal variation in, 165–66;
mid-twentieth century policies, success in reducing, 196–97; percentage
of income received by the top .1%, **6**;
race and, 175–77; in selected developed countries, **160–62**; Social Security and, 186–87; statistics outlining,
3–4. *See also* economic inequality
inequality: in American governance
(*see* government); based on social
characteristics, public opinion regarding, 21–23; economic (*see* economic inequality); effect on public
opinion, 27–28; hurdles to establishing causality related to, 91–93; income (*see* income inequality); participatory (*see* participatory inequality);
political (*see* political inequality); in
political responsiveness, 124–27;
public opinion regarding, 20–21;
public policy and, 156–58 (*see also*
public policy); racial (*see* race/eth-
nicity; racial equality, struggle for);
threat to democracy posed by, 1–2;
wealth, 3–5, 164–65
interest groups. *See* organized interests
Internet, the, political equality and,
68–69, 78*n*64, 217
iron triangles, 106, 109

Jacobs, Lawrence R., 14*n*1, 139*n*19,
140*n*20
Jacobson, Gary, 139*n*12

Javits, Jacob, 97
Johnson, Lyndon, 190
Junn, Jane, 44

Katosh, John P., 74n21
Kennedy, John, 119
Key, V. O., 91, 100–101, 107, 138n4

labor unions, attrition in the power of, 56–57, 59, 198–99
Latinos: economic inequality faced by, 5–6; representation of, 135; unequal political voice, significance of, 42; voting rights of, 193–96
Legislative Demographic Services, 112
life-cycle variation. *See* age
Lindblom, Charles E., 27, 91, 181
Lipset, Seymour Martin, 27
Lynch, Julia, 164

MacKuen, Michael B., 120–21, 230
Madison, James, 29–30, 88
Manza, Jeff, 203n17
Martin, Paul, 107
Massey, Douglas, 176
McDonald, Michael, 76n43
Medicaid, 191–92, 198
Medicare, 111, 136, 186–90, 198, 225
Medicare Catastrophic Coverage Act, 110
Meredith, James, 64
Merriam, Charles, 91
methodological issues: connecting inputs to outcomes, 92; conversion problem, 92; cross-temporal research, need for, 230; nondecision problem, 92; observation problem, 92–93
Mettler, Suzanne, 14n1, 182
Miller, Warren E., 118–19, 126, 197
Mills, Wilbur, 97
money in politics. *See* campaign finance

National Labor Relations Act of 1935, 197
national primaries, public opinion regarding, 25–26
Nie, Norman, 44
Nixon, Richard, 140n20, 192
No Child Left Behind Act, 129

Olson, Mancur, 31
organized interests: AARP, 189; bias of, 53–55; changes in the community of, 55–57; civic organizations, changes in, 199–200; economic stratification and, 10, 216; equal voice in representation, problems of identifying, 52–53; inequality of political voice in, 49, 51; money in electoral politics and, 108; patronage and, 75n34; political action committees (*see* political action committees); public policy and, 108–12; representation by, 51–52; strategies of, 138–39n11. *See also* voluntary associations
Orren, Gary, 20
Ostermeier, Eric, 140n20

PACs. *See* political action committees
Page, Benjamin, 14n1, 121, 158
participatory inequality, 9–11, 32–34; among campaign contributors, 33–34; change over the last generation: conflicting expectations regarding, 44–45; change over the last generation: evidence regarding, 45–49; explaining group differences, 39–41; group differences and, 34–39; high and low income groups in various political activities, **35**; organized interests and (*see* organized interests); policy outcomes and, methodological difficulties in linking, 91–93, 138n8; public opinion regarding,

participatory inequality (*continued*) 25–26; public policy, shaped by (*see* policy feedbacks); reasons to be concerned about, 10–11, 28–30; socioeconomic class and, 215–17; understudy of by political scientists, 90–91; in voting, 32–33. *See also* political voice

partisan differences: conditional party government and, 104–6; polarization of the parties, 95–99; the policy approach to, 101–3; post-World War II, 103–4; the process approach to, 100–101; redistributive policies and, 99–104. *See also* political parties

patronage, 75*n*34

Pell grants, 171

Pierson, Paul, 181

Pinderhughes, Dianne, 14*n*1

Pitkin, Hannah, 223

policy feedbacks, 157, 179–80, 224–26; future research directions regarding, 226–27; the G.I. Bill, 183–86, 225; mid-twentieth century policies, cumulative impact of, 196–96; on political voice, 197–201; Social Security and Medicare, 186–90, 225; study of, 180–83; the Voting Rights Act of 1965, 192–96; the War on Poverty, 190–92

political action committees (PACs): campaign contributions, effects of, 116; campaign contributions, patterns of, 96, 114; growth in corporate associated, 56; strategies of, 138–39*n*11

political inequality: economic equality and, 7; federalism and, 127–29; interest groups and, 109–11; political responsiveness and, 124–27; political voice and concerns regarding, 29–30; political voice of the satisfied and in-

different, questions regarding, 30–31; popular sovereignty and, 129–31; public opinion regarding, 8, 25–26; racial inequality and, 131–32 (*see also* racial equality, struggle for); through representation by organized interests, problems in determining, 52–53

political parties: class interests in party conflict, 61–63; conditional party government, 96–99, 104–6; decline and resurgence of, 94–96; demobilization of citizens, recent, 58–61; distributional politics and, 106–8; elite issue activism, rise of, 63; the enfranchisement of women and, 76*n*41; functioning of the political system and, 93–94; geographic reshaping of, 194; income level of recruitment targets, **60**; participatory inequality, intensifying of, 216–17; partisanship and implications of partisan differences (*see* partisan differences); people/interests represented by, 61; political voice and, 57–58

political representation, 117; descriptive and substantive distinguished, 131–32; descriptive and substantive in racial, 132–36; empirical studies of, 117–19; inequality and popular sovereignty, 129–31; of minorities, 132–34. *See also* responsiveness of government

political science: behavioral research, frontiers of, 217–19; democracy, responsibility to conduct research on the state of, 231–32; new challenges facing, 214–15; public policy, future research directions regarding, 226–27; responsiveness of government, directions for future research regarding, 221–24; society-government links, need for research encompassing the big picture regarding, 227–31; understudy of inequality in contemporary, 90–91

political voice, 19–20, 69–70; equal, reasons to care about, 28–30; equal protection of interests via, 29–30, 42; the G.I. Bill and, 185–86; impact of disparities in, 10–11; the Internet and equality of, 68–69; mid-twentieth century policies, success in supporting, 196–97; organized interests and (*see* organized interests); policymakers, what is heard by, 41–44; political parties (*see* political parties); the problem of collective action and, 31–32; public opinion (*see* public opinion); public policy, shaped by (*see* policy feedbacks); the satisfied and indifferent, factoring in, 30–31; social movements, 63–68; Social Security/Medicare and, 189–90; unequal (*see* participatory inequality); value of the act of participation, 19, 28–29; voting (*see* voting); the Voting Rights Act of 1965 (*see* Voting Rights Act of 1965)

Popkin, Samuel, 76*n*43

popular sovereignty. *See* political representation; responsiveness of government

pork-barrel politics, 106–8

Presser, Stanley, 73*n*21

private property, public opinion regarding, 23

professionalization of politics: in electoral campaigns, 59; participatory inequality and, 45

protesting, socioeconomic status and participatory inequality in, 35–36

public opinion: aggregate and public policy, 119–22; of economic inequality, 7–8; effect of inequality on, 27–28; as effect rather than cause, 26–28; egalitarian or antiegalitarian policies and, 28; exclusion bias of surveys, 26, 217; future directions for research on stratification in, 217, 219; of inequalities based on economic characteristics, 23–25; of inequalities based on social characteristics, 21–23; of inequality, complications in determining, 20–21; manipulation of, potential for, 27; of political inequality, 8, 25–26; responsiveness of public officials to (*see* responsiveness of government)

public policy: addressing economic inequality, public opinion regarding, 23–25, 71*n*6; aggregate public opinion and, 119–22; campaign finance and, 115–17 (*see also* campaign finance); citizenship and, 199–201; distributional politics, narrowcasting of, 106–8; education and economic inequality, 170–72 (*see also* education); egalitarian *vs.* antiegalitarian, public opinion and, 28; future research directions regarding, 226–27; the G.I. Bill, 183–86; government-enforced discrimination, public opinion regarding, 22; health care (*see* health care policy); income and wealth effects of (*see* redistributive policies and politics); inequality and, 12, 156–58, 172–73; organized interests and, 108–12; participatory inequality and, methodological difficulties in linking, 91–93; partisan differences and, 99–104; political effects of (*see* policy feedbacks); processes and institutions in the

public policy (*continued*)
formulation of (*see* government);
pro-integration, public opinion regarding, 22; public input and (*see* political representation; responsiveness
of government); redistributive (*see*
redistributive policies and politics);
the "rights revolution" (*see* "rights
revolution"); social policy of the
welfare state (*see* social policy); taxation (*see* tax policy); the War on
Poverty, 190–92

race/ethnicity: computer ownership
and, 78*n*64; economic inequality
and, 5–7; educational inequality and,
170; equality, struggle for (*see* racial
equality, struggle for); explaining
participatory inequality associated
with, 40; inequality in political voice
and, 20; participatory inequality associated with, 36–39; political activities by, **36, 38**; political party polarization and, 95–96; the "rights
revolution" and, 173–75; voting
rights and, 193–96. *See also* African
Americans; Latinos
racial equality, struggle for, 131–32; descriptive and substantive representation, synergy of, 135–36; descriptive
and substantive representation, tension between, 132–35; post-World
War II, 174–77
redistributive policies and politics:
comparative perspective on, 158–69,
199; conditional party government
and, 96, 104–6; income inequality in
selected developed countries,
160–62; inequality and, 156–58,
172–73; partisan differences and,
99–104; public opinion regarding, 24;
redistribution, limited evidence re-

garding, 158; social policy of the
welfare state (*see* social policy); Social Security and Medicare, 186–88,
225 (*see also* Medicare; Social Security); tax policy, 169–70 (*see also* tax
policy); the War on Poverty, 190–92
responsiveness of government, 219–20;
aggregate public opinion and public
policy, 119–22; congressional responsiveness to income classes, **126**; empirical studies of, 117–19; federalism
and, 127–29; foreign policy preferences of government officials, influences on, **125**; future directions for
research regarding, 221–24; image
responsiveness, 140*n*20; inaction and
selective responsiveness, bias toward, 220–21; inequalities in, 11,
124–27; inequality and popular sovereignty, 129–31; trends in, 122–24.
See also political representation
"rights revolution": economic inequality and, 2–7, 173–74; gender inequality and, 177–79; racial inequality
and, 174–77
Rohde, David W., 76*n*45
Rosenstone, Steven J., 42, 75*n*28, 76*n*45

Schattschneider, E. E.: federalism, concerns regarding, 129; inequality and
American democracy, tradition of investigating, 91; organized interests,
class bias of, 53, 55; policy creates
politics, suggestion that, 180; responsible party government, call for, 99
Schlozman, Kay Lehman, 14*n*1
Schneider, William, 27
Schumpeter, Joseph, 223
Scovronick, Nathan, 170
segregation, racial, 176–77
Serviceman's Readjustment Act of
1944. *See* G.I. Bill

SES. *See* socioeconomic status
Shafer, Byron E., 77*n*58
Shammas, Carole, 164–65
Shanks, J. Merrill, 197
Shays' Rebellion, 63
Silver, Brian D., 73*n*21
Skocpol, Theda, 14*n*1, 48
social movements: Civil Rights movement (*see* Civil Rights movement); economic inequality and, 67–68; political voice through, 63–65; possibilities and limits of, 66–67; private behaviors, potential for changing, 65–66; women's/feminist movement, 65, 173
social policy: income inequality and, 159–64; intertemporal variation in income and, 165–66; mismatch of risks and benefits, inequality and, 166–69, 199; wealth inequality and, 164–65
social science: democracy, responsibility to conduct research on the state of, 231–32; society-government links, need for research encompassing the big picture regarding, 227–31. *See also* political science
Social Security: benefit rates, 198; policy feedback effect of, 186–90, 225; public opinion regarding, 24–25, 72*n*10
Social Security Disability Insurance (SSDI), 182
society-government linkages, need for research encompassing, 227–31
socioeconomic status (SES): health and, 172; participatory inequality and, 34–39; political activity and class stratification, changes over time, 46–49; voting stratification and, 45–46. *See also* class, socioeconomic

Sorauf, Frank, 113
Soss, Joe, 182
Stehlik-Barry, Kenneth, 44
Stimson, James A., 120–21, 230
Stokes, Donald, 118–19, 126
substantive representation, 132–35

Tarrow, Sidney, 77–78*n*60
tax policy: distribution of the tax burden, 169–70; Earned Income Tax Credit, 92, 104, 167, 178, 199; estate tax, repeal of, 112; future research directions regarding, 226–27; partisan effects on, 102–4; payroll tax funding Social Security and Medicare, 186–88; policy feedback effects of, 199; political restraints on nonprofits via, 54; progressive taxes, wealth inequality and, 165; public opinion regarding, 24, 71–72*n*9
Traugott, Michael, 73–74*n*21
Truman, Harry, 97

Uggen, Christopher, 203*n*17

Verba, Sidney, 14*n*1, 20
Vieth v. Jubelirer, 195
voluntary associations: changes in political voice and, 48–49, 216; civic organizations, changes in, 199–200; decrease in membership/increase in organizations, 55; significance for political voice, 46, 48. *See also* organized interests
voting: changes in stratification over time, 9, 45–46; exclusion of felons and ex-felons, 203*n*17; generational cohorts and, 197–98; participatory inequality in, 32–33, 215–16; registration and turnout across social groupings, 33; socioeconomic status and participatory inequality in, 34,

voting *(continued)*
73–74*n*21. *See also* elections; political parties
Voting Rights Act of 1965: enfranchisement of African Americans, 45, 131, 173; majority-minority districts as response to, 133; as part of the War on Poverty, 191–92; policy feedback effects of, 192–96; substantive representation, advances in, 135–36; voting stratification, mitigation of, 9

Wallace, George, 102, 192
War on Poverty, the, 190–92
wealth inequality, 3–5, 164–65
Weir, Margaret, 181
welfare reform, 128–29, 167, 199
welfare state: anomalous characteristics of American, 181; policies of (*see* redistributive policies and politics; social policy)
Wilensky, Harold, 158
Williams, Linda, 191
Wilson, Woodrow, 91
Wolff, Edward, 164
Wolfinger, Raymond, 42
women: advances for upper income, 174; equality and representation of, 131–32, 134; G.I. Bill, impact of, 185; income inequality and, 177–79; organized interests representing, 55; political parties and the enfranchisement of, 76*n*41; the "rights revolution" and, 173–74; Social Security and Medicare, benefits of, 188. *See also* gender
women's/feminist movement, 65, 173
Wuthnow, Robert, 74*n*26

In the twentieth century, the United States ended some of its most flagrant inequalities. The "rights revolution" ended statutory prohibitions against women's suffrage and opened the doors of voting booths to African Americans. Yet a more insidious form of inequality has emerged since the 1970s—economic inequality. Though the Supreme Court has affirmed the principle of one person, one vote, economic inequality appears to have stalled and in some arenas reversed progress toward realizing American ideals of democracy. In *Inequality and American Democracy*, editors Lawrence R. Jacobs and Theda Skocpol headline a distinguished group of political scientists in assessing whether rising economic inequality now threatens hard-won victories in the long struggle to achieve political equality in the United States.

Inequality and American Democracy addresses disparities at all levels of the political and policymaking process. Kay Lehman Schlozman, Benjamin I. Page, Sidney Verba, and Morris P. Fiorina demonstrate that political participation is highly unequal and strongly related to social class. They show that while economic inequality and the decreasing reliance on volunteers in political campaigns serve to diminish their voice, middle-class and working Americans lag behind the rich even in protest activity, long considered the political weapon of the disadvantaged. Larry M. Bartels, Hugh Heclo, Rodney E. Hero, and Lawrence R. Jacobs marshal evidence that the U.S. political system may be disproportionately responsive to the